Brothers on Three

Brothers on Three

*A True Story of Family, Resistance, and Hope
on a Reservation in Montana*

Abe Streep

CELADON
BOOKS

NEW YORK

www.celadonbooks.com

Photograph on page 313 courtesy of Jordan Lefler

Designed by Michelle McMillian

Library of Congress Cataloging-in-Publication Data

Names: Streep, Abe, author.
Title: Brothers on three : a true story of family, resistance, and hope on a reservation in Montana / Abe Streep.
Description: First edition. | New York, NY : Celadon Books, [2021] | Includes bibliographical references.
Identifiers: LCCN 2021015634 | ISBN 9781250210685 (hardcover) | ISBN 9781250210678 (ebook)
Subjects: LCSH: Families—Montana. | Communities—Montana. | Teenage boys—Montana—Conduct of life. | Basketball players—Montana. | Basketball teams—Montana.
Classification: LCC HQ555.M9 S77 2021 | DDC 306.85092/2786—dc23
LC record available at https://lccn.loc.gov/2021015634

Our books may be purchased in bulk for promotional, educational, or business use. Please contact your local bookseller or the Macmillan Corporate and Premium Sales Department at 1-800-221-7945, extension 5442, or by email at MacmillanSpecialMarkets@macmillan.com.

First Edition: 2021

10 9 8 7 6 5 4 3 2 1

For my mother and father
And for Stephanie, who just knows

Contents

A different time will come, *declared the mud.*

—D'Arcy McNickle

After a while, however, I realized that they were saying a great deal, and that on questions of human behavior much that sounded old was so old that it was new again.

—Eugene Kinkead

Brothers on Three

I'll Be There

March 8, 2017

The boy and the old woman let the silence gather. He was used to her talking with her hands and cracking jokes over French toast. Now she was quiet and still, a hospital gown hanging off her shoulders. From the second-story window at Providence St. Patrick Hospital, in Missoula, Montana, Will Mesteth Jr. could see low clouds clinging to the timbered hillsides. Soon it would snow. He looked down to the parking lot. The bus was due any minute. When his *túpyc?* eventually spoke, she told him to go, that she would be fine, the same thing he had heard his whole life: *Don't worry 'bout me.* She always said she was tough enough to handle anything the world could offer, and he had no reason to doubt her. But there was something different about her stillness, and the space between her words. He felt weird. Frozen, almost.

In front of Sophie Cullooyah Stasso Haynes were two versions of her great-grandson. On the wall of her hospital room hung a poster of him in the air, moving toward a basketball rim in his red-and-white Arlee Warriors jersey, mouth agape, the memorial tattoo for his *sínce?*—his brother Yona—visible on his muscled left shoulder. Seated in front of the image was the child she raised, William Mesteth Jr. He was sixteen now, about five foot nine and solidly built, with the first wisps of reddish brown hair sticking out of his chin and the last of his baby fat clinging to his cheeks. His hair hung to his shoulders. She called him Willie.

He was a quiet kid. In class he didn't say anything; girls thought he was shy, and teachers wondered what was wrong. His mother, Chasity, said he was just quiet. His father, a policeman whose name he took, worried his son had trained himself to disappear. With Sophie it was different. She had raised him from birth. Will and his *túpye?* talked about everything: hunting, the past, trucks, his siblings, his dreams. He called her "the most kindhearted person you'll ever meet." Other family members saw a different side of her. "Mean," "strict," and "o'nery"— those were the words more often used.

Will grew up on seventy acres of the Jocko River Valley in Arlee, Montana, near the southern end of the Flathead Indian Reservation. The property was a tribal allotment with horse pastures, a neat family cemetery, and multiple homes. Sophie lived near the entrance, in a warm wooden house where she raised Will. Chasity resided just up the way, in a newer modular home. Beyond that were places belonging to Sharon, Chasity's mother and Will's grandmother, and various aunties and uncles. Everyone just called it Haynesville, and there was little doubt as to who was in charge. Chasity was a teenage mother, so when Will arrived Sophie took him in. She spoiled him, giving him Cream of Wheat, pancakes, or burgers whenever he wanted. It was as though his arrival had given rise to some soft new hope. Later on, when he heard thumps in the house, he rushed to Sophie, knowing she had fallen. He helped her up, then she got back to whatever she had been doing. "Pretty tough woman," he said.

Beeps and hushed voices filled the hospital. Along with Will's *yayá* Sharon and aunties, Chasity sat in a nearby waiting room. She was thirty-two now, a working single mother of six with long hair, well-kept nails, and a cluster of tattooed stars descending from behind one ear. She wouldn't interrupt. "When he comes," said Chasity, "we let them have their time." But the women in the waiting room all wanted Will to leave when the bus arrived to drive him to the state tournament, which was to take place over the next three days. In the past year, he had transformed from a failing student and potential dropout to a star shooting guard on a dominant team. People now put him on posters and talked about him in barbershops.

Down below, Broadway was busy, cars kicking slush to the side of the road. Beyond it, the Clark Fork River carried ice toward Idaho. In March, western Montana combines the cold of the Northern Rockies with the moisture of the Pacific Northwest. It's a season of low skies, heavy snow, perilous roads, and radio announcements imploring basketball fans to drive safely. In Montana, March means frenzied travel over icy passes to high school tournaments. The bus was coming to pick up Will for the most consequential of them all.

In rural Montana, on the weekend of the state tournament, small towns evacuate, their residents filling arenas designed for rock bands and college teams. The Warriors competed in Class C, the division representing the state's smallest schools, where basketball occupies emotional terrain somewhere between escape and religion. Arlee, Montana, has an estimated population of 641, if you choose to believe the US Census, which no one locally does. That weekend, Will was scheduled to play in front of a crowd approximately ten times that size in Bozeman, two hundred miles to the southeast. Despite years of high expectations, and despite the presence of one of the state's most dynamic players, Will's cousin Phillip Malatare, the Arlee Warriors had never won the state championship. Will's addition had turned the team into something formidable, a pressing, blitzing group that outscored opponents in dizzying runs. Will's sudden ascendance brought his family intense pride. Chasity filmed each contest on a smartphone, while Will's father, Big Will, took his place by a large drum alongside the boy's grandfather and uncles, singing before the team took the court.

Twenty-five miles north of Missoula, in Arlee, people made last-minute preparations, painting truck windows with the names of players and trying to book hotel rooms in Bozeman for the three-day tournament. For the Arlee Warriors, the pride of the Flathead Indian Reservation, state was not just a matter of boyish fun. The previous year, they had made it to the championship but lost. They'd entered this season hoping to avenge that disappointment, but by now, it had taken on an entirely different significance. To the Warriors' coach, Zanen Pitts, a thirty-one-year-old rancher with a shock of reddish-blond hair, ruddy cheeks, and cutting blue eyes, the trip meant something so great it was almost ineffable. "This is your opportunity to relieve the pain," he said, of the boys. "This is your guys' calling."

Two weeks earlier, on Wednesday, February 22, word of a death had rippled through the Jocko Valley. The deceased, Roberta Roullier Haynes, was an aunt of Will's and a foster mother, with a kind smile and long auburn hair, who often organized community events. She and her husband, TJ, a tribal policeman, were close with many of the Warriors, and the boys grew up playing in their yard. The cause of death was suicide, but Will did not know that at first. His family initially kept it quiet. It was not the first such tragedy to strike Arlee that season. Since the fall, the community had been in the midst of what public health officials called a suicide cluster, a darkness that spasmodically took its toll. Roberta's passing had been a jolt to the heart of the team. "She was family," Will said. He had wondered if he should skip the next games, the divisional tournament preceding state, to be with his family. His cousin Phil, the Warriors' electric point guard, was particularly close to Roberta; to him, she was "like an auntie." When Phil's parents shared the news, he padded downstairs in his socked feet and shut the door to his room, closing himself in among the basketball jerseys and tournament brackets. But that same afternoon, Phil was at the gym, preparing for all that was asked of him. For him, to miss a practice would have been impossible. "It was time to get down," he said.

That weekend, the Warriors had blitzed their opponents. Over a three-game span, Will scored 49 points, Phil, 67. Then, on the Monday following the divisional tournament, and less than two weeks before state, there followed another death by suicide. The deceased was an uncle of a talented sophomore on the team named Lane Johnson. A wiry, shy kid who was all eyelashes, Lane missed practice that week. At practice, Zanen and the boys started calling out the names of those they were playing for. It was a wild, building feeling—"like cooking with jet fuel," according to a senior named Ivory Brien. "We're not just playing for ourselves, we're playing for this community. And *specific members* of the community." Phil's father, John Malatare, told his son and nephews that when they played, they allowed people to briefly forget their worries. Lane Johnson returned to practice on Friday, March 3, to ensure his eligibility for state. "I knew," he said of his uncle, "he wouldn't want me to miss out."

Only Will's attendance was unassured. Just a few days before the team was to leave for Bozeman, Sophie suddenly lost the ability to form words. She was rushed to the hospital, where it was determined she'd suffered a mild stroke. Will disappeared from both the school and the team, planting himself in the recliner next to her hospital bed. Coach Pitts brought the poster of Will to cheer Sophie up. He assured Will that his *túpye?* would want him to play, as did Chasity, his *yayá* Sharon, his aunties, and Big Will. Will loved and trusted them. But they were not in the hospital room, just as they had not been there on the summer mornings when Will learned to shoot.

Back before anyone put Will on posters, Sophie drove him north from Haynesville on US 93. They'd pass through Arlee and go to the Bison Inn Cafe, at the head of Ravalli Curves, or farther up the hill to Old Timer Cafe in St. Ignatius, at the foot of the whitecapped Mission Mountains. They'd order French toast—he with sausage, she with bacon. They'd head back south toward Arlee in her white Buick, the Missions receding behind them, the Jocko River and the railroad off to the right. A little farther south and they'd emerge into the Jocko Valley, Schall Flats spreading beneath tawny hills. Out to the west, near the river and the railroad, was his grandpa Allen and grandma Kelly's house. And in front of them, at the foot of the valley, was the place where the timber on a mountainside opened to reveal the shape of a heart. Not a Valentine's heart but the kind that pumps.

They would find a court. Maybe the one the boys called the Battle-field, by the junior high, or the Lyles courts on Pow Wow Road, past the community center. Sophie sat in the car while Will hopped out with a ball and walked onto the blacktop underneath backboards that read IN MEMORY OF THOMAS LYLES, honoring a ballplayer who passed away young. Will curled his little body together, gathering energy, then flung himself upward, snapping his left wrist. The ball rose toward the rim. Most of the time it clanged off and he ran to retrieve it. But sometimes it ripped the net. Will imagined doing that at the state tournament to the sound of a thousand voices.

That day had now arrived, but he wasn't sure he could go. The prospect of something happening to Sophie in his absence caused a discomfort that was almost physical. Down below, he saw the bus pull into the parking lot. The boys rode the silver travel rig with dual rear tires and, on the side, a spear piercing the word ARLEE. The windows were painted with their names: MALATARE BOLEN SCHALL FISHER. And he could see his name, too: MESTETH #3. He wanted to go with them. But he also kind of didn't. The doubt that filled him was fresh and strange. Gray light filtered through the room, and Sophie smiled with arcing eyes. "I'll be there," she said. "I'll be there." That settled the matter. Will hugged her and walked to the bus. "My gramma'd never lie to me," he said.

Three nights later, on Saturday, March 11, he looked up into the darkness and felt the eyes. Cameras lined the floor of Bozeman's Brick Breeden

Fieldhouse; above them, a human galaxy in red-and-white shirts extended to the top of the gym. Half of Flathead Nation, it seemed, had made the three-hour-plus commute. A dapper former Tribal Councilman held a homemade scorecard, as had been his practice since the 1980s. Nearly all of the members of the girls' basketball team, the Scarlets, were in attendance. Chasity sat in the second deck with her five younger children, one of them wearing face paint on his forehead that read, simply, WILL. And in front of them, in the handicapped section, as promised, sat Sophie Haynes.

"Ladies and *gennnnnnntlemen!*" boomed the announcer. "We are Montana Class C! We are one hundred and three schools strong! And this, this is our 2016–2017 Montana boys basketball state *chhhhhhhampionshhhhhhhhip!*"

The fans supporting their opponent, the Manhattan Christian Eagles, had a shorter commute, one of about twenty minutes. Manhattan Christian was a private school affiliated with the Christian Reformed Church in Churchill, an unincorporated community just twenty miles from Bozeman. The area was settled by Dutch farmers in the late nineteenth century, and some players had names that reflected that history. But the surrounding region was quickly changing, with out-of-state wealth coming for low taxes, a burgeoning tech industry in Bozeman, and Montana's natural splendor. The man with the microphone introduced Manhattan Christian first. Then he said the word *Arlee*. The sound was strange, a live thing rumbling from the court to the top row. Will felt as if he had occupied someone else's body. He took in the vastness of the crowd and stepped onto the floor.

Part One

You're never promised tomorrow.
—Sophie Cullooyah Stasso Haynes

1

We Just Know

Early Years

US 93 transects the mountainous part of the state of Montana west of the Continental Divide in a line that moves more or less south to north. At the Idaho border it drops from steep mountains into the Bitterroot Valley, a verdant river corridor between two ranges. The word *frontier* is popular here. Between the towns of Hamilton and Stevensville—known locally as "where Montana began"—you can find Frontier Guns & Ammo, the Frontier Cafe, Frontier Lighting, Frontier Windows and Doors, Frontier Office Plaza, even Frontier Internet. Past the town of Lolo, US 93 rises with train tracks toward Missoula, a quickly growing college town. The road crosses through an expanse of malls and past a golf course near ground that was once full of bitterroot, a medicinal tuber capped with a striking pink flower. Here the road passes Interstate 90, near where a sign advertises Glacier National Park and Kalispell, prominent northern points on the tourist map. It makes no mention of the places in between.

Past a cluster of hotels and gas stations, 93 curves around a hill. The timber closes in, then opens to reveal a field bordered by an aspen draw.

Above it, to the north, shines Gray Wolf Peak, rising white out of the Mission Mountains. This is Evaro, the southern entrance to the Flathead Indian Reservation. Two hillsides push in on the road, funneling it toward a narrow point, and the mountains briefly disappear. A casino glints on the left; beyond it a bridge for migrating wildlife creates a small tunnel over the highway. Just past the tunnel the land yawns open to reveal jagged peaks, rolling hills, and handsome ranchland in the Jocko River Valley. Small roads jut like tributaries into 93, bearing names such as McClure Road, Couture Loop, and Lumpry Road. To visitors, they mean little; to residents, they speak of family. For about a quarter of a mile the highway briefly splits to accommodate Arlee's downtown. A handful of businesses line the northbound side of the road: a huckleberry-themed restaurant and coffee shop, a feedstore, a pizza joint, a bar, and Wilson Family Foods, or, as everyone calls it, the Store. Visitors do not always realize they are guests of a sovereign nation: the Confederated Salish and Kootenai Tribes (CSKT). One mile later Arlee is gone.

Two blocks to the east of the Store sits Arlee Schools, a series of one-story buildings spread between fields and basketball courts where kids study from kindergarten to twelfth grade. Many of the buildings are modest, built with asbestos decades ago. But one structure catches the eye first: a $3 million gymnasium with a peaked roof rising into the sky. The gym has retractable baskets that descend from the walls with a push of a button and a high-performance floor that refracts the light pouring through tall windows. You can look down and see your reflection. The school doesn't often hold graduation ceremonies inside, out of fears that high heels might scratch the wood. Zanen Pitts, the Arlee Warriors coach, usually walked into the gym as though he were entering a film set. He often wore cowboy boots. "I believe," he once said, "you can't stop me."

He took coaching very seriously. His team was made up of many

boys, each of whom had his own choices and stories. Two of those players were cousins whose names rhymed, and they would shape the path
of things. Until high school, they rarely hung out off school grounds,
but at recess, in the fields and on the courts at Arlee Schools, they
connected. Whether they were playing football or basketball, they always ran one play because it was so fun, and because they were so fast:
the Hail Mary. One of them would glance briefly at the other, and his
cousin would take off, sprinting past everyone, then looking back for
the long, soaring pass. "Me and Phil," Will said, "we just know."

Will Mesteth Jr. was a child of the new millennium who owed his ex-
istence to the game of basketball. His parents met in middle school on
the courts outside Arlee Schools. Chasity Haynes had an astonishing
smile and the kind of presence that intimidated girls and attracted boys.
Séliš[1] and Navajo, she grew up in Sophie and Tapit Haynes's home
with an appreciation of history. She also inherited from Tapit, her *síle?*,
a love of old cars; from both her grandparents, a love of sports. Some
in the family thought she was coddled because she was a good athlete,
a guard with a smooth outside shot. During coed three-on-threes, she
found herself drawn to a gregarious jock named Will Mesteth. A Séliš
and Oglala Lakota kid, he was stocky and drove with power to the
basket. Even then, classmates called him Big Willie. In the hallways

---

1 In this book I'm using the tribe names preferred by the Séliš-Q'lispé Culture Committee, a
governmental body established by the Confederated Salish and Kootenai Tribes in the 1970s. The
spellings of Séliš and Q'lispé you see here are the ones used by the Culture Committee in ongoing
projects and publications related to language, history, and ethnogeography. When citing or quoting
individuals from other tribes, I defer to them. Some people prefer Indigenous names (for example,
Diné, Amskapi Pikuni, or Apsáalooke). Some people prefer anglicized ones (Navajo, Blackfeet, or
Crow). Some people—and nations—prefer the phrase "tribal citizen"; others, "tribal member." For
my own part, I use Séliš rather than Salish and Q'lispé rather than Kalispel (or Pend d'Oreille)
in accordance with what I've learned from the community. For other tribes, I'm using anglicized
names until I learn more. Given the diversity of perspectives in tribal communities, I've tried to ask
whenever possible.

he was a joker, once leaving a roadkilled squirrel in a friend's locker. At home he carried grief at having lost, at age twelve just years earlier, his father in a car accident. The football field and basketball court were his outlets for expression. He and Chasity started playing together and hanging out. When he was fourteen and she was fifteen, she dove across a volleyball court and felt a pain. That was how she discovered she was pregnant.

Chasity was still living at Sophie's when Will was born, in August 2000. For the first fifteen months of his life, little Will followed Sophie's husband, Tapit, around like a deity, crawling after him. The old man passed in November 2001, and from then on it was Sophie and Will. At home she only spoke Séliš; he didn't start regularly speaking English until age five. They sat together on the bleachers in the old gym at Arlee High School, the one with dead spots on the floor, Will watching studiously while his mom played high school ball. Chasity thought that, had she stayed in school, she might have had a chance to play in college. But, she said, "I still wouldn't have been able to choose that path because I had a little guy at home." She dropped out, entering a job-training program.

By that point, her relationship with Big Will had gone the way of most teenage romances. He became a football star, running over people's backs and fielding interest from Division I colleges. He didn't do a lot of parenting back then, even when he moved to Missoula to play for the University of Montana Grizzlies. On the weekends when he was to care for his son, he'd drop the boy with his mom, Kelly Pierre, and her husband, Allen, and take off. Kelly was strict and worked for the CSKT Tribal Health Department; Allen Pierre, Will's papa, was a respected cultural specialist who stayed up late making art and regalia, bustles and jingle dresses and bonnets. "This thing called time," he once said, "I got no use in my life for time." Allen, Q'lispé and Kootenai, sewed little Will's regalia and they sat up together, listening to drum groups on a cassette tape. Allen's voice sounded as if his throat were full of marbles, and Will Jr.'s emerged throaty and deep. In the summer they traveled from Browning to Usk, Washington, for powwows, and Allen gave the boy the claw of a black bear, for protection.

When Will was five, a group of Arlee parents started a youth basketball program called Little Dribblers. The setting was the Arlee Community Center on Pow Wow Road, which the Tribes had recently opened. If you went to the center on any given Saturday, you'd smell fresh fry bread—Indian tacos were a regular fundraiser—and hear a chorus of rubber soles and laughter, then enter to find about 130 kids tearing around the court. Kids on balance beams, kids hopping on one leg, to develop agility and balance. Even back then, when the kids were waist-high, one of them stood out from the rest, on account of his quickness. He was Will's cousin. Everyone just called him Philbert.

Phillip John Malatare had an imprecise memory and little desire to look into the future. Even as a boy, his ascent to stardom seemed a foregone conclusion. Whether he was tearing around the house with a blue light-up sword or hitting rocks with sticks in the yard, he showed an easy coordination. He ran at full speed in the sort of loops a child might draw if asked to represent the movements of a bee. In baseball he struck everyone out; in soccer he scored goals at will, once causing his mom, Becky, to scold him for making others feel bad. Her husband, John, a Séliš and Cree wildland firefighter, told her not to hold him back. When Phil was six, he told his parents he'd be a professional athlete, so they wouldn't have to work anymore. Phil's dad, John, just laughed, but those words stayed in his mind. "Dream big," he said.

Phil was John and Becky Malatare's youngest child. His older sisters both had dark hair. Phil had a sandy cowlick jutting from his forehead. Following Phillip's birth Becky's grandmother said that at last one of the kids resembled their side, because Becky was white, tall, with sandy hair, descended from Norwegian homesteaders and raised in Hot Springs, on the reservation's northwestern side. But when Becky looked at her son, she saw a small version of her husband: the smile, the motion, the drive.

When Phil was born, the Malatares lived in a trailer on leased tribal land in Evaro. Money was tight then, back before they were established in their careers, John fighting fires and Becky handling accounts for a Missoula hospital. Timber closed in all around, casting shadows. Shortly after Phil's birth, Becky saw a bear in the backyard and announced she would be moving. John convinced the Tribes to let him switch leases, and soon the couple moved closer to Arlee, near his sisters and their children. They sold the trailer and bought a modular home, placing it on lease ground not far from a road sign that bore his mother's maiden name. They owned the house but not the ground; that belonged to the Tribes, which provides leases of communally owned land to enrolled members. John and Becky planted a garden that was more like a farm, with squash and strawberries and tomatoes. The couple's two incomes and a loan enabled them to build a foundation underneath their house. They lifted it off the ground, creating a two-story place in the world. Out front they erected two basketball hoops near a pasture big enough for soccer. "The field of dreams," they called it.

John made his living as a sawyer for the US Forest Service, using hand tools to clear understory down to the mineral soil in order to cut off or redirect wildfires. Back then, he was one of the few Natives on the job, and his position represented a complicated mobility: economic opportunity that also meant uncomfortable distance from home. He had family spread throughout the Jocko and Mission Valleys. His *túpye?* had fifty-two great-grandchildren and said that made her the richest woman on the reservation. He loved his home, but he also resolved that his kids would never know the taste of commodity beef, the fatty canned stuff the government provided tribes. To prove he belonged on the job he outworked his colleagues. "I'd like to get to the thickest, the heaviest patches I could get into," he said.

John and Becky had connected through softball and shared a deep love of athletics. "We're sports junkies," she said. In the early days of their marriage, when they were still getting to know each other, sports was a unifier. Becky did not intuitively understand the complex web of familial relations on the reservation. She knew little about Séliš traditional practices, the way wakes went on for days, with food and singing. John was patient with her, but he was also gone in the summers, sleeping in fire camps across the West. Upon his return, he'd show photos from the fire line. "I'd be like, 'Great, it was nice talking to you about your trip,'" Becky said, "'but I don't give a shit. I gotta go to Costco. Spend a day, rest up, then contribute to the family.'"

But they had sports. In 2005, when Phil was five, they partnered with other parents to start Little Dribblers, to give kids something to do on the weekends. "All of a sudden," said John, "it went off like a fricking rocket." John bought a book on basketball technique. Early on, he and the other coaches focused on fundamentals: chest passes and defensive posture. They did not run plays, save for one: the full-court outlet pass. At a young age it was simply the heave and sprint, later, the coaches taught the finer points of the play. How to contest a shot, then release and look back just as the rebounder secured the ball, whirled, and sent it flying.

The following year, more courts arrived in town, this time on account of tragedy. That March, in a car accident on a country road, a boy named Thomas Lyles died. He was a basketball player who loved the game and thought about it like a coach. Following Lyles's death, the community raised funds to put outdoor courts near the entrance to the Powwow Grounds. Often, people saw Phil there, his cowlick leading the way as he tore around with cousins, dribbling for hours. And sometimes, at night, people saw a white Buick by the courts: Sophie Haynes, sitting with the engine running as Will hurled shots into the night.

When Chasity was twenty-three, she bought a modular home she placed near Sophie's. By then she was working a full-time job in the CSKT enrollment department, a position that offered stability. Near Chasity's place was a trampoline between two baskets where Will and his cousins went at it. The family ate together, and every summer Will accompanied Chasity to Spokane Hoopfest, America's largest three-on-three tournament, to watch her play ball.

But Will slept at Sophie's. "I knew that they had a close bond," said Chasity. "So I let him stay with her then." Sophie taught the boy his history—about how an aunt had accompanied the great chief Charlo on the forced march north from the Bitterroot Valley. She taught Will round-dance songs on her hand drum, and he learned to store knowledge precisely in his head. He didn't talk much. During lunch at Arlee elementary, he often wouldn't eat with the other kids. Whenever he got off the bus at the end of the day, Sophie was waiting with Cream of Wheat, his favorite. They shot baskets together on a minihoop in the house. And at night, before bed, his *túpye?* prayed, first in Séliš and then in English, giving thanks for the day and saying, "You're never promised tomorrow."

"Mom!" said Phil's sister Whitney. "There's a hole in the window!" Phil was about nine, and with John gone during the summer, Phil had taken down his BB gun and shot out the front window of the house. Then, as if on cue, his cousin Alex Moran, who lived down the way, did the same at his house. Al was a son of John's sister Lynette, and he and Phil did everything together back then, along with another cousin named Tyler Tanner. Al and Ty were both stocky ranch kids. The three boys were inseparable, all of them dribbling to one of the hoops in town and returning only for meals. Ty was of Filipino and Finnish and Séliš descent, and had an air of quiet responsibility. Alex was quick to laugh with those he knew well, but sometimes carried anger, because his mom had been diagnosed with leukemia when he was young. On the court, the three boys learned to anticipate one another's movements. Before they were out of elementary school, Phil, Ty, and Al twice won their age division at Spokane Hoopfest. Lynette loved to watch those games, sometimes coaching, sometimes videotaping and calling out traps. She promised the three boys that they would one day win state together.

The Malatares eventually took in the Morans' dog, a black Lab named Pepper, because Lynette couldn't have it in the house when she was sick. John took Pepper hunting and the dog hid when he shot a gun. Phil took Pepper hunting, shot his first grouse, and Pepper brought the bird right back to his feet. "Just like in a storybook," Becky said. After that, Pepper was Phil's.

Around 2009, Thomas "Bearhead" Swaney, an elder to Phil, fell ill with cancer. Swaney was a former Tribal Council Chairman who'd fought to preserve the reservation's wildlands. He also loved basketball— but only one kind. He often said he couldn't stand white man's ball. He and John's father, Bear, were best friends, and Swaney was a grandfather of Thomas Lyles, the boy for whom the courts on Pow Wow Road had been named. Before he passed, Swaney announced that he wanted his .220 Swift rifle to go to Phillip. John asked Swaney's son, Bill, why the old man wanted Phil to have the gun. In John's recollection, Bill Swaney said, "I can never answer that question for you."

Two years later, Al's mother and Phil's auntie Lynette passed away. Al watched old videotapes of Hoopfest, hearing his mother's voice calling out traps, remembering her promise that he and his cousins would win state. Shortly afterward, when Phil, Al, and Ty were in junior high, John drove them to watch the state tournament in Billings. There, in the Metra, an arena that holds ten thousand, John walked them out under a human roar and told them they would one day bring Arlee its first state championship.

In junior high Will walked dirt roads at night with a group of cousins. "Full-on rez kid," he said. "Huh-*heh*!" In class he found a place in the back. He heard China was directly beneath White Coyote Road, where an organization funded by a hotel heir had bought up a sprawling property to build a spiritual retreat called the Garden of One Thousand Buddhas. He learned that land was more valuable than money; Sophie made it clear to her family that Haynesville was not to be sold. One summer Will walked the entire Jocko River with a fishing rod. Even though Will didn't live at Chasity's, he thought of himself as the man of the house. Once, Chasity dated a man whom Will really liked. But then the man left. It was not a good split. Will texted the man, telling him not to return. "He just at times wasn't being a man," Will said later. "He was being immature. That's all I gotta say about that."

Will thought he knew what it meant to be a man. He'd learned from his papa Allen Pierre. Will listened when Allen talked about the importance of art and culture. Will watched the way Allen prepared to dance at powwows. The seriousness of his expression, the silence as sweat beaded on his brow and he arranged his regalia. He listened when Allen talked about how alcohol could haunt you. Will learned to hunt from his uncles, including Big Will's brother Sean, who knew pretty much everything about whitetails. But Will wished his dad would take him to chase those big bucks.

Then, when Will was in junior high, his dad showed up. They went hunting in the hills, driving around in Big Will's truck. It was fun, and they kept doing it on the weekends. Big Will had a good job by this point as a policeman on the Tribes' force. One day, they rolled around looking for whitetails by Saddle Mountain. Up high, snow was on the ground. Big Will felt something bubbling up inside him. He wanted to tell his oldest child that he was sorry—that he had not been ready. That he had grown up without a dad, too, and that it had been hard. That as a teenager he was overwhelmed by what he once called "just pain. Just that." His dad was left-handed, too, and loved soda; Will Jr. looked a lot like him when he smiled. Big Will wanted to say that he was going to try to make it better. How it all came out was another matter. Later on, Big Will just remembered saying, "You don't want to mess around with girls like that. Could you imagine having a child?" His son didn't react. They cruised the hills, looking for bucks.

Phil darted over the snowdrifts. He was thirteen and finally starting to grow. He'd been tiny forever, so small he'd worn the same Halloween costume—a ninja—for three years running. When he was a boy, Becky had to hide the butter knives. Otherwise, Phil would saw the legs of chairs, mimicking his dad skinning a deer. Phil grew up hunting and fishing, shooting his first bull elk at age eleven. Now John wanted to get him into horn hunting. John was nearly fifty, his close-cropped hair silver, a goatee flecked with red hugging his chin. He had hunted for antlers for years, walking the hills to find the sheds that bull elk drop every spring, then selling them to supplement his income. John loved the cold in his lungs, being away from the noise of the world, seeing the land as it thawed and before everything turned fat and green. Although middle age had brought with it a new paunch, he could still outhike firefighters in their twenties. Sometimes he crunched through the snowy crust. His son just floated over the top, easy as anything.

They hiked over frozen brown hillsides and through mud and into draws where the snow was still drifted, until they reached a hill thick with larch and fir. A little ways farther and they dropped into a secret place. There, the tines glinted, ridged and chocolate brown. John saw the first antler. A short way away Phil grabbed the other one, completing the set. They named the bull "crab claw," because the antlers were all crooked. When Phil got excited about something, he focused obsessively. He took photos with the antlers, looking tough, mouth pursed. And then he smiled, angular features all turned up, a smile to change the weather.

Phil loved the woods. That was his escape, one he increasingly sought. The Malatare house was full. When Phil was in junior high, John and Becky took in foster children, three boys and a girl who were related to the family through John's mother. Phil's foster siblings were astonished to see that he had a television in his bedroom. The middle boy, Darshan, was a year younger than Phil, quiet and sweet and fastidious, always showering and changing clothes. He, too, was an athlete, a talented football player who also shot hoops. Becky suspected that was in order to be close to Phil. Sometimes Phil took Dar to the woods. "He found the elk sheds," Dar said. "I think he gets lucky." When the Malatares sent Phil to the river for a dinner trout, he rarely came home empty-handed. And on the court, he blazed past everyone. "Different," said his best friend, Ty Tanner. "Phil's different."

In August 2013, when Will was thirteen, Chasity's younger sister died in a car wreck on a country road. The Haynes family went into mourning. Chasity got a series of stars tattooed on her neck, representing her children; next to them was a shooting star, for her sister. Almost exactly one year later, an uncle of Will's named David passed away in a similar accident. For many in the family, it was almost too much to bear. But Sophie knew what to tell Will about death. "She always told me not to be afraid of it," Will said. "It's nothing to be afraid of." It was almost time for high school.

2

They're Following You

2013–16

Zanen Pitts grew up in Dixon, on a ranch by the Flathead River, with a keen sense of the importance of sport. His parents were both coaches. His father, Terry, had led the Arlee Warriors basketball team to their first state finals appearance in 1995. Terry often said, "More is better"—more jump shots, more time on the track, more hours on the horse. He felt the world contained two kinds of people: entertainers and those who were entertained. The Pittses fell in the former category. That meant late nights watching *Rocky* or discussing the exploits of Zanen's grandfather, who had run track at the University of Wisconsin. Zanen's older brother, Zachary, was a meticulous reader who woke up at 4:00 A.M. to play basketball, later becoming an all-state player. Zanen was obsessed with film, especially Westerns. He treed bears, raised a pet bobcat and a red-tailed hawk, and announced at age eleven his plans to own his own herd of cattle. Zachary's athletic prowess earned him a pass from teasing. Zanen, who was tiny and had asthma, experienced no such reprieve. Certain words echoed through him—*Smelly Stinky Pitts! Stinky Arm Pitts!*—to the point where his parents considered pulling him out of school. But the teasing gave the younger boy a reflexive brashness. In track, he ran until he passed out. On the court he did not possess his brother's precise skill but wore kneepads because he slid around so much, eventually winning a college roster spot through effort. Zachary was, in Terry's words, "a little too modest." Zanen did not suffer that affliction. He put his name on everything from T-shirts to text messages to turn the yoke of it into an advantage, like the Boy Named Sue. "I had a mindset," he said. "Everyone's gonna remember that name. When I die, I want people to remember the name."

Terry helped Zanen get an assistant coaching job at Arlee in 2012, when he was twenty-six. At the time, the community's emphasis on basketball was beginning to show results. According to available records, the Warriors went 88–34 from 2009 to 2013, twice advancing to the state tournament but never winning the championship. The girls' team, the Scarlets, meanwhile, excelled from 2011 to 2016, going a reported 105–39, with Phil's older sister Whitney leading the way early on. A skilled guard, she earned a scholarship to the University of Montana Western, which competes in the National Association of Intercollegiate Athletics, or NAIA. During those years neither the Warriors nor Scarlets won state, but expectation followed success. In 2012, a school board member formally apologized after cursing at the coach over her son's lack of playing time. A longtime educator named Tammy Elser, who designed Arlee's literacy program, said, "We had a school board that was focused almost completely on basketball."

In 2013, after one year as an assistant, Zanen was hired as head coach, inheriting a team that had finished third in the state. He envisioned a program built off defensive effort, agility, and accountability. He often opened the gym at 6:00 A.M. for early workouts, and on game days he had the Warriors wear collared shirts or bow ties. For big games Zanen wore all black, explaining, "It's their funeral."

But during his first year as head coach, the Warriors failed to qualify for the state tournament. Then Phil and Will entered high school. By mid-December, Phil was promoted to varsity. He whipped passes around his back, driving the crowd into convulsions. As a freshman he scored in double figures for a team that lost just one game before the state tournament. The nickname Philbert waned. People started calling him Phillip the Man. The state tournament that year was in Billings, at the Metra, where John had told the boys they'd one day win. Phil couldn't believe the surging feeling when he walked out and heard his name called underneath that sound. Arlee made it to the semifinals. In the final seconds Phil brought the ball up, down by two, and threw a bad pass. The Warriors lost. The five-hour bus trip home was eternal. He crept into his parents' room and wept. He blamed himself for letting the crowd down. John told his son he was a primary reason the Warriors had made it so far. Phil fielded hundreds of Facebook friend requests from girls, which his sisters promptly deleted.

Then the hills melted out and John and Phil pulled on their boots and walked for miles. John punched through the occasional drift, while Phil floated over the top. They dropped into a draw and, sure enough, found crab claw's antlers. Phil smiled, cold air stinging his nostrils. Back at home he put a newspaper story about the loss on the wall of his bedroom for motivation. He watched the game tape over and over. "Phil must have watched that fifty times," said Becky.

Will did not experience that ecstasy or devastation. Early in the season he had played well on junior varsity, but by January was off the team on account of his grades. He couldn't find his way in earth science. He took world history and didn't care. He wished he'd taken Native American history, but nobody had talked to him about that option, at least not in a way that got through to him. At lunch, he often called Sophie, and she came to get him.

Chasity said he was kind of shy, but wondered if he was being over-indulged. When Will started failing classes, she took away his cell phone, hoping to kick him into gear. That just pissed Will off—he did have a temper—and made him feel alone. "I think he learned to kind of hide his emotions," said Big Will, "or maybe feel like his emotions aren't important." An uncle on the school board tried to pay him to raise his grades, but that didn't work. After his freshman year, Chasity decreed that it was time for him to move in with her and her younger kids. "I said, 'Enough is enough,'" she recalled. So, one day that summer, he carried his clothes and video games up the driveway, his face all turned down and glowering, Sophie by his side, helping.

Sophomore year started. Will drove his siblings to school in Chasity's Durango, even though he didn't have a license. When he came home, he saw Sophie sitting in the window. She waved at him, and he at her, and everything changed. She suffered heart ailments and lost weight. It was as though, after she finally came to a reluctant agreement with the inevitabilities of age, centripetal forces made up for lost time. A new confusion drifted in and out of her sharp mind. The Tribes provided a caretaker to help around the house. It was no longer Will picking her up when she fell.

At school, Will took more classes he didn't care about, such as biology. Once again he had multiple failing grades, and it looked as if he'd miss basketball. In the fall, the school had him tested for a learning disability. If the test determined that he had one, he might retain eligibility for basketball despite his low grades. Big Will was opposed. He thought the school was sending his son down the same route he'd experienced: preferential treatment for a good athlete that would, in the long run, prove a hindrance. He wanted his son to be held accountable. "He's a lazy kid," Big Will said. "That's all it is."

But Chasity felt the test was worth pursuing. For Will, it presented a possible route to solving one of life's great obstacles: his inability to play for the Warriors. Big Will recalled his son saying, "They said that's what I am. And if I'm that, then I can be eligible." The boy took the test, discovering he did not have a learning disability. In fact, he scored high on memory. He was once again ineligible for the team.

Meanwhile, rumors began to circulate about Phil. People wondered if he might transfer to Hellgate, a larger school in Missoula, to increase his exposure to the Division I University of Montana Grizzlies— known as the Griz. He even thought about it. "Everyone knows," said Becky, "Hellgate's the gateway to the Griz." But John's feelings were complicated. He believed in bettering yourself and could be critical of those who didn't chase ambitions. In his career, he said, "We heard a lot of 'What are you Indians doing here?' I had to work extra hard to prove I could do the job." But he never wanted to live off the reservation and had passed up career opportunities that would have necessitated a move out of state. He wanted Phil's recognition and opportunities to extend beyond Arlee, but the pride he felt at his son's accomplishments was tied up in community. The way he figured it, if Phil was good enough to win at home, he'd receive the college offers he deserved. Phil's grandfather Bear, John's father, said that if Phil transferred, he'd regularly be playing in Billings, a six-hour drive away. Some Arlee fans had the funds to travel across the state. Some did not. "You look at that crowd," Bear said, "They're following you." Phil thought about his auntie Lynette's promise that he and Al and Ty would win together. Phil stayed, and that winter he was a wrecking crew of a point guard. John tried not to show it, but he felt, in his words, "like a big ole peacock" when he watched Phil dominate. John and Becky sat apart at games. "It just works better," she once said. "I like to kind of breathe. Not John." Phil did aerials. Once, in a gym, John heard a fan say, "That's the best move I've ever seen in my life." On another occasion, a boy yelled, "Phillip Malatare touched me!" The Warriors advanced to the state championship against Box Elder, a team from the Rocky Boy's Reservation. Phillip scored 33 whirling points. When he fouled out, his opponents stopped the game to individually embrace him. One fan said it was the most remarkable thing he had seen in sports. But the Warriors lost by 22 points. Something was missing.

Will didn't see that game. He spent afternoons at the community center, shooting as though hoping for some gift to follow the ball down. He thought about dropping out of school. "I kinda felt left out not doing sports," he said. "That's been a main part of my life. Just made me feel different. I didn't like it, and I didn't wanna be around the school." He figured he'd just shoot hoops and fish and take care of his *túpye?*. Back in Haynesville, Sophie gave him her hand drum.

3

We Need Her

Fall–Winter 2016

In school, Will moved with his head down, eyes darting, and one Air Jordan out of the classroom door. Jennifer Jilot recognized something in the way he carried himself, and she was also familiar with the language used to describe the boy. Over and over she heard the same word: *lazy*. She hated that word. "Why is that everybody's answer for everything?" she said. "No. There's foundational issues, reasons why kids don't want to do certain things." An enrolled member of the Chippewa Cree Tribe of the Rocky Boy's Reservation and a single mother, Jilot was a proud progressive and often felt like an outsider in her work. At another school, she had once been chided for teaching Christopher Columbus's journals, with their florid descriptions of assault. "People know as soon as they meet me," she said, "that I'm an advocate for kids and an advocate for Native people." But from the moment Will met her, she was mostly a pain in his ass. "I'm nosy," she said. "I'm going to go to bat for you. But you're going to have to get used to me."

Jilot was the first hire of Arlee's new superintendent, David Whitesell, and during Will's sophomore year they had made a plan for the boy. Whitesell was a tall navy veteran with green eyes and curly hair.

He'd grown up near various reservations, as his father, a citizen of the Standing Rock Sioux Tribe, worked in Indian schools around the West. "I like leaving," David once said. He wore a bemused smile that some found to be a sign of intellectual confidence, others of haughtiness. Among Whitesell's goals at Arlee were to increase the staff's diversity and awareness of intergenerational trauma. Upon taking the job, he had the staff—including its two principals, who were white—take what was called an adverse childhood experiences (ACE) quiz. It contained ten probing questions, among them:

Before your 18th birthday, did you live with anyone who was a problem drinker or alcoholic, or who used street drugs?

Before your 18th birthday, did a household member go to prison?

Before your 18th birthday, was a household member depressed or mentally ill, or did a household member attempt suicide?

Answering yes to a question added a point to your score. According to ACE data collected between 2015 and 2017 from twenty-five states, 39 percent of participants reported no adverse childhood experiences, while 15.6 percent reported four or more "yes" answers, scores that were linked to increased health and behavioral risks. When the Arlee test results came back, Whitesell was amazed by how many teachers and staffers had scores of zero. "This is foreign to them," he said. "I scored a seven." Many Arlee students, he said, might register near there.

When Whitesell took the job, the school, like most in Montana, was well down the path of the No Child Left Behind Act, dividing kids based on standardized-test performance. Whitesell wanted to re-establish a less rigid, more flexible reading and writing system. When Will and Phil were in early elementary school, Arlee had a progressive foundational literacy program. Coteaching reduced student-teacher ratios, and the kids wrote about their lives in a literacy lab, disregarding grammar and punctuation. "It was raw," said Becky Malatare, "but it helped them express themselves." She kept a folder full of her kids' journals, including Phil's writing about visiting Lynette in the hospital. Will wrote about hunting with uncles or going to powwows with his papa Allen. In the spring of 2008, according to the Montana Office of Public Instruction, 50 percent of Arlee's third graders read at advanced levels, compared with a statewide figure of 42 percent. Arlee's Native American students scored highest, with an advanced reading level of 58 percent—compared with a statewide figure of 20 percent. But following the implementation of policies designed to accommodate No Child Left Behind, the literacy lab became a tech room, and Arlee implemented an evaluation system that, in the eyes of some educators, had the effect of separating children based on achievement. Shortly afterward, in a cost-cutting measure, Arlee adopted a four-day school week. The vaunted literacy program cratered, with the drop-off most acute among Indigenous students. By 2012, the percentage of advanced Native American third grade readers had fallen more than fourfold, to 13.

One hire couldn't fix everything, but in July 2015, Whitesell led a panel interviewing Jilot for a literacy-coach position. She had just completed a master's degree at the University of Montana, and she outlined a philosophy of culturally sensitive, individualized learning. "I said, 'We need her,'" Whitesell recalled. At first, Jilot did not teach. Her job was to work with students needing individual attention. Will was one of the first kids she focused on, with Whitesell's blessing. As an educator, Whitesell saw sports as a leverage point—a way to get vulnerable kids, and boys especially, to care about school. He wondered if Arlee could turn Will around; if, rather than becoming another statistic, he might emerge as a model of a different kind of success, a Native boy who would graduate with the support of an educator who understood him.

But Will didn't think he needed a teacher telling him what to do. He used a familiar word to describe his academic performance: "I was too lazy." He kept driving his siblings to school. Jilot followed him to class. Before long, she realized what he was doing in the back of the room. He didn't tune out. Rather, on his laptop he searched for the definitions of certain phrases his teachers used, trying to catch up rather than ask for help. In Jilot's estimation, "it was shyness because of lack of confidence because he didn't think he was good enough."

Will would never admit to that. But when Jilot said she wanted to accompany him to speak to his biology teacher, he agreed. *Whatever.* She asked the teacher, who also coached the girls' basketball team, Will's questions while the boy sat silently. They worked on the assignments until, eventually, Will gained the confidence to ask questions himself. One day, the teacher rushed to Jilot to say that Will had asserted himself in a group workshop.

Still, his grades were too low to allow him to play in his sophomore year. And he soon found himself with more urgent worries. That January, just before she was due to have a baby, Chasity lost the child. Overcome with grief, she went on a wild drive to Washington, then returned home and spent a week at a facility where she spoke regularly with counselors. Later on, she thought back on that time as though it were some spell that had fallen without her participation. "It's scary," she said, "because you technically don't even know you're there." Will took care of his siblings while she was gone. He could not drop out. "I have to keep a good example," he later said. He kept working with Jilot, eventually raising his grades enough to regain his athletic eligibility. By fall of junior year, he was starring on the football team as his father once had. At the games, both Chasity and Big Will walked the sidelines. Will broke the pinkie on his shooting hand but kept playing, wearing a smile. His grades rose. Chasity started to brag about her son being a 3.0 student. "My oldest," she called him tenderly, thinking about how he held the world together when it had almost spun away. In school, Will walked the halls with his head up.

Basketball season began. In November, Zanen announced that Will would start, alongside Phil and Ty. If Phil was the team's engine, Ty was its rock: solid, patient, always good for a clutch play. Zanen referred to them as "the three-headed monster." The fourth scoring option was Greg Whitesell, the superintendent's son, a slight sophomore guard with a fine shot who was enrolled Diné (Navajo). Greg had moved from Polson, at the north end of the Flathead Reservation, a few years earlier, and upon arriving had resolved that he'd one day be better than Phil. Outside of ball, Greg liked going to Missoula for sushi and playing video games, copying the ball-handling moves of avatars. He wrote, ate, and dribbled with his right hand, but had taught himself to shoot lefty to emulate the NBA player Brandon Jennings. He had big emotive eyes and curly hair and was particular about who cut it. Off the court he was sweet and kind; on it, vicious. Being the superintendent's son was no fun, if you asked him.

The team's rotation evolved over the season. A couple of guys quit before the end of the year, paving the way for Alex Moran to take the final starting spot. He shot three-pointers as though trying to put out the lights and threw forearm shivers into the chests of bigger kids. Ivory Brien brought size off the bench, fighting for rebounds and taking charges. He was about six-three and looked like a movie star. Ivory was Amskapi Pikuni (Blackfeet) and Apsáalooke (Crow) and came from a family with interests that were more cerebral than athletic: his mother the guidance counselor at Arlee High School and his father an archaeologist and instructor at Salish Kootenai College (SKC), the higher-education institution in Pablo. Ivory had also taken part in other sports—soccer, cross-country, martial arts, and baseball—and was taught not to focus too much on one thing, so he'd have balanced interests. He worked in a fish hatchery and participated in Reservation Ambassadors, a cross-cultural education program with other schools. He had good grades and was focused on studying wildlife biology once he graduated. He had played ball because he'd looked up to the previous generation of Warriors. But, he said, early on, "I sucked," and he spent long hours in the gym, often waking at 5:00 A.M. He improved, learning, in his words, that "as long as I'm working, I can do whatever I want."

Younger players filled out the bench. Lane Johnson, the lean sophomore, was a ranch kid who was extremely shy off the court, starting most sentences and some text messages with "Umm." But he was athletic and tough. Zanen was close with Lane's father and had always thought LJ—as he was known—had the potential to be a star. Isaac Fisher was a six-foot-seven sophomore with ever-present glasses, athletic as all get-out and just as quiet. There were also three boys who treated the basketball court like a football field: Darshan Bolen, Phil's cousin who now lived with him; Chase Gardner, the stepson of the school board chair; and Lane Schall, an outgoing kid descended from ranchers who had homesteaded in the Jocko Valley and befriended the Séliš. Lane trained hard for football, working out with a personal trainer, but on the basketball court he had certain limitations. Sometimes, when he dribbled, his father could be heard yelling, "Oh, Lane, jeez!"

The first games took place at a tournament three hundred miles to the northeast, in Havre. Temperatures sat around zero degrees. Chasity drove with Will's younger siblings, then filmed the games on her smartphone for everyone back home. Arlee went undefeated. Over the next three months, from December to February, the Warriors lost just one game, against a team called Plains, from just off the reservation.

During that game, Phil scored nine points in just over thirty seconds, but fouled out on a questionable call. He put a newspaper story about the loss on his wall, next to all the others. He liked to remember the times he'd been down. Will got a new tattoo, in honor of Yona, his brother who had passed away the previous year. MY BROTHER'S KEEPER, it read.

4

This Crazy Feeling of Infinity

March 9–11, 2017

After promising Will she'd make it to the tournament, Sophie's energy surged and her speech soon followed. On Thursday, March 9, she surprised everyone with her strength at physical therapy. Chasity was shocked. She packed up her car and Will's five younger siblings and headed to Bozeman for the tournament's first game. There, Arlee beat Plenty Coups, a team named for the great Crow chief. Phil's stat line looked like a typo: 32 points, 15 rebounds, 9 assists, 6 steals. "Malatare was everywhere—shifting, gliding, leaping, lurking, shaking and baking," boomed the *Billings Gazette*. On Friday morning, before the state semifinal, the doctors said Sophie was free to leave. One of Will's aunties planned to drive her home. But Sophie announced that she wanted to go watch some basketball. A nurse who saw the images of Will said he was handsome. Sophie said, "I know." A few hours later, she rolled into the gym in Bozeman wearing black slacks, a pink fleece, and a pin bearing Will's likeness. He was not even a little surprised to see her. Then he poured in 28 points, firing shots from absurd distances and sending Arlee to the championship.

That night, Zanen sat in his hotel room, stewing as though preparing to enter a fight. He had grown up with a painful understanding that his family had yet to win on the state's largest stage. He called it "the Pitts curse." His mom, Crystal, had come in second while coaching track at Ronan High School. His brother, the all-state guard, had scored 35 points in the state championship in 2002, but lost. And before that came the defeat that Zanen remembered most.

In 1995, Terry Pitts, Zanen's father, coached the Arlee Warriors to the state tournament. Zanen was nine. He remembered walking into an arena in Great Falls and hearing a noise he thought would cleave his chest in two. He remembered the astounding feeling following a victory in the semifinal, against Lodge Grass, out of Crow Nation; he remembered being so happy he didn't care when one of the Warriors gave him an atomic wedgie. His big brother, Zachary, spent that weekend alongside their buddy Thomas Lyles. Smart beyond his years, Tom was a thoughtful poet in school. He also loved basketball, knew every set. That weekend he introduced Zachary to a chant: "Nuts and bolts, nuts and bolts, we got screwed!" Zachary loved it. "Nuts and bolts!"

In the championship, Arlee had lost to Fairfield, a team from across the Rockies. Arlee Schools treated it like a success, with a motorcade leading the team bus home. In public, Terry said the right things: the boys had given it their all and learned about teamwork. But back at the Pitts ranch, there were long, long silences. Nothing was worse than second place.

Zanen now had a chance to redeem that loss. He knew what to expect from his opponent, Manhattan Christian. Their coach, Jeff Bellach, ran a motion offense, baseline screens, and plays designed to get the ball to towering post players or to create space for his son, a slashing sophomore. It was methodical and disciplined and utilized size: two of the Eagles starters stood six foot four or taller. Both of those players had transferred into the school. Arlee's tallest starter was Phil, generously listed at six feet. Zanen ran few offensive plays, instead relying on elaborate presses to force turnovers. The defensive rotations were fast and coordinated, requiring a deep understanding between players and the ability to read passing lanes. Ty anchored it, calling out rotations, while Phil, Will, and Greg brought speed. The defense slowly wore the opponent down until the boys unleashed, leaving the other team gasping for air and the scoreboard lopsided. Zanen suspected that Bellach would use a zone defense to slow the pace, force the boys to attempt long shots, and stifle Phil's acrobatic drives. On offense, the Eagles would likely try to attack Phil, hoping to get him in foul trouble and force Zanen to ease off on defense. Arlee had lost just three games in the previous two seasons. During each of them, Phil had fouled out. "If you get in foul trouble and they get in zone, we will not win," Zanen said. He kept repeating two words to his wife, Kendra, that night: "unfinished business."

His promise to his family hovered in his mind, as did the date. The championship fell on March 11—the anniversary of Thomas Lyles's death. Zanen always remembered the way Tom had supported him as a young basketball player. He remembered telling Tom, as a teenager, that he'd one day marry Kendra. He remembered where he was when he heard about the accident that took Tom—on a bus to a college basketball tournament. With crackling grief setting in, he'd wanted to come right home. But someone had told him, then, that Tom would have wanted him to play. So he did. For Zanen, the basketball court was almost sacred. He thought about all the community had been through in recent weeks, and the names they called out in practice. He had unfinished business.

In the seconds before the Warriors took the court, the boys hopped around in the tunnel. Ivory Brien thought about his job. He had to box out and take a charge. Strange butterflies filled him. He rushed off and vomited. The noise thundered. Greg Whitesell tuned it out, a trick he'd learned from his father, David, the superintendent. Then he let it back in. In the stands, Becky worried. Phil had said he was ready; before the game, John had told his son and nephews this was the moment they'd been preparing for since age six. He'd told Becky to think positive thoughts, but she couldn't help but wonder, *What if they lost?*

From his seat, David Whitesell tried to quiet the worries that lurked in the back of his mind. He knew that suicide is unfortunately common in Montana, and more prevalent still within Indigenous communities. In 2016, Montana had the nation's highest suicide rate. Native youth were by far its most vulnerable demographic. In the event of a loss, he planned to increase counseling resources at the school. "It's a lot to place on the shoulders of a bunch of adolescent boys," he said. But he also wore his son's jersey on his back that night. The superintendent recognized basketball's complex effect, the pride and pressure it brought. "I see both sides of it," he once said. "I love it."

The crowd was simply huge, nearly filling the Brick Breeden Fieldhouse. That same weekend, in Great Falls, two hundred miles north, the Class A boys' tournament brought in $57,000 in ticket sales. The boys' Class C tournament brought in $106,000. At center court, Tyler Tanner lined up for the opening tip-off against a six-foot-five boy. Phil raised his arms, urging the crowd on. The ref threw the ball up, and despite the height differential, Arlee corralled the opening tip. Al came down with it and kicked it to Phil, who made a move everyone knew was coming but few could stop: he crossed over, then quickly spun. But his shot clanged out of the basket, and Manhattan Christian pushed the ball to Caleb Bellach, the coach's son, an athletic six-foot-three kid one year younger than Phil. He drove and Phil tried to close for a block. He fouled Caleb, who muscled the ball into the hoop. This was Zanen's worst fear: Phil receiving his first foul just seconds into the game. Caleb missed the free throw, long. One of Manhattan Christian's tall forwards came down with the rebound and flipped it in. It was 4–0. Phil drove and passed to Greg, who saw an opening, split a double-team, then shot a right-handed floater. It bounced off the front rim. Manhattan

Christian grabbed the rebound. Caleb Bellach, on the wing, drove, took off, and leaped under the basket, laying the ball in. Manhattan Christian was up 6–0. Zanen liked to think of himself as a master of mind games. He was often calm during tense moments. Now, though, he thought, *We're going to lose this game.* He called time-out and came undone.

Ty scored out of the time-out, showing up as he always did when it mattered most, and Arlee started to trap. Greg stole the ball and kicked it to Will, who in one motion dropped it to Phil, streaking up the court for a layup. It was now a close game, but Manhattan Christian's size kept them on top for the first half. Early in the third quarter, Arlee trailed, 37–32. Then Phil saw something. As one of Manhattan Christian's tall players grabbed a rebound, Phil's eyebrows arched. He reached in and seized the ball. The other kid easily outweighed him, but Phil ripped it away and scored. Back on defense, Phil collapsed to the middle of the floor to stop Caleb Bellach's drive. Caleb whipped the ball to the corner, where a tall, thin wing player named Parker Dyksterhouse caught the pass and released a three-pointer. But as he did so, Phil took two long steps and launched into the air. At the apex of his leap he blocked the shot; the ball floated like a shot bird. As Phil soared out of bounds, Ty recovered it, brought it up, and passed to the far corner, where Will waited. His three-pointer snapped the net, tying the game. John Malatare's voice cut through the gym: "Here we go now!"

With five minutes and twenty-seven seconds remaining in the season, the game was tied. Phil brought the ball up, defended by Caleb Bellach. Phil drove right, then crossed to his left. Caleb followed, but when Phil crossed back to his right, the defender briefly lost his balance. Phil brought the ball up, a pump fake. Caleb overcorrected just enough to allow Phil to pull the ball down, duck underneath, and scoop in a left handed layup. Zanen yelled. It was time.

Arlee's devastating press hadn't yet fully materialized, but at the end of the third quarter, Zanen had run time off the clock, letting his team rest to prepare for one great surge. Now, as the Eagles inbounded the ball, Ty Tanner and Alex Moran dropped back toward the far basket. Greg and Will stayed up near the inbound line. Greg fronted the point guard, denying the entry pass. Phil shadowed Caleb at midcourt, threatening to intercept a lob to him while still maintaining position to descend on the point guard should he break free from Greg. Will offered a small amount of room to Parker Dyksterhouse—a trap. The Eagles inbounded the ball to Parker and Will was everywhere, his hands like windshield wipers. Parker dribbled from side to side, looking for an opening. As he turned, Will poked the ball away, back toward the basket. He grabbed it and jumped, laying the ball in. Four-point game. Phil and Greg trapped again, forcing a turnover; Alex dove for a loose ball; Tyler spun for a layup, then Alex shot a great arcing three-pointer and ran up the court, thinking of his mother's promise and knowing it would rip the net.

The pass came with two minutes remaining in the season. The Warriors had a nine-point lead. Phil darted toward the corner, chasing a rebound. Out at the three-point line, Will raised his arm, then put his head down and sprinted toward the far basket. His hair tailed behind him and his arms chugged in a stiff way, the tattooed wings on his left shoulder a blur.

Phil chased down the loose ball, drawing two defenders. Before they could trap, he made a brutal and swift motion, at once controlling the ball, whirling, and cocking his arm. His face took on its most clear expression: eyebrows arched, cheeks drawn, eyes hard. On the bench, Zanen knew what was coming and that he was powerless to stop it. The full-court Hail Mary brought mayhem under normal circumstances. To throw it with the season on the line was borderline insane. The noise in the gym was a boiling roar. Phil snapped his arm, sending the ball toward the gym's roof. The sound flattened out, thousands of eyes followed the orange sphere's path, and underneath it, Will ran.

Phil threw the pass intending for a final, decisive blow. It crested, tumbled, and landed in Will's outstretched hands just beyond the three-point line. The crowd detonated. He moved to his left, one dribble, then two, and launched off his right leg, mouth open, just beyond the defender. He flipped a layup off the backboard with his left hand. The ball rolled around the rim and fell out. Caleb Bellach grabbed the rebound and took off. Will tailed him, almost out of air. Caleb pirouetted through the defense and scored. Seven-point game. Zanen wanted the boys to bring the ball up slowly, to force Manhattan Christian to foul. They only needed patience. But Will once again saw an opening at the back of the defense. Again he took off, head down, a half step ahead of everyone. From behind the baseline, Phil arched his eyebrows, pursed his mouth, and reached back. Zanen could not believe it. Phil let it fly. This time the ball moved in a low plane, hard and fast. When it smacked against Will's outstretched hands, it seemed to propel him. He planted his right foot ahead of the defender. He flung the ball upward; it floated off the backboard; his body crashed to the court, where it stayed, spasming. Zanen and Greg ran to him and pulled him off the floor. His sweat left a trail on the wood, and he smiled, because the ball had fallen through the hoop.

With fourteen seconds remaining, the game stopped. On one end of the court, most of the players stood with their hands on their hips or knees, waiting for Ty Tanner to shoot a free throw. On the far end of the floor, Phil's attention was focused elsewhere, looking for a face to match to the voice in the crowd. He had first heard it coming from the stands moments earlier, following an inbound play during which he and Caleb Bellach shoved each other: *Redskin.*

Phil stalked away from his teammates with an elastic gait, brow down, mouth small, eyes hard, and glared into the seats.

John's voice boomed through the gym: *"Phillip! Phillip! Phillip!"*

Phil never reacted to the crowd. But that word was different; it severed some internal cord. He yelled into the stands.

"Too close!" yelled John. *"You got fourteen seconds left! Fourteen seconds!"*

Lane Johnson loped across the court and put his hand on Phil, offering deep teenage wisdom. In his recollection, he said, "Who cares about them?" Phil gave a final long look and returned to the game.

Will went for a steal and committed a foul. During the free throws, Phil stepped in to box out Caleb, who stood at least three inches taller than him. Caleb could dunk; Phil could not. But when the shot bounced off the rim, Phil maintained his position, elevated, and grabbed it with one hand. He pulled it down as Caleb returned to the floor. Caleb fouled Phil and hung his head. Phil stalked to the far foul line. Greg came to slap his hand, but Phil took it and held on as though offering a gift. Then he made the free throw. The clock ran out, the buzzer sounded, Ty hurled the ball in the air, and the town of Arlee rushed the court. Zanen held his wife and wept. Then he turned to Thomas Lyles's brother and they embraced. Lane Johnson put on a vest that had belonged to his deceased uncle. David Whitesell went to Greg, worried that his son's tears were ones of relief rather than joy. Alex Moran wept for his mother, Lynette. Ivory felt something large rushing through the place, something he called "this crazy feeling of infinity." Phil turned toward the voice in the crowd, flexed his skinny arms, and roared. Then he buried his head in John's shoulder. Will wandered in a daze, a feeling of warmth flooding him. High above, in the second deck, Sophie Haynes left the confines of her wheelchair. She stood.

Part Two

―――――――

Sometimes I have to remind myself they're just seventeen.
—John Malatare

5

Keep Up

Spring 2017

A couple of weeks after the championship, I drove north from Missoula on a reporting trip. I ascended Evaro hill and timber closed in. I passed under the bridge and the land opened, revealing stunning hills. In Arlee, on the right side of the road, I saw a small wooden sign. It read:

2016–17 ARLEE

BASKETBALL

WARRIORS—

STATE CHAMPIONS!

SCARLETS—

STATE RUNNER-UP!

2015–16 FOOTBALL

STATE RUNNER-UP!

At the time I was temporarily living in Montana, a place I loved and thought I understood. I wound through Ravalli Curves, near where the Jocko River pours into the Flathead, taking all that snowmelt toward

Perma. I knew nothing about Perma; I had not yet read the great Séliš novelist Debra Magpie Earling. Up a hill, the National Bison Range emerged tawny and rolling, then the Mission Mountains rose sharp and white above St. Ignatius. Farther north, the flat wetlands of Charlo were lush and muddy. Past Ronan, then Pablo, and the Confederated Salish and Kootenai Tribes' governmental headquarters. To the east sat Salish Kootenai College; to the west, a tribally owned company that builds computer materials used for military equipment. Polson arrived in the windshield and, beyond it, the vastness of the lake. I crossed the bridge over the Flathead River, not far from the great dam, once an affront, now property of the Tribes. To the north, past million-dollar vacation homes, rose the whitecapped peaks of Glacier National Park, where in college I had pumped gas. Back then I drove out with a friend from my hometown, a New York suburb rife with contradiction. Nyack is named for an Indigenous word referencing a location on Long Island. According to the US Census, the town's Native population is 0.0 percent. During my childhood Nyackians prided themselves on diversity and liberalism and a state-champion high school football team called the Indians, with a cheer squad called, shamefully, the Indianettes. I had since left the East Coast, for Montana, New Mexico, Wyoming, and now Montana again; and still I knew nothing.

I drove to Kalispell, a rapidly growing city that is, by some accounts, named for the Q'lispé, one of the Flathead Reservation tribes. Kalispell is 93.5 percent white, a demographic that has attracted a number of far-right ideologues. While parked in a fairgrounds, I looked up the Arlee Warriors and came across a *Missoulian* story about Phil that mentioned his outlandish statistics and the presence of a coach from the University of Montana at one of his games. I later read a recruiting website where Phil had written, "I want to be the first boy in my family to go to college on a scholarship. I live on a reservation so not many kids make it out of here and go to college, I want a better life for myself once I'm out of high school."

Maybe, I thought, Phil was economically disadvantaged. Maybe he wanted to leave home and go to college, seeking migration and economic prosperity, those most American aspirations. I knew nothing. I wrote to an editor at *The New York Times Magazine* proposing an article about the team and Phil as he pursued college. I also reached out to Zanen Pitts. The coach responded with excitement. He said Phil wouldn't be available for a while, as it was horn-hunting season. (Phil, when told about my interest, had apparently said, "What the heck's *The New York Times*?") But Zanen and I began to correspond, his text messages always arriving with a signature: *ITsThePITT$*. In the first week of April we arranged to meet at the Cenex in St. Ignatius. I had been there before when I was just out of college. My job then had been to write about an Amish restaurant for the *Missoula Independent*, a weekly paper since shuttered by Lee Enterprises, the Iowa conglomerate that owns much of Montana's media. Shortly after my flattering story about the food was published, I contracted salmonella. That restaurant was now gone.

I was early, so I went into the convenience store and bought a copy of the *Lake County Leader*, adorned with a photo of Tyler Tanner. The accompanying story recounted the championship in granular detail, focusing on Zanen's decision to spread the court in the third quarter. The article said that Zanen had run into Jeff Bellach, Manhattan Christian's coach, on a scouting trip prior to the championship. According to the *Leader*, Bellach had told Zanen that, when the teams had played earlier in the season, Zanen's use of the spread offense had left Bellach bewildered. The story's implication was clear: Zanen had outmaneuvered his opponent.

Zanen arrived in cowboy boots, jeans, and a hooded sweatshirt. "There he is," he said, with a winning smile. His cheeks were ruddy, his handshake firm. Pen marks covered the back of one hand. We spoke about the championship: the parade, the victory dinner at Olive Garden—how he'd told the hostess they'd won state, and she kept the place open past regular hours. He spoke quickly, using his hands to describe specific plays, flicking his wrist or clapping and shooting one hand out as he exhaled, *"Whoooeeet!"*

He told me a story: he had traveled eight hours to scout another team prior to state and had run into Jeff Bellach, where they discussed Arlee's spread offense. I'd already read as much, but didn't say so. Zanen excused himself to hug a rodeo buddy, then returned and apologized: "You don't understand. Every day I'm still getting emails."

In advance of our meeting, Zanen had told me, "It's rez ball. We're Indians. Don't be politically correct." Now he instructed me to buy a tribal conservation permit, to allow me to travel on certain CSKT lands: "You're white. So am I." But he was technically a first-generation descendant of the Tribes—the child of an enrolled member. He said that the Flathead Allotment Act of 1904, which had enabled his great-grandfather's arrival, had "devastated the rez"; that his family was mostly German, but that his tribal affiliation was Pend d'Oreille (Q'lispé). He told me that he had served a mission in Colorado for the Church of Jesus Christ of Latter-day Saints. He had to go. He was busy with his day job, checking property lines for the Tribal Lands Department. First, though, he said, "Our boys like pressure. They get dunked on, they'll come back and wrap it around your head to try to make you look stupid."

He said that Phil was "the fastest kid in the state without question," called Will "a stone-cold killer," compared Isaac Fisher, the tall sophomore, to Dirk Nowitzki, said Greg Whitesell was a superstar in the making, and added compliments about Lane Johnson and Darshan Bolen. "They're good kids," he said. "Really good kids." He told me about his family's second-place curse that was finally broken. He wanted the glory to carry forward. Immediately following the victory, Zanen had told a reporter, "This was not for these boys, the boys said this was for everyone on the reservation and every kid around Indian

Country." Now he envisioned a billboard reading BALL IS LIFE AND LIFE IS WORTH LIVING. I had many questions, but started with an obvious one: Was Ty, who had been honored as the state tournament most valuable player, going to play in college?

"No one will recruit that kid," he said.

I asked why.

"Unless you actually coach him, you don't even know he scores thirty some nights."

He said college coaches perceived Ty's first step to be slow, that they didn't understand his strength. Zanen didn't mention the unspoken shadow that damaged the prospects of basketball players from reservations, an assumption held by some coaches that Native kids might not stay in school. I asked Zanen if he had any questions for me. He smiled and said, "Just keep up."

About a week later, I pulled into the parking lot of the Store and waited for Phil, a practice I'd soon grow accustomed to. Eventually a mud-spattered white Dodge pickup with a four-wheeler strapped to the bed pulled into the parking lot, and here he came. He walked over in muck boots, moving in a direct line with an elastic gait. "Thank you," he said. He appeared taller and stronger in person than he did in photos, where he looked perilously skinny. I introduced myself and, after a long pause, complimented his truck. Someone came by and grabbed him and asked what he was doing in town. "Can't find no horns down here!" the guy cracked. Phil's angular face turned up into a huge smile. I said I'd love to go horn hunting. In a long, slow voice, Phil said, "I can't take you horn hunting."

Someone else came by, a middle-aged man speaking quickly. He wanted to know if Phil had read the letter to the editor the man had written in the *Missoulian*. "No," said Phil.

The man said his letter had likened the boys' season to *Blind Your*

Ponies, the Stanley Gordon West novel about Montana high school basketball. The man also complained about the *Missoulian*'s coverage of the boys. In a story about the championship, a reporter had made the curious choice to emphasize the age of the team's bus. Phil stood quietly, air passing by. The man asked if Phil had taken his ACT test, one of the prerequisites to a college career.

"No," said Phil. "Not yet." The man said Phil had to take his ACT. That it was important. Then the man shared some anecdotes about his own playing days. Phil stood silent and still. After the man left, I asked what Phil was thinking about college. He said he was looking at Arizona. He'd heard it was warm there. Also, he mentioned, his girlfriend went to school there. He had to move some cows. "Thank you," he said, and was gone.

A few weeks later, I pulled into the Huckleberry Patch in Arlee. Near bags of candy and T-shirts decorated with bears, Becky Malatare met me with a warm smile, her hair pulled back. Phil's mother spoke about all the courts in town, her cadence quick and digressive. John Malatare's manner was more laconic. He sat at a table, intensely playing a board game, his jaw rotating. I introduced myself and made small talk, saying I'd seen a little grizzly bear recently in Arlee. John chuckled. "It's a black bear. It's a cinnamon black bear. He hibernated in a culvert that run underneath the highway. We had so much moisture it flooded him out. He lives just up the road, really near Will Mesteth." I asked about all the travel that basketball must necessitate. "Oh, we never miss a game," John said. "Never miss a game."

The Malatares were clearly both wary of and excited by the attention on their son. Becky mentioned that she'd heard from three Division I colleges. "My daughter and I went to Costco," she said, "and the guy looked at my Costco card. He goes, 'Malatare. Phillip, is that yours?'

I said, 'Yeah.' He holds up the card, says, 'This is Phillip Malatare's mom and sister!'" She told me about the rumors in town about Phil transferring in pursuit of what Becky called "the big ticket." John said, "He doesn't need to go anywhere to get recognized." But, John added, "He's seventeen years old, just going with the moment right now, and it really hasn't sunk into him that he has an opportunity to go to do real super stuff."

When I asked about the team's prospects for the coming season, John stated, "We'll be back at state." But when I asked if they'd be favored to win, he looked a little weary. He said that was unfortunately the case. When I asked about Zanen's coaching style, Becky said the boys liked his energy. John said, "Rather not comment." Something made him uncomfortable. He asked me, "My question really is, what is this story truly really all about?" He said, "It happened all about the time we were having some major suicide going on. And we're still continuing to have major suicide." John said, "We made it a lot about giving some relief to these families who had lost people in these suicides, these tragedies. And we kind of took away from those boys, by putting all that publicity on how much of a relief they were for the grieving families. And I don't know if we really let those boys celebrate what they had just accomplished. Because it was about those boys. It wasn't about Zanen Pitts, it wasn't about the Flathead Reservation. It was about these boys from Arlee."

Over the coming years, when I got lost, when any concrete sense of time eluded me, or when I wondered what I was doing here, I came back to that: it was about these boys from Arlee. As people throughout Montana and the country asked the impossible of the Arlee Warriors, seeking bold-font answers where few existed, looking for some clean, bright redemption, John's words returned. It was about these boys from Arlee. What they had done and what they would choose.

During that first meeting, John said, "They're kids." And for the moment, that was true.

The Pitts branding was scheduled for the middle of April, and the coach recruited just about all the boys to help him. On the morning of the event, a half-moon hung above the mountains at Ninemile. In the predawn, Zanen loaded up boxes of ear tags and pour-on applicators, a dart gun, and an electric brand. He hustled in and out of the barn at his parents' ranch in Dixon, a town named for the legislator who helped open the Flathead Indian Reservation to homesteaders. The house was set on Zanen's grandfather's old calving grounds, which had for years served as a base for the Pittses' expansive cattle operation. The barn was old and warm, smelling of hay and animal breath, with ropes, saddles, and bridles hanging along one wall. Outside, Zanen loaded up a Chevy pickup with dual tires and a custom hydraulic bed. An eagle feather hung from the rearview mirror. Zanen started the engine as a cattle dog named Koda jumped onto the bed. As Zanen pulled out, past the river, the truck produced a great creaking sound. "Dang it," said Zanen, "that's the belt for this HydraBed. Gotta get that figured out." He pulled across the railroad tracks and drove west, toward Perma. He sometimes said he had only four goals in life. Three he had now accomplished: winning the tie-down roping at Crow Fair, as his father had done; breaking the Pitts curse by winning state; and marrying Kendra Wabaunsee. He pointed to the shadow of a mountain silhouetted black against the lightening sky. "In that peak there in the snow that's disappearing in the clouds, that's where I asked her to marry me."

A little farther on, and he nodded to the south and a high meadow full of bunchgrass, land that once belonged to his grandfather. He didn't like to think about it and couldn't stop himself from doing so. "See all that grass? See that cow pie? That was me. Now they got it all." This was the fourth item on his list: Zanen wanted a ranch. Like some who came before him, he sought both land and influence. His great-grandfather was named Virgil Lee Pitts, a white man from Missouri who ran away from home and moved to the Flathead Indian Reservation as a teenager, around the time of its opening to homesteaders. He trapped on the Jocko River and married a tribal member named Geneva Houle. The partnership didn't last and Virgil raised their children, including Zanen's grandfather Eugene, who was enrolled in the Tribes and received a land allotment as a boy.

Since the early twentieth century, the Confederated Salish and Kootenai Tribes have, like many tribal nations, defined their enrolled membership by using blood quantum, a specious colonial concept. For centuries blood quantum had been used to preserve the property and power of those with light skin, and it followed the settlers overseas. In colonial states, tribal ancestry was seen as a taint on white settlers; in eighteenth-century North Carolina, those with "mixed blood" were prohibited from testifying in court.

That wasn't how the tribes traditionally handled matters of kinship and belonging. According to Thompson Smith, coordinator of history and ethnogeography projects for the Sélis-Q'lispé Culture Committee, both oral histories and the written record show that, during the nineteenth century, the Séliš nation included people who were in part of Nez Perce, Iroquois, Delaware, Shawnee, French, and German descent. But blood quantum accompanied the fur trade out West, and it was used in conjunction with land allotment to destroy tribal lifestyles. In 1893, the federal government created a commission to break up the land mass of tribes that had been removed to Indian Territory, which would later become Oklahoma. The Dawes Commission used blood quantum to define who was and was not Cherokee, Choctaw, Chickasaw, Creek, and Seminole. Those determinations were often based on appearance. "The Dawes rolls were based on blood, but only on how blood 'looked'," wrote the Ojibwe author David Treuer in *Rez Life*.

"From the beginning, the rolls were flawed and were designed to cheat Indians."

Blood quantum was a means of reducing the number of recognized Indigenous people on land that settlers craved. In some parts of the West, "mixed-blood" Natives could sell allotted land, while "full bloods" were permitted to do so only should the secretary of interior deem the sale "for the benefit of the respective Indians." Despite its ever-changing and opaque nature, blood quantum became widely accepted as a method for determining tribal membership following the passage of the 1934 Indian Reorganization Act. A card identifying a person's quantity of "Indian blood" was then, as it remains today, a requirement for many tribes. In 1960 the Confederated Salish and Kootenai Tribes updated its constitution, requiring that new members have one-quarter combined Séliš, Q'lispé, or Kootenai blood to qualify for enrollment. Blood quantum's math is grim. But in the twentieth century, the Tribes needed a means of protecting natural and cultural resources. "They had to adopt their conquerors' idea of what an 'Indian' is," wrote the scholar Ronald Trosper, a member of the Confederated Salish and Kootenai Tribes.

Eugene Pitts was identified as "Indian" on his draft card and "white" in other military records. He led an adventurous life: running track for the University of Wisconsin, fighting fires as a smokejumper, and serving in World War II with the US Navy as a fighter pilot. According to an account he once gave, he survived amid circling sharks after being shot down in the South Pacific. After returning home he opened a saw-mill that employed many tribal members. He was known as generous and a good boss. He also owned and leased a great deal of land, which his tribal membership helped him acquire. In Zanen's words, he had a "little empire."

But generations and familial strife had winnowed it. Zanen had hoped to one day buy his grandparents' ranch near his parents' place, but an uncle who was the estate's executor sold the property to someone else. Zanen's parents now owned approximately twenty acres near the Flathead River as well as an eighty-acre allotment on Camas Prairie, on the reservation's west side. Some of the land was trust ground, meaning the US government controlled the deed for the Confederated Salish and Kootenai Tribes and its members. Terry, Zanen's father, could pass that land down to documented descendants for two generations, after which ownership would revert to the Tribes. Furthermore, much of the Pittses' ranching operation depended on lands that the Tribes leased out to members. Terry was enrolled and had served on Tribal Council. But in accordance with the 1960 constitution, his sons were not enrolled. Zanen was in a complex historical bind: to carry on the legacy that meant so much to him, he had to compete with the influx of Hollywood stars and captains of fracking buying up pieces of the so-called Last Best Place. "It's the hands we were dealt," he once said, "so no point complaining about it. Just figure it out." He and Kendra lived in the downstairs of her parents' home and checked real estate listings constantly. He could not drive by his grandfather's old ranch without feeling a pang. He said, "I don't hold a grudge. But that one I do."

Soon we passed the place where, the previous year, he had broken his leg when his horse rolled on him. A couple more miles, and he told me the story of the other time he broke a leg, when he was training for the Indian National Finals Rodeo. During a dismount, his rope had bounced and caught on his boot. By the time Zanen realized his foot was trapped, his horse had already turned around. Caught underneath, he was kicked for two minutes straight. "My strength and my weakness is I'm not very patient," he said.

Zanen drove through a gate and up a steep two-track. We arrived at the branding site, a high meadow under the timberline with an old wooden corral. About ninety cows and calves stood within a temporary fence line Zanen had constructed. A small creek flowed out of the woods through the pasture, fast with snowmelt and bordered by aspen and willow. Far down below, the Flathead River folded around islands and reflected low clouds. Zanen finished banging in some posts and the sun rose. Kendra arrived in a diesel truck pulling a black trailer stenciled with the words PITTS QUARTER HORSES. She wore a hoodie and bejeweled jeans, and had brought a grill and burger fixings. The mountainside filled with pickups, some of which carried the Warriors: Lane Schall in a state-championship hoodie and Greg Whitesell in a Carhartt vest. Ivory Brien rode a horse, as did his father, Aaron, the instructor at Salish Kootenai College and a member of the Apsáalooke (Crow Tribe). Zanen wore a white straw hat and rode a palomino named Cowboy. When he was a boy, Gene Pitts had used a calf table for branding. But after Gene passed, the Pitts branding evolved into a different kind of event, with men on horseback roping calves. "He's turned it into his dream," said Zanen's mother.

First, the men separated the cows from the calves. Then Zanen whacked cows, pushing them through the chute. At the headgate the cattle received shots and pour-on parasiticide. One cow had a nasty boil on her mouth. Zanen suspected she'd eaten cheatgrass, an invasive species he loathed. He sometimes checked his boots to make sure he didn't spread those seeds.

More pickups rolled in, bearing more families. The calves were sent one by one into the fenced corral, where men on horseback roped them and the boys wrestled them to the ground. Then others ran in, giving the calves three shots, applying a pour-on dewormer, and branding them. Once the calves received an ear tag with a number, they were free to go. Ivory, a thoughtful and sensitive kid, was either tentative, early, or gentle with one calf, and it got up. Zanen wrestled it to the ground and stood on its neck. It quivered when the brand hit. Lane Schall grabbed the next one, his blond hair flopping. He was neither tentative nor gentle.

Zanen yelled, "Why can't you rebound like that?"

At lunch, the kids moved toward the burgers. Greg hung by Lane. The two had been close friends ever since Greg moved from Polson in junior high. He hated when people reminded him that he was "not from Arlee." But Lane Schall was welcoming, a joker who brushed by negativity. Lane often invited the boys to his family's ranch, to eat steak or sit in the hot tub. Now Ivory joined them by the burger fixings. He was preparing to head to the University of Montana to study wildlife biology. The three boys started to talk about other teams in the area. They liked the players on Hot Springs and also St. Ignatius, the Class B school everyone called Mission. "Full of good people," said Ivory. Charlo was a different matter.

"They're the white team," said Lane Schall, who was white. "It'd be different if they weren't so arrogant and rude."

Greg just rolled his eyes. "It's the stereotype of jocks." A few years earlier, Greg's father, the superintendent, had told some Charlo fans to stop performing the tomahawk chop at an Arlee volleyball game.

Lane shook his head. "There's nothing to say to 'em."

They started to talk about state, the unbelievable sound of the gym. Ivory talked about the nerves he could not control. Greg remembered the end of the game, when Phil took his hand, before the clinching free throw. "He said, 'State champs, baby,'" Greg recalled. "That's burned into my brain."

The boys had heard rumors that some ballplayers wanted to transfer to Arlee to chase a ring.

"We got our eyes on who we want," said Greg. "Good role players."

"If I was them, I'd be transferring," said Ivory. "I'd be working."

Zanen hollered, "Okay, let's get it done!" and the boys were up after the next calves. Terry Pitts showed up, taking photos and recounting the championship in a discursive manner. The key, he said, was when Zanen had spread the floor. That was to rest his players, Terry said, and also to mess with Manhattan Christian. "The coach panicked," he said.

"He went to man-to-man and started the fourth quarter, and that's why we win the game."

A figure in a Chicago Bulls cap appeared on the hillside, zooming down from the timberline on a four-wheeler. Everyone started to laugh and holler, *"Will!"* He had come from Ravalli on dirt roads and two-tracks.

"Will's Will," said Greg.

"Just give him the ball," said Terry. He had told his barber that Will was the secret, the final ingredient: "They don't know about Will." The boys tore off, their laughter ringing over the whine of the engine, and soon Ty arrived, too. But one kid was conspicuously absent.

6

Never Do It for Yourself

April–May 2017

That weekend, somewhere outside Seattle, Phil stole the ball and took off, leaving everything in his wake. He sprinted down the court, his coach screaming for him to stop. That didn't happen. He stopped midsprint and feinted the ball up. A defender flew by and Phil calmly made the layup, sealing the game.

Phil missed branding to play with a team in the Amateur Athletic Union called the Idaho Select. In a series of spring and summer tournaments, the AAU offers a showcase for prospects, where college coaches examine kids' speed, height, and explosiveness. Parents fork over thousands of dollars in hopes that a child might be deemed suitable for the for-profit business that is Division I basketball. Phil had never played AAU before. He liked to fish in the summers. The Malatares were a two-income family, but they also had five kids to support. This year, though, they thought AAU might be worth the effort. When Phil found some nice antlers he sold them, making about $3,000, enough for his AAU fees and travel.

John and Becky couldn't make it to Seattle that weekend, so Phil's older sisters, Whitney and Morgan, accompanied him. Whitney wanted seafood from Pike Place Market. But Phil wanted a quesadilla from a chain found in Montana, so they went there. On the court, Morgan thought everyone was trying to show off, and the games took on an individualized flavor. It took Phil a minute to get comfortable. But on one play he drove, stopped short, and performed a crossover dribble. His defender slid across the court. On another occasion, an opponent said to Phil, in his recollection, that "Indians don't do nuthin'." So Phil provided evidence to the contrary. His sisters couldn't help but notice that whenever Phil made his signature spins or whipped around-the-back passes, he got in trouble with the coach, a man named Clint Hordemann. It was as though Phillip was being asked to transform. Phil turned the ball over a couple of times, and Hordemann put him on the bench. Even so, during the tournament, a number of colleges in Oregon and Washington reached out to Hordemann about Phil. They had no idea who he was. "He was completely off the grid," said Hordemann, "which was unique for a player of his caliber."

What most astounded the coach was Phil's endurance—the way he defended full out all game. "He never gets tired," said Hordemann. "I don't know how he does it. He doesn't pace himself really." On defense, the coach said, "It's not like he's picking up at the three-point line. He's covering the whole court." It was almost as though he were playing a different game.

Shortly before the turn of the twentieth century, a young Blackfeet teacher named Josephine Langley moved home to Montana from the Carlisle Indian School in Pennsylvania. Her destination was a new boarding school set at an abandoned military fort on the plains east of the Rocky Mountains. Around 1896, at the Fort Shaw Industrial Indian Boarding School, Langley started teaching basketball to Native girls from Montana and Idaho. The sport was young then, at least in Western eyes—James Naismith had been credited with its creation in Massachusetts in 1891. But scholars have noted basketball's similarity to games played by Indigenous peoples in Mesoamerica, and tribes from the high plains and Northwest plateau had their own sports involving balls and hoops. Maybe the game was familiar; maybe the court was just a rare place where traumatized kids could be kids at a time when boarding schools took extreme measures to "civilize" Indigenous youth.

The Indian boarding-school era was brutal, designed to forcibly assimilate Native youth through the extirpation of language and culture. Songs were forbidden, hair cut. Richard Pratt, the founder of the Carlisle School, described his plan as to "kill the Indian in him, save the man." Forced integration into American society was his goal, and most boarding schools followed Carlisle's lead.

But when it came to basketball, the Fort Shaw girls did not assimilate, beating college teams in Montana. Langley was a player-coach during the team's early years, and Fred C. Campbell, Fort Shaw's superintendent, eventually coached the team. The girls proved so successful that they were invited to the 1904 World's Fair in St. Louis, where their duties extended beyond the court. In front of white crowds the girls played violins to illustrate the efficacy of Fort Shaw's reeducation programs and recited passages from Longfellow's *The Song of Hiawatha* while wearing buckskin. Linda Peavy and Ursula Smith, the authors of *Full-Court Quest*, a book about the team, wrote that they were "objects on display and full participants in a grand adventure." Peavy told me that, from interviews with the girls' descendants, she understood the players to be savvy about those performances. "It wasn't that they were always happy with how things were going at the school," she said. "What they did was turn adversity into opportunity." The girls furthered a complicated tradition of living Native theater that was widely known from the painter George Catlin's fundraising tours of Europe and Buffalo Bill Cody's Wild West shows. The latter events featured defeated chiefs and warriors, performances that demanded the reduction and romanticization of a lifestyle for the entertainment of those bent on its elimination. But over time, the form evolved. "As the nineteenth and twentieth centuries unfolded," wrote Philip J. Deloria, a citizen of the Standing Rock Sioux Tribe, in *Playing Indian*, "increasing numbers of Indians participated in white people's Indian play, assisting, confirming, co-opting, challenging, and legitimating the performative tradition of aboriginal American identity."

On the court, the Fort Shaw girls set their own terms of engagement, playing with such dominance that they were proclaimed world champions. Around the same time, other Native teams took the court in Lawrence, Kansas, in Oregon, and across Montana—especially in the plains. Their game was noted even then for its quick pace and long shots, according to Wade Davies, author of *Native Hoops: The Rise of American Indian Basketball, 1895–1970*.

Montana is home to twelve individual nations, comprising eight federally recognized tribes. Seven of these federally recognized tribes are seated on large reservations. (The Little Shell Tribe of Chippewa Indians does not have a land base.) For much of the twentieth century, those nations' citizens were overrepresented in the state's prisons and poverty indexes; they were underrepresented in its universities, media, and halls of political power. Montana is 89 percent white. But on the court, none of that mattered. For thirty-two minutes, kids who possessed enough skill and effort could flip colonial hegemony on its head. In 1934 and 1935, Poplar, a team from the Fort Peck Indian Reservation, won back-to-back high school state championships. Another Fort Peck team, Wolf Point, won four titles between 1941 and 1953. In 1957 a Crow star named Larry Pretty Weasel averaged 32 points in a state tournament. He turned down universities like Utah to attend Rocky Mountain College, in Billings, but left early. Willie Weeks, from Wolf Point, averaged 18 points per game in two seasons at Montana State. He would later write, "Alcohol and drugs, however, cut my career short as, after several knee operations, I sought relief and false escape."

In 1967, Don Wetzel, a Blackfeet guard and graduate of Cut Bank High School, enrolled at the University of Montana, where he would play four years of Division I basketball. When he was on the freshman team, he snuck into a varsity scrimmage against the orders of his coach and, in his words, "kind of lit 'em up." That was the first time he heard one particularly vicious racial slur starting with the word *prairie.* "I took it as a compliment," he said. "I was so focused." He outworked teammates, playing through injuries, and won the team's MVP award. He went on to coach at Browning, on the Blackfeet Reservation. During the American Indian Movement, Wetzel's team took the court in war bonnets, in a show of performative defiance.

The state awards four championship trophies per year to both boys and girls. The Class AA schools come from the cities—Missoula, Bozeman, Kalispell, Billings. The smaller divisions—A, B, and C—consist largely of teams from ranching and mining towns and Indian Country. Between 1980 and 1990, boys' teams from reservations won eight championships and finished in second place six times. In a state with a reported Native American population between 5 and 7 percent, reservation teams comprised 18 percent of those competing for boys' state championships. Throughout the eighties, one team reigned above the rest: Lodge Grass from Crow Nation. With a fast-breaking style that thrilled crowds and left opponents gasping for breath, Lodge Grass dominated Class B and just about anyone who dared play them. Their star was Elvis Old Bull, a clutch guard who could shoot, defend, and pass. He won three consecutive state tournament MVP awards. When he entered gyms, announcers boomed that Elvis was in the building.

In 1991, Gary Smith wrote about Old Bull and the Hardin star Jonathan Takes Enemy for *Sports Illustrated.* The piece, "Shadow of a Nation," examined the players' generational talent, struggles with alcohol, and the apparent limits that had been set—by history, hegemony, or both—on Native ballplayers in Montana. Smith quoted Herb Klindt, the former coach of Rocky Mountain College, in an unvarnished moment. "Well, I tried to work with Indians," said Klindt, who in 1968 left one position of power for another, as a state senator. "I tried to keep them in college. But I got to a point where I just threw up my hands in disgust and gave up, and most of the other coaches did, too."

Since then, young Indigenous women have made significant inroads in the state's Division I basketball programs. In 1992, Malia Kipp (Blackfeet) entered the University of Montana, starring for the Lady Grizzlies. "I felt if I didn't succeed," she once said, "others wouldn't get the opportunity." She played all four years and graduated. Afterward the Lady Griz's coach, Robin Selvig, recruited extensively on reservations. Over the next two decades he signed nine Native players on athletic scholarships. Those teams made ten NCAA tournaments.

But for Indigenous men in the state, progress was slower. In the 1990s, JR Camel, from the Flathead Reservation, starred for the Griz, setting a steals record; he and Kipp later married. In 1999, Pete Conway, a Blackfeet guard, joined the Montana State University Bobcats. He publicly suggested he might leave the team after his coach, Mick Durham, said to *The New York Times*, in 2001, "Have you ever been on a reservation? There's hardly any green grass. They park right in front of their front door. That's always amazed me. There's no self-pride in having a nice house and taking care of it. They don't care if they have five cars broken down, sitting in the yard." Durham subsequently apologized and suggested his quotes were taken out of context, saying "a very narrow portion of that conversation made it into print." Conway stuck it out and averaged more than 14 points in his senior year. A few years later, Mike Chavez (Northern Cheyenne/Crow), a stunning talent who attended high school on the Blackfeet Reservation, signed with the University of Montana. During his freshman year, in 2003, he was arrested for driving under the influence of alcohol. He left school under intense scrutiny. Then he returned, played two more years, competed in the NCAA tournament, and went on to play professional basketball after being drafted by Justin Wetzel, a Blackfeet coach. Of Chavez, David Whitesell told me, "He fixed it, came back, and graduated." Since then, no Montana tribal members have played on basketball scholarships at the state's Division I men's programs.

At a lower level in the state's athletic hierarchy sit Montana State University Billings, a Division II school, and six programs that compete in the Frontier Conference of the National Association of Intercollegiate Athletics, or NAIA. In 2017–18, those seven schools' men's basketball programs' rosters listed twenty coaches, recruiting coordinators, operations managers, and graduate assistants. Not one hailed from a reservation. "It's a good old boy industry," said one Native coach, who left the state to pursue his ambitions. "People aren't going to usually relinquish that." Absent diversity, stigma lingered. Zanen said that, during one player's recruitment, three coaches asked if the boy was tribal, implying a concern he might not stay in school. "Those coaches need to do a better job of sustaining them," Zanen said. "They need to understand what they're coaching."

Don Wetzel, the former Griz star, was tired of hearing the same story, ad nauseam, about Native boys going home. In 2007, Wetzel and his son, Don Wetzel Jr., an educator and athlete who goes by Donnie, cofounded the Montana Indian Athletic Hall of Fame, partly to correct a record they saw as deeply flawed. Donnie Wetzel, an Amskapi Pikuni (Blackfeet) first descendant, was now the American Indian Youth Development Coordinator for the state's Office of Public Instruction. Out of high school he had been recruited to Montana State University Billings, but left after having a child. He also found the basketball challenging, its own unspoken form of assimilation. The stands were empty, and on the court the game was less fluid and connective, instead an ordered sequence of plays, many of them isolations. Donnie Wetzel said, "You're not taught to be like that." He added, "It's conformity." One coach told Donnie he'd been 0 for 12 in recruiting and retaining Native boys. Whose fault, Donnie wondered, was that? How did leaving a system built for and by others constitute failure? "People from outside Indian Country," he said, "they think that everybody needs to chase their ideals." Around 2010, seven tribal colleges—Salish Kootenai included—started a basketball league, giving athletes an option that didn't involve so much culture shock. But sometimes those programs didn't have enough players to field teams, and Donnie sought larger change. He noted that some state universities have improved recruitment and retention of Indigenous students; he wanted to see that happen on the basketball court. He imagined programs hiring tribal coaches, establishing thoughtful support systems for Indigenous student-athletes, and recruiting multiple kids at once: "I've always said if you're recruiting Native players recruit two at a time."

His father pointed out that roads run both to and from reservations. "We're always talking about the way out," said Don Wetzel Sr. Coaches, he said, "gotta get out to the rezzes. You gotta feel that, what goes on there." Wetzel Jr. envisioned a kid like Phil taking college teammates home, to show them the richness of the place. Lacking substantive institutional change, it fell to individuals who had to get out and, it was so often framed, make it—whatever that meant. "I wonder if it gets in our children's heads that 'If I don't make it,'" Donnie said, "'I'm just another one of *these*.'"

Zanen prayed.

Our most kind and gracious Father in heaven,
*Our Creator, K*ʷ*lncutn,*
We are very grateful for this opportunity

To gather together as a family and as a community
And to take an opportunity to rejoice
In all the great moments that we've had throughout our lives.
We ask your blessing, Father,
For all those that are traveling
That they may travel here safely.
Please bless the hands that prepared the meal
And the animals that gave their lives so that we can partake.
Bless our loved ones, and we say so in Jesus Christ's name, amen.

It was a month after branding. The boys' and girls' teams had gathered for an awards ceremony in Arlee's old gym, the one with the low ceiling and a curtained stage behind a basket. About 150 people attended, and everything smelled wonderful. At the front of the room were a taco bar and two cakes. Phil and Ty sat together in the bleachers. In the previous weeks, Ty had finally received three college offers. One was a partial scholarship at Rocky Mountain College, in Billings, whose coach, Bill Dreikosen, had a good reputation in Montana for recruiting tribal players. Ty said he also had a similar offer at Montana State University–Northern, in Havre, and a scholarship at Dawson Community College, a two-year school by the North Dakota border that competes in the National Junior College Athletic Association. He wanted to study agriculture business, as he planned to work his parents' ranch after school. He came off as pragmatic and measured. Unlike his best friend, Phil, he planned into the future. Still, he didn't know what to do. At Rocky, Ty's offer was to join the junior varsity, and the school was private, with tuition, room, and board fees approaching $40,000 per year. The scholarship would not cover all that. Northern also offered a partial scholarship, but it was cold as anything in Havre, and money was an issue there, too. Ty was a Séliš descendant, not an enrolled tribal member, and did not meet the blood-quantum requirements to qualify for the tuition-fee waivers available at Montana's public universities. Dawson offered a scholarship covering his tuition and books. But it was way out east where it was flat as a court. "It's been kinda stressful," he said.

By his side, Phil wore a stony expression and, on his right foot, a walking boot. "Just my Achilles," he explained, as though it were nothing. He turned to Ty. "Hey, you wanna go hop in line?" They moved toward the tacos, Phil clanking around.

During the AAU tournament in Seattle, Phil's sisters had noticed that he wasn't moving right. He'd tweaked his ankle during the playoffs and had a pain at the back of his right foot, some strange burr. The weekend after Seattle, John and Becky had flown with Phil to Las Vegas for another AAU series. He stole the ball on successive possessions at the end of one game and played well enough that Vanguard University in California offered him a scholarship, just like that. Three years earlier, the school had won the NAIA national championship. Phil was polite, but California sounded pretty far from the Mission Mountains. Besides, Phil's ambitions exceeded the NAIA. But the deep pull he felt toward Montana left him with precisely two paths to reconcile his Division I dreams: the Griz and the Montana State University Bobcats. He said, "It's just nice being near home."

After the game, his ankle hurt so much that he couldn't walk. When the Malatares returned to Montana, they took him for an X-ray. According to Becky, the doctor said Phil had injured his posterior tibial tendon, which runs from the calf to the inner ankle. But Becky wasn't sure. The X-ray also revealed a hook on the back of his heel that could have been a bone spur, or some buildup from all that stopping and spinning. "They were kind of worried about an Achilles tear there, too," Becky said. "They're not sure what exactly it is." An Achilles injury is not a minor matter; an Achilles injury can mean a different relationship with sport. Becky wondered if Phil might need surgery. If so, she wanted to do it sooner than later. For the moment, she said, "We'll leave him in the boot. Without complete rest it won't heal."

She walked around the gym, trying to get the kids to autograph posters. Greg sat with Dar and Lane Johnson, the Séliš ranch kid. The Fisher boys, Isaac and his little brother, Billy, stuck together. Isaac was now six foot eight, and had the build of a fence pole. "He don't have a lot to pack," said his auntie, Roberta Lafley. Billy was about six feet tall, with spiky hair and a huge smile. First descendants of the Tribes, the boys were always together, under the careful supervision of Roberta and her partner, Les Fisher, their uncle. Roberta was mostly known by her nickname, Inj. She worked for the Tribes, caring for the elderly, while Les cut wood and played basketball and raised the kids. Isaac had grown up with a love for skating, but both boys had taken up basketball with Les as their coach. They spent many days at Missoula's outdoor courts, working on Isaac's dunks. "We go Lob City!" Isaac said.

Will walked around with a crooked pinkie. The Warriors' assistant coach, Francis Brown LoneBear—known as Franny—pointed it out. Franny was a large, warm single father who was enrolled in the Northern Arapaho Tribe and was a Séliš first descendant. He cooked for Nkʷusm, the Séliš language school, by day. "He broke his pinkie again," he said to Zanen.

"How'd you do that?" Zanen asked.

Will mumbled something inaudible.

"You tell him you went off?" Franny asked.

"Nah."

"He went off," said Franny, describing Will's performance at a recent tournament in Idaho.

"He don't talk to me anymore," Zanen said. "Once he got his title and his recognition, only person that texted me is his mom trying to figure out where he is." Zanen smiled. "Went off, huh?"

Will didn't say anything.

Franny boomed, "Probably had forty-something! Threes every-where!"

After everyone ate, Zanen announced that a suicide prevention pro-gram called Reason to Live Native had supported the awards banquet. "They're going to start trying to be a part of all the community activities," Zanen said. "Not just athletics. But also academics." The suicide cluster had not abated, but had spread widely among youth. Shortly before the awards banquet, a relative of Will's who played for the Two Eagle River School, in Pablo, died by suicide. In the shadows, other attempts fol-lowed. Among young people, suicides often come in waves, as happened in 2013 and 2014, in the Gila River Indian Community in Arizona; and in 2015, on the Pine Ridge Indian Reservation in South Dakota. In 2014, according to the Centers for Disease Control, Native women between the ages of fifteen and twenty-four died by suicide at a rate of 15.6 deaths per 100,000 people, or three times the rate of white women and five times the rate of Black women of the same age. Young Native men had a rate of 38.2 deaths per 100,000 people.

But the shattering data can only say so much. That spring, across the reservation, kids and adults made attempts on their life. The com-munity reeled, trying to survive and heal even as the fallout continued, and the Tribes responded by increasing wellness outreach among young people. Zanen said, "We just want to have them more involved, so ev-eryone knows that there are people that are willing to listen, especially family, and that we all go through struggles."

He turned to the boys. He said the team had two mottoes: "Never do it for yourself" and "Ride each other's waves." He said the coaches couldn't decide who deserved the Sixth Man of the Year award, so they split it between Ivory and Lane Johnson. Of Ivory, Zanen said, "It's hard to be able to find words for when a kid accepts his role, he knows exactly what it is, and he's totally positive." He touted Lane for hitting a clutch three-pointer in the championship, then talked about Greg shelving his ego: "It gave me goose bumps thinking about what you did for the team." Zanen apologized for carrying on—"I can sit here and talk about 'em all night long"—then carried on some more, about Dar, Isaac, Will, Alex, Phil, and Tyler. "This title," Zanen said, "would not happen without all sixteen boys." The kids stepped forward to receive their rings. Phil kissed his. Someone cued up a highlight video. It showed boys laughing, joking, having fun—all except Phil, who just destroyed opponents with a hard expression. I asked what it was like to watch it.

"Sucks," Phil said.

Why?

"'Cause it's over."

7

Almost Exactly the Same

June 2017

O n a practice court at the University of Montana's Dahlberg Arena, tall Canadian boys moved briskly through layup lines. They had come to Missoula for an event everyone called Griz camp. Every June, the University of Montana basketball program holds a showcase during which high school teams from around the Pacific Northwest and Canada pay a fee to compete in front of Griz players and coaches. For the Griz, it's a recruiting tool. For the high schoolers, it's a taste of what could be.

The Canadians looked down to the far side of the court and found it empty. They seemed puzzled. Twenty minutes remained before game time; then fifteen. Still no opponent appeared. With just a few minutes remaining before tip-off, Lane Johnson and Isaac Fisher and two freshmen rolled in and flung up a couple of shots. Greg walked in and tied his shoes. Then Phil entered, hair plastered down on his forehead. He had taken his walking boot off well in advance of the six-week mark recommended by the doctor, explaining, "I think it's pretty good."

Zanen was tied up with a summer job teaching horsemanship to youth at a camp back on the reservation, so Franny Brown, the assistant coach, was in charge. One of the Arlee boys pointed out that only six players were present. "If Will gets here, be seven," Franny said. "You can only play five at a time anyway." Will strolled in and eased onto the bench. "Here's where we get people overconfident," Franny said. "Look like a buncha jokers." He flashed his big smile and his state championship ring. Then Travis DeCuire entered the gym. In the hierarchy of basketball in Montana, DeCuire, as the head coach of the Grizzlies, sat at the top. The first Black head coach in the program's history, he had grown up in Seattle and starred for the Griz at point guard—Phil's position. He was hired by his alma mater in 2014 at a difficult time for the athletic department: multiple sexual assault cases involving football players had made national news and contributed to an eight-year span of plummeting enrollment. DeCuire's program was a needed bright spot. He talked about character, respect, and competing through adversity. He also wanted to win. "I'm trying to make my stamp with recruiting," he once said. "I want to put more talent on the floor than anyone has ever done at the University of Montana."

In his first season, in 2014–2015, the Griz were picked to finish in the middle of the Big Sky Conference, but advanced to its championship game. In his second year they repeated that performance. Just one of DeCuire's first eight recruits came from Montana. The coach did, however, eventually make room for two walk-on in-state players with ties to the program: a Billings West graduate whose father starred for the Griz, and Zachary Camel Jr., the son of the coach at Salish Kootenai College and a nephew of JR Camel, the Griz star. "To me it was bringing family to be part of what we were building," DeCuire said. In high school, Zack competed at Polson for three years and Arlee for one, where he played for his uncle JR, who was then the head coach. The team came in third that year and Zack received all-state recognition, averaging 12 points and 10.5 assists per game. After two years at Salish Kootenai College, where he played for his father, he transferred to the Griz. He expressed an interest in one day coaching and transitioned into a managerial role, hoping to eventually lead a Division I program.

During Arlee's game, DeCuire took a seat in the corner. I introduced myself, and he made it clear that he could not speak about specific players, given the National Collegiate Athletic Association's rules. But his eyes seemed trained in one place. DeCuire said Griz camp was designed in part so that he could evaluate local talent: "The state's so big, and these kids are so spread out, that you don't get to see them all." He characterized Montana's level of high school play as "not great." DeCuire continued, "It's hard to evaluate a kid for if he's a college player if he's never playing against anyone."

Out on the court, Arlee had taken a commanding lead, the opposing coach calling time-out with a bewildered look on his face. If DeCuire was impressed, he did not let on. "You find that, with some of the Montana kids, that you can dominate and be one of the top players in the state and play as a part-time job," he said. "But when you get to Division I basketball, these kids, it's been a full-time job for their entire life." DeCuire noted that many Montana kids didn't play AAU ball. Within Arlee his assessment was correct. Ty had never played, since he worked the ranch during summers. Phil hadn't either prior to his brief foray with the Idaho Select. Only Greg had regularly participated, in Las Vegas. It was fun except when kids asked if he lived in a tepee and rode a horse to school. "You can't get away from it," he said.

In recent years, the AAU circuit has come under increased scrutiny as it's been revealed that top players and coaches have received improper benefits. Jeff Bellach, Manhattan Christian's coach, also pointed out that a concentration of urban tournaments can put rural players at a disadvantage. Ranch kids have to work, whether they're from Arlee or Churchill. That's before you consider the impacts— both physical and emotional—of such specialization on sixteen-year-olds. "Too much of anything is probably not great," said Bill Dreikosen, the coach of Rocky Mountain College. "I like kids to still be able to be kids."

But DeCuire occupied a more ruthless stratosphere. In Division I, basketball is business, and too much time spent ruminating about the essence of sport means someone else is eating your lunch. In his program, he said, six to eight hours a day were taken up by "class, weight room, study hall, practice, individual work, and then time on your own. And if you don't put that type of time in, there's just no way you can succeed." He added, "The biggest thing for us is just trying to find guys that actually live basketball more so than love it. They need to love it, too. But it's more important to be able to live it. You can love it and be able to play and want to go out and have fun. But if you're not willing to live it, you're not going to be successful."

Once, I asked Big Will what he thought that word—*success*—meant. He said that, to him, it was having a job that helped his community—making home better. He also said he knew once-great athletes who slid by in life thanks to fading adolescent achievement. "It goes away," he said. "Sometimes they just don't get over that hype. That's it. They expect life to be that easy and that hyped up for them for the rest of their lives and then pretty soon reality hits and nobody gives a shit." John Malatare's version of success was also simple: "a family and a job."

On the court, Phil threw an around-the-back pass, and Arlee scored, widening the lead to 39–18. DeCuire asked, "How many of these kids you think when they're done with this game are going to go home and watch the NBA Finals tonight? Probably none of them." DeCuire had one question about recruits: "What are their habits?" He asked, At 5:00 P.M., "what do you do? Do you play Xbox? Do you get on Twitter? Or do you grab your ball? The guy that grabs his ball, that's the one that can be the starter. The one that gets on Twitter for fifteen, twenty minutes, gets on PlayStation for twenty, thirty minutes, goes to see his girlfriend, sits on his couch and watches the latest TV show but the NBA is on and college is on and he's not watching it? Low ceiling." On the court, one of the players on the Canadian team dunked, drawing a loud response from the crowd. Phil pointed at the lopsided scoreboard. DeCuire chuckled: "You gotta have a little shit to you to be good." In the game's final seconds, as Phil dribbled out the clock, a defender made the unwise choice to attempt to steal the ball. Phil cocked his head as though mildly amused, then performed a crossover dribble with such speed that the defender backpedaled and whirled his arms, losing an embarrassing battle against gravity. The crowd exploded, the buzzer sounded, and Phil walked slowly off the court, leaving the ball bouncing. He pulled on a shirt that said ARLEE WARRIOR BASKETBALL THIS IS SACRED GROUND and left.

That afternoon, Will stood in Missoula's McCormick Park, watching an uncle play softball. Will wore wraparound sunglasses, bright Skyn Style shorts, his flat-brimmed Bulls cap, and, on one finger, his state championship ring. He peered into his hand. Gleaming back through the cracked glass of his phone was a blue Dodge Ram with 145,000 miles on it. Chasity had bought it for him just a few days earlier. For Will, that truck represented freedom and manhood and hunting in one four-wheel-drive package. "New tires on it, too," he said, grinning. He was just two months away from his seventeenth birthday, and that he didn't yet have a driver's license didn't bother him in the slightest.

The spring had been cool and wet, the Clark Fork River surging brown with runoff. Beyond, to the east, cranes hung above nascent hotels. Missoula had grown by more than 20 percent in the previous two decades, to a population of nearly seventy-five thousand. Kids played on a new jungle gym, and young adults in breathable polyester clothing ran on a manicured riverside trail decorated with signs informing passersby about the various ways in which the built world imitated the natural. For example, one sign said wind turbines move like the fins of trout. Will didn't read those. He talked about hunting: whitetails and elk. He knew a lot about whitetails, from the trips he took with his dad and his uncle Sean, but he needed to get better at elk hunting. In the fall, elk came down to the hills behind his papa Allen and grandma Kelly's house. Last year another uncle had taken Will to shoot his first buffalo near Yellowstone National Park. The snow was hip deep, and about nine guys had waited for the herd to cross out of the park boundary. He recalled, "As soon as they all crossed, we all picked a couple out and *bwooh bwooh!* Shot 'em." Then came the processing. "They're pretty fun to gut, though, because you basically gotta crawl inside there." He added, "They're nice and warm, too, in that cold weather."

The Arlee boys had another game that evening—they would play a total of seven over the three-day event. Will's back hurt: "If I bend down, I lock up. Start cramping. I don't know." Chasity thought it was all the Mountain Dew he drank, so he was trying to cut back, but that was hard. Will understood that the Division I Griz remained a long shot. But, he said, "I wouldn't mind any college that wants me for basketball. Montana Western, or, like, Carroll." The University of Montana Western was Zanen's alma mater, and Whitney Malatare had played there; they use a block schedule in which students take one class at a time. Carroll College is a Catholic private school in Helena with a reputation for excellent academics and a lackluster record for athletic recruitment from reservations. During the previous two seasons, its men's and women's basketball teams included seventeen players from Montana, according to the teams' rosters. None had come from reservations. Will was planning to play AAU ball like Phil in hopes of increasing his college chances. His parents had separately begun raising money to support the effort; the possibility of leaving home in search of some distant achievement rose fresh and new and uncomfortable.

On one hand, leaving would mean Will was special. But on the other hand, he loved the reservation. "My whole family is there," he said. "I've thought of it, I'd miss huntin' and fishin'." Whenever he left, even for a day or two, he felt a longing. Ty was doing it—leaving. He'd finally decided on college, taking the offer at Dawson, way out east. Will said, "I don't even know where Dawson is."

It was one of those Montana spring afternoons when clouds close in over brilliant light, causing everything underneath to refract—especially, it seemed, the gems and metal in the warrior head on Will's state ring. Will asked if I'd hiked up to the *M*. He nodded to the east. There, just above the university, was a green hillside decorated with a white-painted *M,* a homey brand seared into the land. Looking at it, Will was reminded of something. "I'll have to show you this picture," he said. "It's way back when, like, our tribe used to live here. When they were coming from Stevensville. And that same exact hill. It's without the *M* and stuff, but you can see this river and, like, all the tepees and stuff."

The photo was black, white, and full of shades of gray. "And," he said, "you can see that exact mountain. Almost exactly the same."

Everyone on the Flathead Indian Reservation felt the reverberations from the time when the US government forced the Bitterroot Séliš out of their ancestral homeland. But Sophie was one of the few living tribal members who experienced the first aftershocks. For thousands of years the Séliš, a semi-migratory people, lived in bands extending from the Pacific Coast to far east of the Continental Divide. During the summer and fall the Séliš traveled from western rivers full of salmon to the plains, but returned to the Bitterroot Valley in the spring to pick a pink-flowered tuber they called *spéƛm*: the bitterroot. The Séliš traded with the Nez Perce (known to them as Saảptnišả), who lived to the west, across the Bitterroot Range; the Q'lispé, whose bands spanned the Northwest; and the Kootenai (Sql'sé in Séliš), a northern tribe with a distinct language.

Archaeological research in western Montana has shown evidence of inhabitation dating back to the end of the last ice age.

The Q'lispé and Séliš often intermarried. In the pre-smallpox era, the Tribes numbered in excess of twenty thousand. But by the early nineteenth century, the Séliš had been decimated by disease and felt pressure from the Blackfeet, who had brought guns from the north. In *The Salish People and the Lewis and Clark Expedition*, the Séliš-Q'lispé Culture Committee wrote that, by the turn of the nineteenth century, "Our people moved their headquarters into the Bitterroot Valley and the western portion of the overall aboriginal territory." In September 1805, a few hundred Séliš were at fall camp in the southern Bitterroot Valley, preparing to hunt buffalo on the plains east of the Continental Divide, when they saw a group of haggard travelers on sorry horses approach: the Lewis and Clark expedition, scouting the American West following the Louisiana Purchase. Taking pity, the Séliš gave the men good horses. Captain William Clark appeared to have misinterpreted the gift as a shrewd purchase and a member of the expedition misnamed the Séliš "a band of the Flathead nation." During the brief visit, according to tribal history, Clark conceived a child with a Séliš woman. The Séliš headed east to hunt buffalo, and Lewis and Clark traveled west into the Bitterroot Range, where they survived by eating a number of their colts.

Following the passage of Lewis and Clark's "corps of discovery," increasing numbers of trappers and traders arrived. As the French, British, and Americans competed for turf in the Pacific Northwest, Christian influence spread. Early fur traders noted with hope a similarity between some tribal and Christian spiritual tenets—especially variants of a story, shared by inland Northwest tribes, of coming ecological destruction followed by a period of rebirth.

In the early nineteenth century, Iroquois fur trappers moved into the region, intermarrying with the Q'lispé and joining the Séliš. One Iroquois, Ignace LaMoose, or Big Ignace, told stories of Jesuits from the east who wore black and carried strong medicine. The Séliš were intrigued, as this story aligned with something they'd heard before. Around the turn of the nineteenth century, as smallpox took its spasmodic toll, a prophet named Shining Shirt had foreseen a time when men in black robes would bring new knowledge to the region.

In 1831, a group of Indigenous men traveled from Séliš and Nez Perce territory to St. Louis, searching for the famed Black Robes. Two of the men died shortly after reaching Missouri. Word of their journey spread, and in 1833 a New York publication called the *Christian Advocate and Journal and Zion's Herald* published a sensationalist account that read, "May we not indulge the hope that the day is not far distant when the missionaries will penetrate into these wilds where the Sabbath bell has never yet tolled since the world began!"

Before long, wrote the historian Alvin M. Josephy Jr., "volunteer missionaries stepped forward for the glorious task of saving the Flatheads' souls." The Séliš, meanwhile, sent more groups east to retrieve the Black Robes. Big Ignace himself led two of his sons in 1835. Still no Black Robes came. In 1837, Big Ignace set out again and was killed by a Lakota party near the Platte River. In 1839, two more emissaries from the Séliš set out, traveling by canoe with fur traders down the Missouri River. At a Jesuit mission at Council Bluffs they met with Pierre-Jean De Smet, a Belgian priest, then continued on to St. Louis. In 1840, De Smet traveled to visit a large camp of Séliš and Q'lispé west of the Tetons. The next year, the Black Robes finally arrived in the Bitterroot Valley, with De Smet and a small company of priests and laborers building a chapel and log homes. That December, hundreds of Séliš and Nez Perce were baptized. But the priests' dogmatism, along with their efforts to engage with the Blackfeet, strained relations between the Séliš and the Jesuits. Smallpox also persisted. By 1850, the Séliš medicine men had left St. Mary's Mission. "As it was told to me by some of the elders, the intent of bringing the Black Robes here was to add to the powers and the religion that the people here already had," Tony Incashola Sr., the Director of the Séliš-Q'lispé Culture Committee, once said.

Some Jesuits moved west into Washington Territory, where another mission faltered, then returned. In 1854, the fathers constructed a mission called Saint Ignatius some seventy miles north of St. Mary's Mission, in a stunning valley underneath whitecapped peaks in the heart of Q'lispé territory. The following year, Isaac Stevens, the young governor of Washington Territory, convened a council near the Clark Fork River, hoping to secure legal rights to Indigenous land, consolidate tribes on a reservation, and make way for a railroad. The Chief of the Séliš, Victor, believed the gathering to be a peace treaty and wanted protection against the Blackfeet. One Jesuit observer called the proceedings "a ridiculous tragi-comedy," adding, "Not a tenth of it was actually understood by either party."

In the end, the Hellgate Treaty provided the Séliš, Kootenai, and Upper Q'lispé—the band with ancestral roots around Flathead Lake—no guarantee of protection against the Blackfeet. The nations ceded 20 million acres in exchange for the 1.25-million-acre Flathead Reservation. The federal government agreed to pay $120,000 and provide a vocational school, a blacksmith shop, a gun shop, a sawmill, a flour mill, a hospital, and an agricultural store for wagons and plows. Stevens was unable to convince Victor to leave the Bitterroot, and the government agreed to survey the valley and assess whether it or the Flathead was better suited to the Séliš. Victor was under the impression that his tribe would keep their homeland.

In the following decade, as settlers poured into the Bitterroot Valley, the US government acted toward the Séliš, Kootenai, and Q'lispé as it had with countless other tribal nations: it broke its treaty obligations. The government's payments were delinquent and short, and it did not produce the promised hospitals and schools. "It is obvious," wrote the historian Robert J. Bigart, the librarian emeritus of Salish Kootenai

College, "that the Salish and Kootenai were shortchanged, and that tribal leaders understood they had been cheated."

Officials assigned Natives anglicized names. Still, for much of the nineteenth century, people on the reservation lived without overwhelming daily interference, hunting, fishing, and, as the economy changed, grazing cattle. In the Bitterroot Valley, life was different. The government failed to adequately survey the region, but settlers arrived anyway, driving down game populations and surrounding the Séliš. In 1860, merchants opened a trading post near the Blackfoot River, which they would later move to a site called Missoula Mills. It took its name from a Séliš word referencing the water of the Clark Fork River: *Nmesulétkʷ*.

In 1870, Chief Victor died on a buffalo hunt, and his son, Charlo, or Claw of the Small Grizzly Bear—Słm̓x̣e Q̓ox̣ʷqeys, in Séliš— became chief. The following year, President Ulysses S. Grant issued an executive order for the removal of the Séliš from the Bitterroot Valley to the Jocko Valley unless they renounced tribal ties. When Charlo refused, settlers grew paranoid. The Oglala Lakota chief Red Cloud had only recently finished thrashing the US military in the Powder River Basin, where colonists seeking gold broke treaty law to pour in on the Bozeman Trail. In the Bitterroot, militias formed, and in 1872, the government sent the Ohio congressman James Garfield to resolve the matter. He warned Charlo and two subchiefs, Arlee and Adolph, about growing unrest among the settlers. Charlo did not budge; Arlee and Adolph worried that if they agreed to Garfield's demand, history would soon repeat, with settlers coveting the Jocko Valley. Garfield said it would never happen: "We should be everlastingly cursed if we do without your consent."

Garfield offered $55,000 and sixty new houses to be built in the Jocko Valley in exchange for the tribe's removal. Arlee and Adolph signed, and Charlo again refused. But when the agreement was presented to the US Senate for a vote on ratification, the head chief's signature had been forged on it. Arlee left for the Jocko Valley. Charlo, angered, remained in the Bitterroot with the majority of the tribe. Settlers came and came. In 1876, Missoula County proposed taxing his band, which prompted Charlo to deliver a stinging rebuke. That April, *The Weekly Missoulian* quoted him as saying, of the white man, "He spoils what the Spirit who gave us this country made beautiful and clean. But that is not enough. He wants us to pay him besides his enslaving our country. . . . What is he? Who sent him here? We were happy when he first came. . . . To take and to lie should be burned on his forehead, as he burns the sides of my horses with his own name."

Two months later, Cheyenne, Lakota, and Arapaho warriors defeated General Custer's forces four hundred miles to the east. Missoula's settlers clamored for a protective fort. Chief Joseph of the Nez Perce, battling in retreat from the U.S. Army, came east over the Bitterroot Range. Charlo allowed the Nez Perce warriors to pass but stated that the Séliš would not fight the whites. The government expressed its gratitude by banning the sale of ammunition to Native Americans in Montana Territory, interfering with their ability to hunt.

In 1882, senators pushed Chief Arlee and the Q'lispé and Kootenai leaders to allow a railroad through the reservation. Shortly afterward, a Missouri senator met with Charlo, hoping to persuade him to head north. Again Charlo refused. He traveled to Washington, D.C., for an audience with President Chester Arthur, where Charlo reiterated his desire to stay in his homeland. With bison herds dwindling to perilous levels, the Séliš had taken up farming, but a drought in 1889 wiped out their crops. Just days before Montana's statehood and a year before the massacre at Wounded Knee, Charlo finally acquiesced. It was decided that he would reside at the property formerly belonging to Arlee, who had recently died. When the Séliš left the Bitterroot, two years later, in Bigart's account, the men were stoic and the women wept. Charlo rode at the rear of the procession and led prayers in the evening.

Sophie told Will that one of her aunts accompanied Charlo; Sophie's father and uncle, twins named Antoine and Lasso, were orphaned during the relocation period, the first boy settling in the Jocko Valley, the second farther north. On the reservation, some Q'lispé and Kootenai had fared well in developing agriculture, and settlers in Missoula began to look north covetously. In 1904, Congress broke Garfield's word and cleared a path toward opening the reservation to homesteaders. The tool it used to do so was allotment: divvying the land into individual portions, at 80 or 160 acres per family. When it came to destroying the traditional way of life, allotment was a remarkably effective tool, one Theodore Roosevelt called "a mighty pulverizing engine to break up the tribal mass." After each tribal member received property, the government planned to sell off the "surplus" lands to settlers. In 1906, Congress passed an act allowing the interior secretary to deem individual Natives "competent" enough to sell off their own property. Subsequent legislation increased the size of homesteads, making them more appealing, and enabled the government to sell off Indigenous land should the guardians of allottees display "carelessness or incompetency." Finally, in 1909, President William Howard Taft signed a proclamation opening the Flathead Indian Reservation to white settlement.

Fences and irrigation ditches turned the Mission and Jocko Valleys into a land of squares. The government claimed and fenced off rolling, fertile hills near the confluence of the Jocko and Flathead Rivers to create the National Bison Range, where tribal members could not hunt. In a hiccup private property emerged as the governing philosophy. Mercantile owners offered Natives loans secured with the title to their land. For predatory lenders, wholesale theft was a matter of paperwork. For most tribal members, all of this was anathema: the idea of private property, the concept of land ownership, the capital they were told they lacked. To indoctrinate tribal children with Western values, priests and nuns started boarding schools. One religious institution was the Ur-suline Academy, a Catholic school opened at St. Ignatius that started originally as a kindergarten. Later, the Ursulines took in older students, many of them orphans. One boosterish account of the Ursulines' music program cheerily noted that girls were taught to perform a song called "Motherless and Fatherless." Nuns walked the halls with sticks. According to one student, when terrified children wet their beds, nuns forced them to wrap the soiled sheets around their bodies. The influx of homesteaders continued. The town named after Charlo, set in lush wetlands, turned predominantly white. By the time of Sophie's birth in the early 1930s, most of the allotted property had passed into white hands and tribal members were a minority on their own land.

Sophie told Will about what her parents had been through. Her father died young and her mother was killed by a subsequent lover. She told him so he'd understand that things were hard then, so that he'd understand that they were survivors. *Don't worry 'bout me.*

On the softball field, someone hit a home run. Some of Will's cousins picked him up. He had to go back to Griz camp. Maybe a coach there would think he deserved a place in Montana.

The next morning, Phil showed up just before the first game, and the team lost to a large school from Idaho. Becky said, "Phil has to score half their points."

Will had a bloody lip. "I think I'm dehydrated," he said. Maybe it was the soda. Les and Inj, in the crowd, were unimpressed—mostly with how few shots Isaac got. Les thought he should have been starting the previous season, during the championship run. Franny Brown, the assistant coach, wasn't worried by the losses. It was just summer, time for the young players to gain confidence. "Our kids understand it, they're good with it," he said. "It's the parents that can't understand it. We've only had six losses in three years. It's hard for them to understand."

That afternoon, DeCuire floated in and out. A bubble of pressure seemed to engulf John Malatare. Finally, he said, of his son, "He's got to prove to me he wants that next level. He's got a girlfriend, we all did. There was a time he wanted this. Basketball." He added, "This was his dream at one time. He's made an impact on someone else, he has people watching him." Given the history, John couldn't help but wonder if Phil, as a Native, might have a steeper hill than other recruits. He once told me, "A lot of these colleges in Montana will give a Native kid one chance." Had Phil's already elapsed?

But DeCuire was not a member of Montana's old boys network. He once ran a nonprofit focused on mentoring youth through basketball and spoke frequently about racial equity. In his brief tenure, DeCuire had already attempted to recruit a Crow star, RayQuan Evans, and had launched Zachary Camel Jr.'s coaching career. Still, he did not appear to be much for coddling the winds of adolescence. He once described his team-building philosophy in stark terms: "If you recruit to the league, you're not going to win the league." When I asked him about the pull some tribal youth felt toward home, he acknowledged that he was more familiar with the experiences of kids from cities. "I think it's common to all kids," he said. "I don't think that's just a Native situation."

But for Phil, Montana was not just home; it was the only place he felt truly comfortable. He had always articulated a desire to play for the Griz. But then, he'd always been told, by everyone around him, that he was bound for the Griz. In his junior year, he had averaged 20 points, 6 assists, 7 rebounds, and 6 steals per game. For a Division I prospect, he was small and his shot needed to improve. But he possessed elite quickness, endurance, passing ability, and a singular ability to anticipate the outcome of a sequence of events on the floor. Don Holst, a former head coach of the Griz who now worked as an elementary school principal at Arlee, put it this way: "Phil's got this innate ability to see things that others don't see until it happens."

Following his sophomore year, players on the Griz had invited him to summer workouts. He'd declined. "Knucklehead," said Zanen. But, he added, Phil's iconoclastic streak was what made him so good. Zanen also wondered if Phil was scared of confronting what it meant to chase Division I basketball. Becky Malatare said that her kids grew up with the best of both worlds—the connection of the reservation and access to all that America had to offer. But that also brought complications: an expectation that Phil would somehow contort himself to simultaneously accommodate the ambitions of the outside world and the gravitational pull he felt toward home, all while figuring out what it means to be a young man. He was seventeen and changing like the weather, and his place in Montana athletic history paled in comparison with more pressing concerns. Or, as Becky put it, "Honey's home."

Jordyn Clairmont was two years older than Phil, the daughter of one of John's colleagues. She'd grown up in a ranch house near Ronan and played softball with Phil's sisters. Phil was always at the games, smitten. When they started seeing each other—"talking," as she put it— his sisters lent him their cars for dates. Jordyn was a senior then, Phil a sophomore. She called him Phillip; everyone else called him Phil. No one else ever challenged his best friend, Ty Tanner; she told Ty, "You're always stealing my boyfriend." She was open, with a semicolon tattoo indicating a willingness to talk about depression and suicidal ideation; Phil hid his emotions. She knew Phil held his stress inside, and she knew that his greatest fear was disappointing people who looked up to him. When she broke up with him, after leaving for college in Arizona, he paced the house for hours, hoping for a text. But now they were back together. A bonfire and a long drive had done the trick. With her back at home, Phil's priorities had shifted. "Jordyn's his kryptonite," said one Arlee girl.

Jordyn attended the games that weekend, the first time she met Will. She and her best friend tried to get him to talk, but he wouldn't. On

Saturday, the games mounted, and Phil's back started to hurt enough that he sat one out, which turned into an ugly loss. In the crowd, Becky announced plans to book him a massage. She thought he held emotional tension in his back. "Phil should lay down and stretch," she said. A row away, Jordyn chimed in, "He said it was hurting so he wanted me to step on his back."

Becky's head swiveled slowly, and her eyebrows arched. "Don't step on his back."

8

He Don't Like to Go Far

Summer 2017

The land was fat, the hills green, cottonwoods shedding by the rivers and the aspen draws smelling sweet and dusty. Huckleberries grew in thick bunches, deer filled the hayfields in the evening, and the sun set far behind Saddle Mountain at 10:00 P.M. High in the mountains, under dark timber, trout slurped the surface of empty lakes. The boys had names for places that didn't appear on maps. They worried about nothing, except maybe running into a grizzly bear. Ty, the responsible one, summed up their attitude toward the season: "Fuck it, it's summer."

In late June, he, Phil, and Will went to Spokane Hoopfest. There were street vendors, three-point shoot-outs, dunk contests, people walking wires, near fights, short shorts and tank tops, tens of thousands of young people in a labyrinth of rims. The courts spread over forty-five city blocks. Kevin Durant, the NBA star, attended while promoting a new Nike sneaker. I excitedly sent Will a message. Had he seen Durant? He replied, "I was playing in the championship during that time." Phil later clarified, "Winning our own championship."

They drove home. The moment when they passed under the bridge for migrating wildlife near the casino always felt like a transition point from places where they were less understood—"out of bounds," in Franny's words—to a world where they were revered. As if to accentuate the point, a large red-and-white sign hung from the overpass, reading AR-LEE WARRIORS 2017 BASKETBALL STATE CHAMPIONS! In bounds, they could show up to games when they wanted. If their trucks broke down, it wouldn't be long before a friend or relative pulled over to help out. They could move cows with Zanen, or they could blow off his frequent requests. They could crash with cousins, or cousins could crash with them, or they could go to the Schalls' to sit in the hot tub. They could disappear up the Jocko to fish. In bounds, in summer, they lived in heaven.

Phil was hard to find, spending all his time at the ranch or with Jordyn. But a couple of weeks after Hoopfest, he taught at Zanen's summer basketball camp. There, about thirty screaming kids tailed him, trying unsuccessfully to steal the ball as he dribbled with only his left hand, a great smile on his face. Then he disappeared to go meet Ty or Jordyn. Will, meanwhile, participated briefly before leaving to move a body.

He had taken a job at his auntie and uncle's funeral home in St. Ignatius. At first he was responsible for maintenance—mowing the lawn, cleaning the carpets, running a cement mixer. Soon his roles expanded, with his uncle teaching him how to set up for wakes, to clean hearses, to fill in graves, to lower caskets. He got used to seeing bodies—bodies taken by age, by car crashes, by illness, by their own hand. He learned to roll them from a freezer to a room where his uncle embalmed them. He smudged frequently, burning sage and sweetgrass and pulling the smoke over his head, a strong prayer to protect himself. "Dealing with dead bodies is not my thing," he said.

Despite his continued interest in college ball, he decided against AAU. It was just too much time away from home. Big Will was frustrated. In his job as a cop he occasionally responded to calls involving once-great athletes who had succumbed to temptations. He knew all about that trap because he himself had once fallen into it. He had been recruited to the University of Montana's football team, but missed a preseason training camp while on vacation in California. Upon returning, in his recollection, he did some conditioning but partied his way off the team before taking part in a practice. He hated watching the games after that, seeing guys inferior to him running on the grass. He didn't find a home at the university. "I was wasting everybody's time including my own," he said. "I couldn't figure out what I wanted to do." Then his mom got him an interview with the CSKT Tribal Police Department. He wasn't sure he wanted to be in law enforcement—"There was no cops in my family," he said—but he didn't want to let his captain down. Within a year he was working as a patrol officer. Then, when the Tribes assembled a drug task force, Big Will asked to be assigned to it. Busting ill people for possession of minimal amounts of methamphetamine possession did not interest him. He wanted to stop the pipeline of drugs from entering the reservation. He spent long days and nights studying interdiction tactics and philosophies, and he thought of his own father, who had struggled with addiction. He and his wife, Ashley, moved back to Arlee, buying a large house, and he put a tribute to his father on the mantel. He developed a thirst for knowledge at work. He and Ashley started a family. Every Thursday night, he brought his kids to Kelly and Allen's to make art. The Tribes asked him to share his story with youth, and he sometimes did so, with uncomfortable honesty. It became a kind of salve. "It's what I want these kids to know," he said. "You can come from nothing and eventually be something. And when you decide to do it, it gets interesting." He wanted his oldest son to pursue such ambitions; he also wanted Will Jr. to get going earlier than he had. He was irritated by Will's decision to skip AAU. "Two weeks, man," he said. "You're going to have to learn to do this stuff!" Chasity, for her part, just laughed. "He don't like to go far."

Bear Malatare, Phil's grandfather, stood by his motor home, parked by the stick-game pavilion at powwow, holding up a jacket. Red-and-black, it read STATE CHAMPION. Bear had close-cropped white hair, an athletic build, a clean-shaven face, big hands. He looked younger than his seventy-one years except in his face, which hung low in resting moments. Not now though. His smile took off decades.

Becky asked what size the jacket was. She needed to get one for John. "Two X!" Bear said.

"For John? Will that fit John?" Her husband was fighting a fire in Arizona; John had retired from the Forest Service and was now working for the CSKT Division of Fire as an incident commander for an aerial unit that the Bureau of Indian Affairs dispatched around the West.

"I have no idea!"

"Well, is it big on you or tight?"

It looked a little large. But Bear said, "By the time you put a shirt on underneath there, it's just right."

Becky admired it. "That *is* a nice-lookin' coat."

The heat of summer had descended, the temperature approaching triple digits. It was June 30—powwow time. Arlee's *esyapqini* (celebration) is held every year on July 4 weekend, a tradition dating to the turn of the twentieth century. At the time, traditional dance was prohibited, so tribal members told the Indian agent they wanted to celebrate America's independence, then did as they pleased. It was early, before the dancing and stick game started, but the food vendors were already cooking burgers and fry bread. Bear said, "What I really wanted to do is put my grandsons' names on the back. If I could afford it, I'd put the whole team. 'Cause like I say, nine of them kids are related."

He started to count: "So there's Phillip. Ty Tanner. Alex Moran."

Will's grandmother was a Malatare. Dar was related through Bear's wife, Irma. "And then you got the two Fisher boys."

"Their gramma and Bear are first cousins," said Becky.

"They run from that clan right there that's runnin' that concession stand," said Bear. "Okay. Then Lane Johnson, he comes from another side of the Malatare clan."

"The only one that comes from your mom is the Fisher side, right?"

"No. They come from the Malatare side, too. His mom is my second cousin."

"Wait," I said. "Sorry." Until now I'd almost kept up with the galaxy of interpersonal relations, or at least pretended to, but here the tidal wave of aunties and cousins and friends seemed to break.

"The two little Fisher boys," said Bear, slightly exasperated. "They're related to us on both sides. Through the Malatares and the Nomees. Well, the McClures are all my first cousins. They're all my auntie's kids. See, and that's where your Ty Tanner comes from, your Cody Tanner. Oh, that's who we're missin' is Cody!" Here he referenced Tyler's younger brother, a rising sophomore.

"And the twins," said Becky. "The twins. Because their mom comes from ."

By the time they were done counting, Bear and Becky had determined that Phillip was related to eleven Warriors. As Becky often said, it was a small valley. A little ways away, at the pavilion, the dancers gathered in a long line for the grand entry, jingle dresses ringing. The boys walked around the powwow grounds, swerving past iced-drink vendors: Isaac and Billy, together as ever, and Will, leading a group of cousins, in a tank top and wraparound shades, wearing a tough expression. Every now and then, a girl passed and tapped him on the arm.

Phil and Ty stood in the fiery sun in waterproof boots, changing pipe at the Tanner ranch. Wet barley reached above their knees, and a timbered ridge rose behind them. The ranch sat up the Jocko River from Phil's house. When the kids were young, they fished there just about every day. Now they stood in one of Ty's family's fields, figuring out which lengths of pipe needed to go where.

"This line over?" asked Phil.

"Yeah," said Ty.

"Okay."

Phil crouched and lifted the pipe, elbows close to his torso, and walked about fifteen feet forward. When he set it down, the water splashed over his feet. Then they hopped in trucks and drove to the next field. Ty drove Phil's truck and vice versa. Ty's had cracks in the window and a .22, for gophers, in the back. They weren't playing ball at pow-wow. "I just got things to do," Phil said. Besides, he said, "The fricking blacktop burns my feet."

They waded into the field together, pulling lengths of pipe apart, the Jocko snowmelt tipping out cold. Did they have favorite memories, I asked, from the championship? Ty recalled a crossover move he'd made and the bus picking up Will at the hospital. Then he added, in the way teenage boys do, "Phil missing that free throw when we told him not to miss it. 'Cause he's a shitty free-throw shooter!"

Phil, for his part, just said, "Alex," as though his cousin's three-pointer needed no further explanation. They moved through the field in silence, then got back in the trucks. I asked Phil what had happened at the end of the championship, when he walked away from the game. "They were calling us redskins," he said. "Calling me a redskin." It hadn't happened in a while, he said. But one time, when he was playing on another team, with kids who were not from Arlee, Phil mentioned to his teammates that people were being trafficked on another reservation. "Like for drugs," he said. "It's starting to be a big thing. And I was telling some of my teammates about that." A boy asked where this was happening, so Phil told him. In his recollection, his teammate responded by saying, "Oh, yeah, course, it's on a reservation. That's why." So Phil stood up and said something. "I was like, 'Hey, don't talk bad about Native Americans, 'cause you're talking to one right now.' He was like, 'Oh, really, man, I didn't mean to.'"

The kid hadn't known that Phil was Native. As a sports star with state-wide recognition, Phil had to deal with crap like that less frequently than some other tribal kids who were also of white descent. But Phil still heard it: some people thought he looked white. Even I heard it. During the time I spent reporting on the Warriors, two men who were not from Arlee both said that, based off photos, they thought Phil looked white. They had internalized some rigid and entirely visual understanding of what it means to be Native American; an essential part of that, it seemed, was appearing not white. So the ubiquitous photos of Phil in the papers—with his crew cut and drawn face, occasionally pale with exhaustion—threw them off-center. But Phil was a teenage boy. He looked different all the time, depending on if he was inside or outside or sweating or had cut his hair or had shaved off the weird half mustache he sometimes allowed to grow on his upper lip in an effort to impress Jordyn Clairmont.

When it came to the boy on his team, he was not impressed. "You're gonna take it back," he said, "but you'll still say it to anybody else now but me."

Becky stood buffeted by the wind, blowing up balloons to decorate a long trailer with a plastic hoop on it. She wore an Arlee Youth Basketball shirt; her friend Shannon Patton, who helped lead the Arlee Booster Club, wore an American-flag T-shirt. It was 10:00 A.M. on July 4, and the Arlee parade was scheduled to start in less than two hours. The task of assembling a celebratory float for the teams had fallen to Becky and Shannon. Along with John's sister, Phil's auntie Cheryl, they'd spent the previous afternoon getting started, but it was so windy they couldn't affix the balloons. They had considered hay bales, but Dar was allergic. Also, Becky had run to Party City in Missoula to get silver streamers for the American flag. Two girls who played for the Scarlets showed up. "The girls are more apt to help," said Becky. She added, "Boys are the laziest." Dar emerged from the house and announced, "It's too early for this." He often stayed up late and slept in. He always took care to present himself well to the world, and it was hard in the mornings. He looked displeased. But he got to work, doing as he was asked.

"The vision is sparkles," said Becky. She talked about the coming season. "Of course Phillip wants to take 'em to state again this year. They've been there, they've felt that—you know that, what do they call, there's some kind of high." To win back-to-back titles would put the team in rare territory. She shook her head. "I'm not gonna live my kids' glory. I mean, I'm not going to live—I'm not going to live . . . But for some families it meant a lot." Her voice took on a melodious, singsong quality as she referenced Bearhead Swaney, Bear's best friend and the former Tribal Council Chairman: "That was kind of the vision that he had, that they would be state champs one day. And certain families for sure. We've sacrificed. I mean, so our kids can go to camp. Not just basketball or football. We go without new vehicles. Wanna know what my new-vehicle payment is? It's my boys goin' to Griz camp. Or new shoes. Or, like, our house. We can't have a brand-new house. But we choose to route our money through community events and we donate a lot personally. And my in-laws donate. I mean financially. Somebody has to fund it! So anyways, I'm not going to live through my kids' glory. I'm proud of all my kids whether they win a state championship or not."

Just minutes before the parade began, Phil and Ty arrived out of nowhere, the last boys on the float. As the team circled the town, throwing candy to children and water balloons at adults, people chanted, *"Ar-lee War-riors!"* and *"We're number one!"* Phil hopped off the float to grab Zanen's youngest son, a look of joy on his face; Will cradled the state trophy. When the truck made the final turn to approach the school, an old woman jogged after the float, arms upward, teeth to the sky. Then the boys vanished, some to the powwow, some to the lake.

Zanen had missed Griz camp to teach at Horse Camp, a cultural event run by Thomas Lyles's parents. In tents and a field outside a handsome log home, kids learned to bead and to dry deer meat. In the driveway, a couple of boys shot hoops in a soft rain. Zanen walked a horse through a corral, joking, "So do you want to just ride 'em?" A chorus of young voices responded, *"Yeah!"*

"I'm just playing," he said. Then he taught the kids how to safely walk near horses. When he finished, he raced to the Dixon ranch to pick up some calves, then across Perma Bridge and up a winding canyon under fast clouds. He was late for the Homesteader Days rodeo in Hot Springs, where he instructed his sons to remove their hats as an announcer introduced the national anthem as "the greatest song that our world knows."

Zanen was adept at navigating the orbits he traveled in. He loved the Flathead Indian Reservation but he also craved broader recognition. At Hot Springs, he was introduced as a "world-famous basketball coach." But he was not world-famous, and he wished to change that. He was brash and entrepreneurial, with his own convincing truth. During his Mormon mission, in Colorado, he was asked to keep a list of people interested in the faith. "If someone has ten or twenty, that's a lot," said his partner on the mission. "He had a hundred."

Terry and Crystal Pitts had attended a Mormon church in St. Ignatius when their children were young. The faith's emphasis on self-determination appealed to Terry. "To know that no matter who I am, no matter what kind of decisions I've made, I can be forgiven for those through the atonement," he said. "And to understand that we strive to be perfect, we strive to do things right, we strive to be Christlike. But knowing that we're probably all going to fall short in some areas—but I will be judged individually." He also found other aspects of the church clarifying. Since its founding in the nineteenth century, the Church of of Jesus Christ of Latter-day Saints held that Native Americans were descendants of one of the lost tribes of Israel. According to the Book of Mormon, the dark-skinned Lamanites and the pale-skinned Nephites who settled in the Americas shared a common ancestor.

The idea that both Natives and settlers had originally come from the same place offered a mechanism for reconciling Terry's questions about himself. "Things made so much sense," he said. "When I looked at the whole picture, I thought, *Well, that's good.*" As a kid, Terry was picked on for being a pale-skinned tribal member, and he once wrote a paper comparing the experience to Odysseus' trials. "I heard this so many times: 'Well how much Indian are you?' You kidding? It's like, 'Tell me your bank account.'" He added: "You sometimes get tired of the same rhetoric. Someone doesn't know you and that person says, 'Well how much Indian are ya?' I'm an enrolled tribal member."

Zanen's own identity seemed a rare point of vulnerability. When I asked him how he saw it, he said, "I have white skin and grew up around a lot of Indians." He stumbled. "I mean, my family, we have Indian heritage, my wife is Native. I mean." He paused. "If you check a box, I'm gonna check white." But to him, it was more complicated. He camped at powwows. He competed on the Indian rodeo circuit. He grew up hearing certain stories. He told me about his father instructing him to always pick up an elder who needed a ride. He understood the ambiguities of his life and the place he loved, but he also seemed to believe in bright lines. Or maybe he just knew that's what the outside world sought—neat frames and answers. He once said that, when it came to the community's mental health issues, "I don't really know if there's a solution or an answer to it," adding that each individual faced their own complex challenges. But before the Hot

Springs rodeo, while Zanen warmed up, his mind turned again to the suicide cluster that had not abated. Now, he said, it came down to "people not being afraid to teach morals and standards and religion to youth." The rope gathered air, creating small winds. "How's a kid supposed to fix a problem if he doesn't have a belief in something? I mean, you have to have a belief in something, whether it's right or wrong."

Zanen believed in the Holy Trinity, in accordance with his faith. He believed in accountability, in validation through victory, in competition, in sobriety, in removing his hat in the presence of women. He believed bunchgrass was made by God for the buffalo and then cattle. He believed Montana was being overrun by out-of-staters, some of whom, he said, were "actually trying to overtake it." And he believed in basketball. This year the team would be fast—"too fast at times." A lot depended on the juniors. Greg was crucial, but it would come down to the others: Dar, Schall, Isaac, Lane Johnson, all of whom, he hoped, would make a crucial leap. "That's the year," he said. "That's when they become men."

On the court, Zanen's contradictions melted away. There, a different kind of philosophy emerged, a stubbornly optimistic thing that was hard to articulate. He envisioned, through the boys, a better world, one in which everyone thrived and accolades followed goodness. When bad news happened, he spun it. (He called Phil's heel injury a blessing that would give him time to rest.) But sometimes, the forces seemed too overwhelming. He thought about how many people he knew who had died in the past year. He put the figure at more than twenty. "I like to say some of the things I say help these kids. But I really don't know if it does. Because the adversary is so strong."

One evening, we were out by Niarada, zooming back to Dixon from a rodeo, the shadows getting long, when Zanen told me it would be his last year coaching. He said he was doing it for Will and Phil. He

wanted to buy a ranch as well as more vehicles. "I need to buy a Suburban." I asked if he'd ever consider moving to a city, like his older brother, who lived in Kalispell and worked for a company that used artificial intelligence to detect digital fraud. "It's boring," Zanen said. "Look at me, man. I'm flying from a rodeo. Heck yeah. Busy." Around us grass rolled into timbered hills, turning silver and black, no buildings anywhere. "My favorite kind of country," he had said, a moment earlier. "Big elk and lots of cattle. Lots of grass." The light fell as we ascended to a high plateau. "I love it. I love sagebrush." He said he would live here if he could. But, he allowed, it was dry. "You gotta be a little crazy to want to live here. A lotta ticks and rattlesnakes." He was looking forward to when this was his only concern: grass and cows. "I'm excited for the day I'm done coaching. I'll never be on my phone again." He would ride into the sunset, just like in a movie. Night swallowed the shadows.

In mid-July, lightning strikes brought thick smoke and skies the color of trout eggs. With fires extending across the state, John came home. At the end of the month the community held one more celebration for the team, a ceremony called a *syulm*. An instructor at Salish Kootenai College named Shandin Pete was instrumental in the effort, along with Johnny Arlee, an influential elder descended from Chief Arlee. Traditionally, Johnny Arlee said, "Nobody bragged. There was never a time when you said, 'I did this.'" Rather, you waited for someone else to talk about your achievements in a formal ceremony. The *syulm*, a dance for warriors returning from victorious battle, was such an occasion. Pete had spent a long time researching the ceremony. According to him, the *syulm* hadn't been performed in over one hundred years. The boys would gather in a circle while women teased them, playfully hitting them and whooping until one of their relatives presented a gift.

The event came together at the last minute and not everyone made it. But Phil, Will, Alex, Lane Johnson, and Ivory did. About

thirty women danced—among them Chasity—and ten men sang. John Malatare attended, taking a day off from flying from fire to fire. But Zanen was missing, off chasing cows or working a rodeo somewhere. That gave John heartburn. "That *syulm* meant so much," he said. "Zanen wasn't there." Will and Ivory laughed, a little uncomfortable. Phil wore a serious expression, hands in his pockets. John marched out to get him, offering blankets and beadwork, hearing songs that hadn't been given voice in over a century. "Without that language, these traditions," John said, "we're nobody without 'em." Afterward, he tried to impress the event's importance on Phil and Alex. "I get it," said John. "He's seventeen years old. He doesn't understand that that well. So him and I and my nephew Alex, we talked about that after it was all over . . . how important that was. We don't go out and steal horses, we don't go count coups. But being a good man, taking care of your families, being a provider for families. Winning that championship for themselves and giving the community a little bit of release from what we were going through." John hoped Phil and Alex would appreciate the ceremony someday. "Sometimes I have to remind myself they're just seventeen."

For the next month Phil remained elusive. Eastern Washington University, a rival of the Griz, also invited Phil to attend its skills camp, but he decided against that, instead doing Ty's precollege workouts with him. Phil declined the opportunity to join the Idaho Select's summer team. "Basketball takes so much out of him," Becky said. Maybe he needed a break from the immense pressure; maybe it was something more, the beginning of a search for a life outside sport. Or maybe he was beginning to realize that playing Division I basketball would necessitate leaving the places he loved most in the world, the mountains of the Flathead Indian Reservation. John was frustrated every time he saw his son leave for the lake. He tried to confront Phillip: "This isn't the dream you had, son." Phil said maybe it had been John and Becky's dream. One day, Phil went fishing while wearing his state championship ring and it fell in, old waters swallowing the warrior head. In August, he mentioned, almost as an afterthought, that someone from the Griz had invited him to walk onto the team. "He didn't even tell us for a couple days," Becky said. She wasn't sure what the invitation entailed; she thought he'd have to try out. John asked Phil if he was going to blow his opportunity. Then Phil promised to prove his commitment. He went to the gym.

Part Three

Let the refs keep up.

—ZANEN PITTS

9

A Brutal Truth

August–September 2017

Under the sheen of smoke the sun resembled a peach; the moon, a plum. The ongoing wildfires prompted Montana's governor, Steve Bullock, to declare a state of emergency, and an air-quality specialist referred to the smoke as "a hideous brown spiral of misery and despair." Greg Whitesell agreed with that: his summer job had been mowing lawns, and it felt as if he were chewing on the smoke. "Just miserable," he said. He looked forward to football, where he could be around his friends. Most of the boys played. Dar was a star running back and defensive back with straight, downhill speed. "I *love* football," he said with a gleaming smile. Lane Schall and Will competed to be the starting quarterback. Lane worked out regularly with a personal trainer in Missoula and envisioned being a college star. Will had a strong arm and his father's instincts with the ball. Schall won the job, so Will transitioned to playing running back alongside Dar, the two of them tearing through defenders. Greg was a slight wide receiver. That concerned Zanen. "Will's a football player," he said. "I can live with that." But Greg, he worried, was not built for the sport.

Greg, like most teenagers, sought belonging, and sports was where he found it. His first years had been spent in Twin Bridges, a tiny town known for fly-fishing. David, who was superintendent of the public schools, and Raelena—Greg's mom, a Diné optician—raised him and four siblings. Twin Bridges is more than 95 percent white, and from a young age Greg remembered being the only Native kid in class. In pre-school, his teacher asked the students to dress as pilgrims for Thanksgiving. Greg refused, making his parents proud. He spent summers in New Mexico with his mom's family, giving him a glimpse into a more diverse cultural landscape. From Twin Bridges the Whitesells had moved to Polson, the town at the northern end of the Flathead Reservation. David's tenure was contentious. He supported a district-wide powwow and, he said, found himself in a dispute with a parent about why Polson didn't arrange a similar event for students of Irish descent; he pushed for the hiring of a specialist focusing on Indigenous education, a position that was later eliminated. (Polson Schools did not reply to a request for comment, but a longtime principal in the district supported Whitesell's account.) Greg once woke up to GO HOME spray-painted in the snow and FOR SALE signs in the yard.

In 2012, David left the district with a settlement after filing a discrimination complaint. He and Raelena also divorced, and Greg took it hard. Greg felt pressure to be a great athlete and to live up to his older sisters' academic excellence. He'd inherited his love of basketball from his father, who had both played and coached. (David liked to tell a story about coaching in New Mexico, when two fans quit their jobs in order to watch him lose at a tournament.) Following his parents' split, Greg moved with his mom to Arlee, while David took a position in the Bitterroot Valley. Then David got the job in Arlee, hoping in part to reconnect with his youngest child. But he lived in Missoula and commuted. At school, Greg tried to somehow avoid the dreadful tag of being the superintendent's kid. He was a terrific student when he chose to engage, but he often didn't. He was funny and friendly and deeply loyal. He could also be mercurial, one minute attentive, the next off in a silo. He was a little girl crazy. He and a bright student named Tomi Brazill had seen each other on and off throughout high school. That fall, as school started, they were off, a separation that pained Greg. His mom knew something was wrong, but he brushed her off and said he was fine.

In early September, a man who was family to many Arlee students died by suicide. Shortly afterward, an Arlee student took his life. The school arranged more meetings, with mental health experts covering the diagnostic system known as QPR—question, persuade, and refer. By November, the number of deaths by suicide in the reservation-wide cluster would reach twenty, according to Anna Whiting Sorrell, an of-ficial with the Tribal Health Department.

David Whitesell had no answers. "We need to focus on relation-ships," he said. "We need kids that can read, who can figure out their problems. Kids who are college and career ready. We need kids who can survive their past, present, and future." He was in constant contact with the school's therapists and the counselor and psychologist. He held to the increasingly prevalent school of thought, supported by numerous recent studies, that some effects of trauma can be passed through genes. Whitesell was horrified at the normalization of suicide—in response to bullying, loneliness, and, frequently, teenage heartbreak. "It's an option," he said. "It can't be an option." The championship had been astounding. But, he wondered, did it "really solve, resolve, redefine, the issues this community has?"

In September, during a football game, Greg suffered a concussion, his fifth. It was severe enough that he had to stay home from school for a couple of weeks. He struggled to keep food down and had to avoid electronic screens. Not only was he unable to do homework, he couldn't play video games. Isolated from his friends, he slept a lot and thought too much about Tomi. "I wasn't in the right state of mind after the concussion," he said. "And I felt like I just didn't—like it wasn't me. I'm positive all the time, always smiling." Now, though, he felt constantly tired and alone. Raelena kept asking if he was all right, but he lied and said he was fine. "I'd have a bad day," he said, "and it would tear me down mentally and physically." He spent too much time in his own head but didn't want to talk about it. "I was tired of being depressed. You just get tired of everything." That confused him because he was a starter for the state champions. He almost felt as if he had no right to be sad, and that just made it worse. "I don't know how to explain it. But I was looked at as—I don't want to use the word *God*—but people looked up to us. And I didn't want to be, like, letting people down." He said, "I was almost on top of the world. People see me, like, 'He's a state champion.' But they don't really see what's going on in your life." In the darkness of his room, a strange logic set in, one that was appealing in its awful simplicity.

One night he sent a disturbing text to Tomi. "He said something like 'Thanks for everything,'" she recalled. She tried to call but he wouldn't pick up, so she reached out to Lane Schall, who was out with Dar. They were rolling around somewhere in Lane's pickup. Lane had no idea his friend was struggling. Lane's reaction was disbelief that soon turned to anger. He tried to call Greg but couldn't get through. "Wouldn't respond to none of us," Lane recalled. "He kept declining calls." Not knowing what to do, Lane called his mother, who in turn called Raelena. But she was sleeping. Meanwhile Lane and Dar raced along the dirt roads. "It didn't feel good at all," Dar said. "I just knew that I had to be there."

Greg was alone in his bedroom with his thoughts when the head-lights shone into the drive. Lane and Dar came to the front door and started banging. Raelena, groggy with sleep, figured they were just coming to mess around, as they often did, so she opened the door and went back to bed. Lane and Dar stood there, and Greg emerged, a hoodie over his head. Dar gave Greg a hug, while Lane was pissed off, wanting to know how Greg could even think of something like that. What Greg remembered was Dar saying he loved him. "Dar was a sweetheart," Greg said. Dar and Greg sat together while Lane woke Raelena. Soon Raelena came into Greg's room and sat with him. Her son was oddly calm when he told her he was not scared.

Raelena asked Dar to give them a moment alone and the boy walked out, crying. In the bedroom, Raelena told her son he could not talk like that. She remembered saying, "I need you." After some time she called David. By now, Tomi had arrived. She, too, told Greg she loved him. When Raelena told David what was happening, he told her to take the boy to a hospital in Missoula. Raelena drove Greg, keeping calm to be strong for her son, yet feeling deeply alone. When she pulled up to the hospital parking lot, David embraced his son. Meanwhile, David's girlfriend, a graduate student at the University of Montana named Erin, approached Raelena. Before that the two had not been on the friendliest of terms. But now Erin came to the driver's-side window, and Raelena broke down. Erin hugged her long and hard.

Greg soon found himself alone in a bare room with scratches on the walls. He was given a change of clothes—his new outfit was made of something with the consistency of paper, so he couldn't harm himself. "You're in this room and it's just like a hotel bed and the walls are all blank," he said. "It felt like an insane asylum. I felt like I didn't belong there. I felt, 'This isn't what I want to do.'"

The hospital staff kept him overnight, then sent him home. After that, for months, Raelena woke up every couple of hours to check on her son. Greg also saw a therapist. The fog of the concussion eventually cleared, and he returned to school. He didn't talk much about that night, and Lane and Dar kept it to themselves.

When David Whitesell and I spoke, early in the fall, he did not share the whole story, simply saying, "Greg is struggling." His voice was heavy. I asked what he thought the community needed. "You know.

Good question." I asked when basketball started. "Not soon enough." By November, some of the boys had begun to work out without the supervision of coaches. One day, David walked into the gym to find his son, Lane Johnson, and Phil going at each other and talking trash. The juniors took turns on Phil, jawing at him, playing as though it were the last time they would ever see a court. It got so intense that David wondered if he should intervene. Then he thought better of it. He had rarely seen such beautiful basketball. "There's a brutal truth to it," he said, "that you can't teach."

10

Who's Tired?

November 2017

Zanen strode into the gym, a baseball cap on his head and dried manure on his boots. It was 5:00 P.M. and already dark out on November 15, the evening before the first practice of the season. In the gym, the boys horsed around, shooting, playing one-on-one, Lane Johnson and Isaac trying to dunk. Phil kneed Will in the groin. Lane Schall arrived in cowboy boots.

"What's up, baby?" said Phil. "What you doin'?"

"Workin' cows, baby!" yelled Schall.

Thirteen boys were present, a few players absent including Greg, who was getting checked by a doctor in accordance with concussion protocol. Zanen directed the kids to a small room in the back of the gym. "We're here for a purpose," he said. "That purpose is to win a state championship. I'm going to chew on you, I'm going to break you down, I'm going to build you back up." He said he was going to change their lives. "This is so much bigger than you." The championship, he said, was 110 days away. He announced the captains—Phil, Will, Greg, and Lane Johnson—then outlined the rules. Guys who disrespected teachers would not play. Guys whose parents complained about court time would not play. Latecomers would not play. Exceptions would be made only in extreme circumstances: "If you want to go hunting, you've got some huge buck figured out, call me."

Franny interjected, "If you're still hunting, you're a weak-ass hunter."

Zanen cued up the highlight reel from the championship season and strode out of the room. Will had a copy and often watched it late at night. Phil did not. Zanen returned and said, "Here's your captain. Chew some ass." Phil, wearing a camouflage hoodie and a backward hat, walked to the front of the room and announced that his goal was to win every game by 40 points. "We all have each other's back," he said. "Someone says something to you, we're all four of us gonna go after him. Maybe not hurt him, but we're going to score on him. We're going to make him turn it over. He's not going to want to be on the court with us. Everybody's going to be intimidated. And we gotta make them intimidated. And that is going to be how it's going to be." He had one more thing to add: the boys were not to demean their opponents. "We don't have to talk shit. We're the kings." Zanen asked Will if he had anything to add. He did not. Zanen informed the team that the next morning they would run until they puked. "We don't quit," he said. Kendra popped in with root beer floats.

The next morning, at 5:30, sixteen boys were in the gym along with three coaches: Zanen, Franny, and Andrew HeavyRunner, who is enrolled in the Niitsitapi (Blackfoot Confederacy) and the Kainaiwa (Blood Tribe) from Canada. Greg had cleared the concussion protocol. He looked thin. A couple of new kids showed up, including a blue-eyed junior with big earrings named Nathaniel Coulson, known as Nate, who'd grown up walking the streets with Will. While no one would mistake his skills with Will's or Phil's, he was tough and coordinated. When the team won the championship, the previous year, he saw Ty throw the ball in the air and one thought entered his mind: *I want that.* He'd torn an ankle ligament during summer ball, but still came out for the team.

Practice started with plyometrics: boys shuffling side to side and jogging backward. After ball handling they started an exercise called Warrior Drill, a three-man full-court weave designed to facilitate a fast break. It was supposed to be free-flowing and smooth. It was not. Boys stumbled and balls crashed off the walls.

Phil stopped everyone: "Raise your hand if you don't know how to do this. Be honest."

A few hands rose. Will said, "Just talk. If you talk, you make it easier."

"Gonna be a long first week," said HeavyRunner.

On the sidelines, Greg took breaks from the heavy exercise. Bright lights hurt his head, and he struggled to maintain an appetite, with his mom forcing him to eat. He looked much thinner than he had in the summer and had a new haircut: box braids dyed blond. On the court, the team went over basic half-court offenses. Greg thought about what a couple players needed to develop. It wasn't technique. "It's more about heart," he said. "You'll see the other teams on their knees. Phil lives off that."

HeavyRunner and Franny pulled trash cans to both sides of the court. The boys lined up under one basket, each of them with a basketball. While dribbling, they sprinted between the baseline and each successive line on the court. They did not go fast enough. "Back on the line," said HeavyRunner. "Now you're letting the seniors down because you're not busting your ass. Now you got some more running because of it!"

It was time for the drill the boys dreaded more than perhaps any other: seventeens. Everyone lined up along one sideline, took a basketball, and dribbled across the court and back. Each round trip counted as one. They went to seventeen. They ran and ran, and soon the trash can's function became apparent. Two boys moved to one, heaving. Phil, shirtless in a white headband, did not appear tired. "Come on, Sage!"

he hollered. "Come on, Ardon! Come on, Lane!" Two more new kids went to the sidelines to throw up. The gym resounded with the sounds of dribbling, heavy breathing, gasping, spitting, vomiting. "Get down here, everybody!" Phil said, indicating another seventeen. "Bring that garbage can!"

Franny yelled, "You're on the wrong team if you think you're gonna walk!" The exercise ended, and the boys gasped.

Phil yelled, "Who's tired?"

Every hand went up, Will's included.

"Why you guys tired?"

Someone said they were out of shape.

Phil said, "You don't think we did this last year? Well, we did. But this year's gonna be way harder." He said, "Frick, you're gonna run all over these teams. They're gonna be throwing up and you're gonna be laughing at them. You think it's really hard? It's gonna be harder. Every day is gonna get a little bit harder. You think it's gonna be hard?" He pointed to the door. "There's that exit. I don't want any of you to leave, but we can't have no holdbacks this year, okay? There's that door if you wanna go. You don't have to come back tonight. But I wanna see all you guys here every day. If we're gonna make this team better, I gotta make the younger kids better, and we gotta keep building this program. And this is what we gotta do. Just run and you'll be fine."

Greg said, "It hurts now, boys, but once you get to the top—"

"It'll be worth it," Phil said.

They shot briefly, then lined up on the baseline and did a speed dribbling drill, one player taking off about twenty feet ahead of the next. If the first player got caught, he had to run a seventeen. The gym resonated with the hard sounds of dribbling, like hail on the roof. Will ended up on the trash can, arms up, vomiting. After fifteen more exhausting minutes, Phil pulled everyone together. "Brothers on three," he chanted. He counted to three and the boys responded, *"Brothers!"*

They walked out into the predawn. It was 7:00 A.M. Almost time for class.

Franny stood over a hot stove in a hoodie and basketball shorts, cooking Spam and eggs. When not coaching the Warriors, he worked at the Nkʷusm school, a preschool–8 facility that teaches the Séliš language. Will's grandpa Allen Pierre taught there along with Allen's father, Patlik, one of the Tribes' most influential elders. Franny was the cook, feeding up to seventy people at a time. He also studied there, taking adult language classes. He wanted the team to incorporate more tribal culture. "We call plays in Séliš," he said as he cooked. "Orange—*pum*. So the color orange. Which comes from, we used to call it Syracuse." The Syracuse basketball team, Franny explained, was formerly "called the Orangemen." (The name was changed in 2004.) "So we said we'll call it *pum*. The language is hard to match up with English words."

A voice from the door said, *"X̌est skʷẹkʷst."* An older man walked in. He had a strong build, swept-over white hair, and impressive cowboy boots: Pat Pierre, Allen's eighty-eight-year-old father. "Patlik!" said Franny. The elder reached for a coffeepot. As he lifted the glass vessel off the hot burner, the bottom simply fell out of the pot. With a crash the coffee spilled on the floor. "Hi-yo!" said Franny. "You okay? Man!"

Patlik didn't say anything, just wiped himself off and moved along. Now another voice was in the door, similar to Pat's, but less guttural and more gravelly: that of his son, Allen, Will's grandfather. "You wanna ride home and change it?" Allen asked. He had driven his father to the school, as was his practice. Patlik said, "No. It'll be all right."

Franny alternated between asking if Patlik was okay and rehashing the pot's demise: "I just made it and it broke. He just picked it up and it fell out the bottom. Cheap pots."

Patlik was unconcerned. "It'll dry out."

Franny shook his head. "Might have been 'cause it was too hot and

I started it again." I'd never seen him so concerned. Everyone in the room started cracking jokes, easing the moment, then Allen said, "So, when the big boys start practicin'?" He wore jeans, old sneakers, a nice zip-up sweater, and a baseball cap, his long silver hair tailing out of the back. On one forearm, a tattoo read 100%CSKT.

"Oh, we been practicin' two days," said Franny.

"Oh, really?"

"Yeah. We just got done."

"Oh, yeah? How's Will?"

Franny said, "He quit drinkin' pop. So you gotta keep on him. He told me this morning, said, 'Is that huckleberry drink better than pop?' I said, 'Anything's better than pop. It's the carbonation that gets you cramping.'" Everyone remembered when Will had cramped up and been carried off during the state championship.

"Cramping," Allen said. "That's what I been telling him. Even when he starts his conditioning. He's gotta drink a lotta water before that and during that because he don't realize what he's losing when he's sweatin'."

"He's one of the most sweatin'est kids I know," said Franny.

"Yeah. And that's the thing about— I'm always worried, too, about him because it's his senior year," said Allen. "And then he reflects back on what his uncle and his dad did in their senior year." Allen had videos of Big Will's games. "He watches those, and he thinks that they set the bar for him. So he's either gotta meet that or go above and beyond that. And I told him, 'With what you did last year, you shouldn't even have to worry about that. That shouldn't even be on your mind.'"

Allen's voice took on a marching cadence, and the room fell silent. "Just play to the best of your ability. And I said, 'Don't forget you're part of that team, and it's a team effort.' That's why I'm just kinda always on him. And he's like, 'Jeez, Grandpa, every time I come over here . . .'

I said, 'Because that's the way it's gotta be. You can't expect things if you're not gonna work hard for it.'"

Allen went on about Will's grades, his powwow dancing, his love for the mountains, his grades. "I've always told him that, you know, his sports are, you know, they're good. But I need him to get an education because for Native people it's a little bit different when you get out in the mainstream and try to live life." I thought about that phrasing—*I need him*—and all it conveyed. Allen continued, "It's a little bit different and there's more challenges that you run up against. Our children know where they come from and who they are. So it's not only my grandson that I think about when I talk about that way of things. It's almost every Native American that gets put up against something like that. There's just so much that ain't working for them."

The food was ready along with a fresh pot of Folgers. All of them bowed their heads, and Patlik and Allen prayed together, a Catholic prayer in Séliš. Patlik had been an evangelical minister for decades before realizing, in his words, "I'm not that. I'm this." He had retired twice before, after working in the forestry industry and then working for the Tribes. "No more retirement," he said later. "They say, 'How come you don't wanna retire?' I say, 'That's for old people.'" He liked basketball just fine—Will, he said, was "pretty strong in his Indian ways, and he uses that on the basketball court and he's a top man in his field." But Patlik wanted to discuss larger issues. "It's always been us against them or them against us. One way or the other. And so a lot of this reflects deeply on young people. As they're growing up, they're learning that they're different than other people. And because of that they feel inferior to the dominant society." He clearly didn't think the dominant society was much to be envied. But kids didn't always get that. "They feel inferior. And so because of that, that's why the suicidal tendencies come. And, 'What can I do to change? What can I do to be more like them? Or more outgoing?' Stuff like that. They can't find a way. So they become depressed."

I asked if the conflict between Indigenous America and the America begat by my ancestors was inevitable; if it was naive to hope for a more harmonious and just future. "I'm hopeful for it," he said, "but I don't think it's going to happen. There's always going to be that thing there." He had a word for that thing. "It's called greed. Greed. When all the forests, all the oil's out of the ground, all the minerals are taken and there's no more to take, those people that have exploited the earth, they're gonna find they can't eat their money. Gonna have taken and taken and taken, have given nothing back, and they're gonna find out that there's no more. And that's coming. I predict that to be coming." His eyes bored into me. "What's gonna happen is, out there, when the earth becomes desolate, they're going to come and knock at our door. 'Can I have some of what you've got here? How did you keep the place so beautiful? Why is it beautiful when all the rest of it's desolate?'" He answered, "Because we know how to be."

The next morning, Will drove up the mountain, a Dr Pepper between his legs and his loaded .300 Winchester Magnum propped on the center console of his Ram. He and a buddy named Brad were looking for whitetails northwest of Arlee. Will wore sweats and a Steelers beanie. Brad was big, about six foot two, wearing a red shirt and jeans. He spoke softly, his .270 propped next to Will's rifle. Brad had a puppy with him. He was a couple years older than Will. After graduating he had briefly gone to the University of Montana Western to play football but had returned and was now studying at Salish Kootenai College.

The truck occasionally slid on ice, and the dog and guns rattled around. Will rolled through a creek and said, "Valley Crick." He and Brad laughed as if that were the funniest thing in the world:

"Huhhehhuhheh!"

Once you got to a certain point, past the railroad tracks, any small body of water could safely be called Valley Crick. The truck climbed into cedar and larch and ponderosa and the sun rose, reflecting off bright snow in the far hills. Brad hopped out to grab a cedar bough for me. Occasionally Will pulled over to scope. He found some bucks far away, but they were too small. He sipped the Dr Pepper. "First one in a while," he said, as though speaking it into something like truth. He drove straight up for a time, then down a steep rutted road, putting the truck in neutral and letting it roll. The air smelled faintly sweet. Between long silences Will talked about how an uncle boiled deer skulls, to mount them. Brad said that, in his own career, he had been "terrible" at hoops, but Will corrected him, bringing up a couple of games where Brad had played well, the play-by-play precise as ever. "We ain't gonna lose this year," Will said.

I asked how he knew.

"I just know, Abe." He stuck his left hand out the window and flicked the empty soda bottle in the air. It landed square in the bed of the truck next to the severed head of a buck.

A couple of weeks later, Will walked into Jennifer Jilot's classroom, wearing a hoodie with his name on the back and a cap that read FRESH. He walked past the interactive whiteboard and the large table in the center of the room—the kids sat together, rather than at desks—and flopped onto a couch under the window. Jilot's eyes lit up at his entrance, then her expression turned concerned.

"Aren't you doing your presentation?" she asked. He was supposed to be working on a history presentation, with a group, about the anti-Federalists, who opposed a centralized government during the constitutional era.

"Nobody was ready to practice," Will said.

Jilot looked a little skeptical. Will's academic progress was a source

of great pride, but it also drove her nuts. Sometimes he engaged; sometimes he did not. Now he lay down on the couch and hugged the pillow
like a child. She occasionally threatened to get rid of the couch when
she found students dozing there. But when she was out of earshot of
the kids, she said that part of trauma-informed education was "having
a comfortable place like a couch."

Next to the couch was a Denver Broncos pennant. There were other
posters, too: an advocacy board for missing and murdered Indigenous
women, an image of a man smudging, and, above the blackboard, two
identical posters. They showed the previous year's Warriors team in
a huddle, the camera's eye looking up into the boys' faces. UNITY IS
STRENGTH, they read. YOU ARE ALWAYS ONE OF US. EVERY VOICE, EVERY
LIFE MATTERS. I saw pressure in that. But when I asked Jilot about it, she
looked defiant: "It reminds us that no matter what, we stand together."

Her bookshelf contained Sherman Alexie's *Flight*, about a young
man with a large imagination negotiating the thorns of adolescence
and a traumatic background; Lauren Myracle's *Shine*, about a hate
crime in rural America; and Paxton Riddle's *The Education of Ruby
Loonfoot*, about the legacy of Indian boarding schools. "Shakespeare
doesn't really relate to their world," Jilot said.

In her own education, Jilot had often felt adrift. As a child in a suburb of Denver, some classmates war-whooped at her. Others thought
she was Latina. In high school she often drove into the mountains to sit
by a creek. In the summers, she spent time with her family on the Rocky
Boy's Reservation in northern Montana, where she felt, as she once put
it, "more connected than I had anywhere in my life." After high school
she took a winding route—a college in Colorado, then Stone Child,
Rocky Boy's tribal institution—before landing at the University of Montana. There, she felt swallowed in lecture halls. "It's not being the only
brown person." Rather, she said, "You see the world in a much different
way than everyone in the classroom." The ideas that most interested

Jilot—about familial and ecological connectivity—didn't seem to matter in her classes. She dropped out, moved to the Flathead Reservation, and eventually enrolled, at age twenty-five, at Haskell Indian Nations University, in Lawrence, Kansas. There, in a small teachers' education program, she found an intellectual home where her ideas coalesced. After graduating, she returned to the Flathead Reservation to teach in various schools, including Nkʷusm, before enrolling in the master's program at the University of Montana. She remained critical of the university but, during her studies, was introduced to a book that became an ideological anchor: *Power and Place: Indian Education in America,* by Vine Deloria Jr. (Standing Rock Sioux) and Daniel Wildcat (a Yuchi member of the Muscogee Nation). A series of essays, *Power and Place* made a case for decolonized education: "Because people desire just the 'facts' without any understanding of the relations and connections between the 'facts' and the rest of the world," wrote Wildcat, "we have the search-engine model of education." Jilot's copy of the book was worn and marked up with comments: "This is where I'm at!" She spoke of teaching subjects that interconnected, of breaking the addiction to specialized achievement, of indigenizing education: "We have to change everything we are doing in schools. If we really want to change our community, we want to help our kids realize that they don't have to continue this cycle that just keeps going, then we have to make some drastic changes."

She and Zanen were constantly in touch, texting about his players' academics. Seen through one lens, their partnership was surprising. She was a progressive, deeply critical of America's foundational myths; he was a patriotic cowboy. She found Donald Trump abhorrent and openly criticized the president; Zanen didn't like when people did that, believing firmly in the Mormon Church's patriarchal hierarchy. "We can't teach kids to disrespect the position," he said. He called himself a political independent but liked that Trump was, in his word, "real." He said, "He's able to go out and tell people the way he sees it and people don't like that"—Zanen identified with that. But Jilot and Zanen were both dreamers at heart. She talked of building a better world; Zanen believed he'd already done so on the court and just needed everyone to stay out of his way. Jilot was aware of a perception that she paid more attention to certain students. But as a literacy coach, her role was to focus on kids facing specific academic challenges. "I help the voiceless," she said. "Those tend to be Natives." And at the classroom level, "They tend to be boys, for whatever reason." She had heard elders say young men struggled because their societal roles had shifted so drastically in the past century. Lacking purpose, they could fall down bad routes that would affect the entire community. Sports provided an outlet, albeit a temporary one.

Will got up to leave, and Jilot snapped. "Hey! Did you practice this morning? Are you gonna come to tutoring?"

"Yeah," Will said sleepily, shuffling out.

Jilot sighed. "I'm going to be so excited and proud for him to graduate. And then on the other hand, thank God because I'm turning gray."

The boys woke when the stars were bright. Phil drove Dar and two other cousins: little Cody Tanner and David "Tapit" Haynes. Will drove two younger cousins and often took Nate Coulson. More cars arrived in the parking lot: Greg in a Subaru; Lane Johnson, a blue sedan. The Fisher boys came in a red van with a skater decal; Lane Schall in a pickup he called the Batmobile, which featured a paper cutout with a hand-drawn Bat-Signal in one window. The boys parked, engines idling, hoods pulled over their heads. Rising exhaust and falling snow met in the predawn darkness. Then Zanen, Franny, and HeavyRunner arrived and opened the gym. On the sideline, the kids slipped off their shoes and pulled on crisp sneakers—LeBrons, Kyries, Kobes, Jordans. Will estimated he owned twenty-five pairs of those. Only Phil didn't seem to really care about his footwear: "I don't have no twenty-five pairs of shoes. I wear 'em until they go out." Greg cued up the music, Zanen boomed, "Baseline!" And it began.

Over the years, journalists have described reservation basketball as "freewheeling," a "beep-beep blur of legs and arms and sneakers," and, most frequently, "run-and-gun." Don Wetzel Sr., the former Griz MVP, said that, during Lodge Grass' dominant era, some Montanans thought the team just outran everyone. But that kind of assessment, he said, ignored the work done from the shoulders up. Wetzel said that Lodge Grass' coach, Gordon Real Bird, "had a system." So did Zanen. He often said, "There is a structure to our chaos." Arlee's offense was centered on four basic sets: a couple of motions, a dribble drive, and the spread that slowed play down. That was it. Plays were boring. Plays were for those who could not do what they did.

"Our defense is our offense," said Zanen. The defenses were not basic. There was *pum*, the extended two-three zone. There was 10, a half-court man-to-man. They ran a one-three-one defense that extended two thirds of the way down the court. Called 21, this soft press was designed to force the ball to the sideline. Players were not to go for a steal, but rather trap the ball handler, enticing him to lob a pass into the middle of the floor, where Phil lurked. Amoeba was a half-court zone; the team ran three variations of a full-court zone; in another scheme, Greg and Will stunned the ball handler in a quick-hitting half-court trap. Zanen often used those defenses early in games to wear the opponent down before it was time for the real stuff: 30X, a full-court man run-and-jump press, or Dilly Dilly, an all-out man-to-man denial. Whenever a boy got beat, he said one word: "Go." Then everyone rotated hard, the entire defense shifting in a flash.

It was dependent on effort and connection, the defense working as one amorphous entity. "It teaches 'em," said Franny, "not to give up." Once, Phil cut in during a defensive drill to say, "You can communicate, we're all fricking friends. Who cares if you might say some dumb shit sometimes?"

But yelling was hard. They were teenage boys, more comfortable with silence. On the second day of practice, Phil pleaded, "Is it gonna be quiet in here?"

Will murmured, "No."

"Sounds like it," Phil snapped.

In early December, Dar called out a play too softly. "What?" boomed Phil. "Louder!"

But no one was quieter than Isaac. He was long and lean and fast, his legs flying up and down the gym, and he could shoot and dribble adeptly for his size. Because of his height, Isaac's natural defensive role was to occupy the back of the formation, protecting the rim. But that positioning also required him to call out rotations. Isaac was soft-spoken and sweet and seemed to eschew contact. His favorite thing to do was dunk and hang on the rim, way up high, away from everything.

"You still just as quiet as a church bell!" Phil yelled at him.

HeavyRunner said, "We need you to start talking, okay?"

"You ain't gonna play unless you learn to talk," said Greg.

Isaac nodded, looking worried.

Phil softened up: "Just learn how to talk a little bit."

Once, Zanen asked Isaac to speak to the team: "What you got to say, big man?"

"I got to communicate."

"No," said the coach. "To them!"

"Just be supportive and help each other out." An awkward teenage silence followed.

During those first days of practice, Greg rested his eyes on the sideline. He struggled to keep weight on. "With the concussion I had, it messed up my emotions," he said. "I don't feel hungry or anything." He had to force himself to eat. But, he said, "I've been so tired and sore that I just put it off." Sometimes he chewed on his fingernails as he spoke. Zanen sat with him, talking about specific players or inquiring about Greg's new girlfriend from up north. Greg said he used to find Zanen's interest in that stuff "kind of pushy," but he now saw the coach as a big brother. On the court, Greg's personality shone through. He joked around, was quick to pick up a teammate after a fall, and also scolded kids, talking about how easily they used to score a hundred baskets in Warrior Drill or cautioning, "Manhattan Christian's probably working their ass right now, too." He ruled the music, crafting meticulous playlists: Kendrick Lamar, Lil Wayne, Wale, Drake, Migos.

Every practice ended with conditioning. Running, running, running. Franny pointed to Phil: "He's my meter"—meaning they would run until he was tired. There was just one problem with that. "I've never seen him get tired," said Greg. In those early practices, Zanen could be militaristic. When the boys did not show the effort he demanded, he said, "I'm sick and tired of watching you guys run like you're from some other school!" Once, he yelled at the nonstarters, "You're making them weak because you're weak!" He said the kids were playing like "millennials, pathetic city kids." He told the boys to breathe through their noses and out of their mouths when they thought they were going to vomit. "Don't work," said Will.

But just when Zanen's style verged on draconian, he shifted into a more nurturing mode. "I love seeing how you're really trying," he said to one boy. "So thank you." When Nate Coulson hobbled up and down the court on his bad ankle, the coach said, "You're hurting, right? Don't want me to cut you?" Nate said nothing. Zanen told him to shoot standing shots.

Phil, too, vacillated between tough and kind. One minute he yelled, "You boys ready to throw up?" But he also said, "I will help out every little bit I can for each one of you guys," and he tried to offer incentives.

If the boys ran like him, he said, "You could walk them hills, look for deer all day, won't get tired." He taught his younger teammates to cleanly pick crossover dribbles and to bait opponents into passes before darting into the lanes to intercept the ball. "You're reading their eyes," Phil said. "You'll know when."

The distant boy of summer was gone, replaced with an exacting taskmaster. He told Cody Tanner, "You need to run, man." He told a freshman, "You need to pick up on this, okay?" One day he told me he wanted to prove that a Class C kid could make Division I, sounding a lot like his dad. But he seemed most focused on defending the championship. "My best friends were Al and Tyler. Doing it with them last year was so great." He referenced the highlight tape: "That ending when Ty throws the ball in the air . . ." Phil looked at me, exhaled, dropped his hands. "It's, like, really sad."

Will's mode of captainship was less vocal. He rarely spoke, but when he did, the boys listened closely. Once, the coaches said that a missed layup would result in running. Will announced ominously, "Nobody miss a layup." He was constantly dehydrated, despite consuming vast amounts of water. "I try to drink at least a gallon a day. But I like my pop, too."

He also had two lingering football injuries: a dislocated pinkie and a sore knee, from when he'd been speared on the gridiron. He said nothing about it. During a snowstorm, he walked in the gym shirtless, wearing just his Steelers beanie.

Lane Johnson—LJ, as he was known—was held up as an example for the younger players. The previous year, he'd guarded Phil in practice. "He didn't start all year long and he took a beating from all these guys," said Zanen. "I don't know if you guys could handle that." This year, Lane was poised to be the starting power forward, having grown to about six foot one, with the potential for more—he wore a size 13 shoe. Despite his quiet nature off the court, he and Greg were the team's most frequent trash-talkers. He also chimed in as an occasional voice of reprimand for the younger kids. "Last year I busted my ass so hard," he said. "You guys are just fucking jogging."

But it was Phil's team. Save for Will, the boys regarded him with some mix of awe and fear. A freshman was trying to raise his grades just so he could take the court alongside Phil; a junior named Ardon said Kyrie Irving reminded him of Phil. "In my opinion," said Greg, "he's the best player in the state." On the second day of practice, Phil stopped a drill to announce, "Each day that goes by, it's a day off our season. It's a day off your junior season, sophomore season, senior season. And just like this"—he snapped his fingers—"it's over. You'll look back and say, 'Fuck, maybe I coulda done that a little bit better.' So every practice we go hard." He paused. "Could be your last practice. Not maybe tonight." But, he said, "You could get in a wreck the next day. Roads are going to get bad."

Zanen chimed in, "We've all had enough people die in our families. We've all seen it happen over and over and over. Make the most of it."

In advance of the first game, both the *Missoulian* and the *Lake County Leader* ran season previews. The *Missoulian*'s focused on the amount of vomit in conditioning. Greg did not like the article. "They talked about everyone else, they didn't talk about me," he said. "I've always been slept on." He thought that this year, he would finally get recognition, but it hadn't happened. "I was kinda pissed about it but I kinda felt selfish."

The *Missoulian*'s sports coverage was now part of a statewide website called 406 MT Sports, run by Lee Enterprises, which owns Missoula's paper, the *Billings Gazette*, the *Ravalli Republic*, the *Independent Record*, out of Helena, and *The Montana Standard*, out of Butte. Lee has a reputation for cutting editorial costs to turn a profit. But in Montana, its sports press is vigorous. Started in 2015 as an aggregation of the company's existing coverage, 406 MT Sports quickly proved profitable, drawing about one million annual visitors. It competed with another popular site, MontanaSports.com. Like so many others, 406 MT Sports' editor, Jeff Welsch, had moved to Montana after seeing the film *A River Runs Through It*. Welsch said that stories on high school basketball were frequently the site's most popular. "The human-interest feature on the small-town basketball star or track star or football star never fails," Welsch said. "And then there's the additional impact if we go to a reservation."

But 406 MT Sports did not employ a single tribal reporter. Welsch told me that was a deficiency he wished to address, but the coverage of reservation basketball often veered toward simplification. Sometimes the stories tiptoed; rarely did they ask challenging questions, especially when it came to equity in recruitment. That topic had been a third rail in the state since the Montana State University coach Mick Durham made offensive comments to *The New York Times*. David Whitesell said, "It is hard for Native players to get recruited, and there is not a single coach out there that would tell you." Zanen backed up that assessment.

Bill Dreikosen, the coach of Rocky Mountain College, seemed to acknowledge the issue when he said, "You can't lump everybody in there together. We have several kids off reservations playing in our men's and women's programs." But when I asked Steve Keller, the coach of the University of Providence in Great Falls, a top Frontier Conference program, about the steeper hill that tribal boys seemed to face, his answer did little to defuse Whitesell's argument: "I think skill-wise there's really good players. I mean. Yeah. I don't know. Yeah. I'm just not going to comment on that. Yeah. I don't know you very well and there's been—yeah. I don't even want to get into that." Carroll's athletic director, Charles Gross, said it was not his place to tell coaches whom to recruit. When presented with statistics showing a lack of Indigenous representation at colleges including his, he said, "I'm not sure that's an area that I can comment on." When I asked if any Carroll coaches were tribal members or from reservations, he said, "If I were guessing, I would say no."

Discussing white privilege in much of Montana, Whitesell said, was "like saying the sky's blue to someone who's never taken the time to see it before." In February 2017, before the Warriors won their first championship, a radio host in Billings—a transplant from Ohio—suggested the state segregate its basketball tournaments because of "unruly" crowds. The story made national news, reaching *The Washington Post.* In their coverage of the incident, the *Gazette* and the *Missoulian* ran an op-ed by Mike Chavez, the former Griz star, decrying the comments as "toxic." But the papers also published a lengthy story on a small protest of about forty people supporting the radio host. The piece included just one Indigenous voice of dissent.

In Arlee, many people got their basketball news from a Facebook page maintained by Bill Swaney, Bearhead's son. Called Native Hoops Hub, it curated news about reservation teams, posted updates on players bound for college, and provided a forum for fans to discuss travel logistics. Zanen had long felt that his team was undercovered, despite its proximity to Missoula. In the past, he said, "We could upset the number one team in Missoula. We could do anything, any school here on the rez, and the *Missoulian* will never do anything. It'll be in the back page." Only recently, he said, had the attention increased.

For the boys, the *Lake County Leader*'s season preview was thrilling. "Did you see it?" Phil asked at practice. "The paper they wrote? It's like, 'Warriors Preparing to Defend the Title.' It just came out this morning in the *Lake County.* Big. Front page."

Zanen asked, "Who's the picture of?"

"Me."

"Phil's gonna be in all the pictures," said Greg.

"And then you have a quote on there," Phil continued. "It's like, 'We ain't scared. It's like mental, we don't even think about it.'"

This was the actual quote, splashed in bold font beneath an image of Phil flying to the hoop: "Pressure is a weakness of the mind and we don't even talk about it."

The first game of the year was scheduled for Friday, December 8, in a tournament called the Native American Basketball Classic. The event was to be held at Salish Kootenai College—on the boys' home turf. Arlee's first opponent was Rocky Boy, a Class B school that featured a talented six-foot-seven-inch player named Kendall Windy Boy, as well as a quick point guard, Kordell Small, and a shooter named Ben Iron Eyes. "You only get one shot at beating Rocky Boy," said Zanen. Franny warned that Rocky Boy would have studied Arlee's defenses. Once, Zanen stopped a defensive drill when his post players didn't fight aggressively enough. "You guys are gonna get destroyed," he said. "Those northern Indians, they are nothin' like what you guys have played against. They will find you when the ref ain't lookin'. They will fricking turn and shove you."

Phil interjected, "How me and Will are in open gym? That's how they are in the real court. They're . . ." He smacked his hands together: *whunk, whunk, whunk.*

Defensive assignments were discussed at length. Phil decided to take Iron Eyes, while the job of guarding the point guard, Small, fell to Lane Johnson. With his speed and toughness, LJ had emerged as one of the team's top defenders. Still, Greg said, "If that Kordell kid starts making stuff happen, I'm guarding him." But it was Isaac who had to defend Rocky Boy's star. "Kendall Windy Boy," said Franny. "Tough in the post."

"Isaac," said Zanen, "I believe."

Phil said, "You're gonna be nervous, it's your first varsity game starting." Isaac just nodded, glasses bobbing.

Zanen said, "I'm going to tell you now in front of all these guys: if you make a mistake, it's fine."

He wanted everyone to look nice. If they didn't have a tie, he said, Kendra would find one. Just before that, he addressed the younger players who would be on the bench: "Once the ball tips I want you guys freaking nuts the entire game. I don't want you sitting down until the refs tell you." Then he said, "When the ref turns around, you stand back up."

11

This Is the Right Now

December 2017

The locker room was all-white, tile floors and painted walls, the flash from cameras refracting off a mirror decorated with a flyer for a suicide-prevention hotline. All but three of the tags on the bottom had been torn off. Will's hair shone in a double braid courtesy of Chasity. Phil also had a new haircut, a Supercuts fade. He was all wired even though he'd spent the morning hunting deer. Lane Schall pulled the silver cross off his neck and the state championship ring from his finger. Greg sat quietly, headphones on, bobbing his head. He didn't believe in letting the opponent see your feelings. Zanen wore a black shirt and slacks, black cowboy boots with red stitching, and his gold buckle from the Crow Fair. A knife was clipped to his right pocket. He instructed the team, "No more talking, just sit here and think about how you're gonna win." He left. It was silent, save for the click of a camera shutter.

The *Missoulian* was here—a reporter and a photographer—along with me and Jordan Lefler, a filmmaker and Arlee graduate who produced highlight videos for the school's sports teams. Outside the door, the gym hummed with buzzers, whistles, and a couple thousand voices. They had come from as far as the Fort Belknap Reservation, six hours to the east, in the high plains. Becky sat at the front entrance raffling off a handmade quilt for the Booster Club. Next to her was Arlee's new athletic director, Amy Bartels. Raised in Great Falls, Bartels had a master's degree in athletic administration from Gonzaga and was now tasked with overseeing Zanen's basketball program. "I like his enthusiasm," she once said. "I don't ever see him take a break." She did allow that, because of the nature of her role, "I'm always going to drive those guys crazy." John Malatare had assumed his seat by 3:30 P.M., to watch the earlier contests. It was almost seven now, nearly time for the Warriors to take the floor.

In the locker room, Franny Brown broke the spell, bellowing to Isaac, "You ready, motherfucker?"

Isaac bounced up and down, his head nearly hitting the ceiling, saying, "Yeah, I'm ready!"

Zanen reentered, dribbling a ball, the cameras turned on him. "Aight. Sit down and shut up. You good, Will?"

Will messed with a headband. "Should I go under the braid or over?"

"Leave it," said Phil.

"Over," said Zanen.

"Done," said Franny. "Time to play ball."

Zanen went over the game plan. They were to start in a man-to-man half-court defense, then, upon scoring a layup, they would enter a full-court man press. That meant that Isaac had to sprint back after each basket to defend the far hoop against the talented post player, Windy Boy. "Kendall's been balling," Zanen said. Isaac looked a little nervous.

"This is the right now," said Phil. "First game of the season. You're gonna come out nervous, a lot of us are gonna be nervous, but the game is gonna come."

Zanen interrupted. "We're not nervous."

Softly Phil said, "I'm nervous." His palms were sweating. They always did before games. His teammates appeared relieved. The camera shutters clicked. Zanen reached down and opened a box, revealing sleek hooded warm-up shirts, red-and-white, with a warrior head on the chest. The boys' nerves melted away in a chorus of hollering. Zanen choreographed the team's entrance, instructing the boys to fan out onto the floor once Allen, Big Will, Sean, and the rest of Will's family hit the drum. "I want everyone to know," Zanen said, "the champs are here."

The boys fell silent, and Zanen prayed:

Our Father in heaven,
We bow our heads humbly before you
For the great opportunity that we have to play this game.
To separate ourselves from the world.
We ask, Father,
That Thou will bless us with strength and wisdom
And give us the ability to be safe.
Bless our opponents
That they also can come out and perform at their highest potential.
That they can be safe as well.
And most of all,
Let the refs keep up.

Then the drumming started.

For a while, people had said I needed to watch a real game; that it was hard to describe and that video couldn't catch it. David Whitesell's assessment of the game's brutal truth stuck in my mind, and Don Holst, the principal at Arlee elementary school who formerly coached the Griz, told me that the boys would challenge some college teams. Zanen said, "These guys are wicked, they're like wolves, they're like a tuned-up sports car, they're coming at you a thousand miles per hour."

But I was by now accustomed to the coach's hyperbole. Though I had not been around for the previous season's championship run, I had seen the team during the summer and in practice. Phil was dominant, clearly, Will and Greg highly skilled, Lane and Isaac and Dar incredibly athletic. But I had not yet seen Zanen's Ferrari. I imagined the games couldn't be too different from the ones my father coached in New York City public school leagues. My job was to describe the Warriors' play, and that was potentially perilous. Tensions simmered between the community and the press stemming from a history of outside journalists either applying a bore-like focus, without consent, to trauma, or romanticizing the culture. Even in my excitement to see the boys play, I was wary that my characterization of the competition—that my characterization of anything—might prove me to be, as Anna Whiting Sorrell, of the Tribal Health Department, once put it, "another one of those."

Then the ball went up and my heart rate rose as I ran from Malatares to Mesteths to Fishers to Whitesells to Hayneses to Pierres, handwriting shifting in and out of legibility. For months afterward I would look at a recording of the game, hoping to reinhabit the experience with the aid of a pause button. On the screen it looked like nothing much—fast breaks, lots of space, too many turnovers. The distance of the replay obfuscated the way the boys moved at full speed in elliptical, curling lines, rather than the sort of straight routes favored by most coaches. Something else was missing, too, the thing that boys who keep certain feelings inside let out when they discover the right venue. I'd return to my notes and find this:

will steal to phil race back pass to lane 2 will lane take out one guy lane blocked off pass greg all over floor greg from way out isaac out walk not called lane miss 3 will steal will sprint back . . . spinning floating and one steal layup will steal phil give and go phil layup will QB pass phil over back almost its an art . . . i'm screaming

On some fast breaks the ball did not touch the floor, touch passes flying between Greg, Lane, Will, Phil, Dar, and Nate, when he got in the game. Will's shot was off—he scored just 6 points—but his defense was overwhelming. In the second quarter, Phil deflected the ball and took off toward midcourt while Will chased the ball down, caught it, turned, and in one motion fired a crisp pass toward center court. Phil then tapped it up ahead in between three defenders before blowing past two of them, taking off into the air and whirling into a funnel. The crowd gasped. Zanen screamed, "Careful!" A defender hit Phil, and he laid the ball softly in the hoop.

The tape missed the sound Greg's body made when he hit the floor after taking a charge from a larger boy. The heaviness of the thud. I thought about his head, but he was back up in an instant. The tape caught Isaac's dunk—him rising, with the game tied in the fourth quarter, to catch the ball and slam it through the hoop, in a decisive and momentum-shifting play. But it missed the expression on his auntie's and uncle's faces—the way their mouths opened and eyes widened, Les in a backward hat, holding up a video camera, Inj standing with nerves coursing through her. And how, after the game, an eight-point victory, the grown-ups so tenderly converged on the boys, those juvenile constellations of hope. "My boy," said Les, "Isaac." Will hugged his mom and siblings and yayá Sharon and Allen and Kelly. Sophie was not in attendance—she had fallen and broken her elbow weeks earlier and was still recovering. Big Will said, to his son, "You're putting too much pressure on yourself," and the kid nodded silently. Someone complimented Greg on a move he'd made, a floater. He pointed to his father and said, "He taught me that." For a moment, the superintendent's face changed. His expression usually carried a heaviness. Now, all that weight evaporated into some fresh happiness. Zanen approached Nate Coulson, who was alone. Nate had worked hard to become academically eligible. "Glad you're eligible?" the coach asked. "Feels good, huh? You did really good. I'm super proud of you."

In the locker room, Zanen had turned to Isaac and said, of the dunk, "That was fricking crazy, dude!" Franny said they had too many turn-overs, and Phil took the blame for that. Then Phil turned to the starters and said, "You did great, you did great, you did great." To Isaac, he said, "Man, way to fricking grow some coconuts!" Joyful laughter echoed around the room, then someone started to clap. Others joined in, and the sound rose, speeding up, a thrumming crescendo. Phil's voice cut in, "Love you, boys, brothers on three." He intoned, "One, two three," and the team chanted, *"Brothers."*

Will slipped out alone. The *Missoulian* reporter approached Zanen to talk about Phil, who had scored 36 points: "I think I see a D-One player." But Zanen gushed on about Isaac.

Inj approached with a light in her eye. "A long time," she said. "Something that's been waiting a long time, you know what I mean?" She said, "It's finally happening." A freshman named Sage Nicolai said, "Write down, 'Sage is the coolest; Phil is the suckiest.'" So I did.

Then I ran into David Whitesell, the heaviness back in his face. "Very few go undefeated. How do you survive a loss?"

The next morning, the front page of the sports section of the *Missoulian* showed Phil in the air, splitting two defenders, beneath the headline RETURN OF THE KINGS. In the locker room before the next game, the boys were excited about the headline. Phil and Cody Tanner debated who was better, Michael Jordan or LeBron James, and Lane Schall and Dar started cutting up. Will was less psyched after his poor shooting performance. His hair was different today—cornrows—and he'd made a footwear adjustment, swapping out red Kyrie Irving sneakers for retro Jordans. In his pregame speech, Zanen seemed to sense the tension. He made a point to note Will's defense in the previous game. "When you're eighty," he said, "ain't no one gonna know the stats. Every record is gonna be broke. But they'll never get the back-to-back state championships. That lasts forever." Will silently tied his shoes.

Phil said the boys should beat their opponent, a school from near the Fort Belknap Reservation, by 20. Zanen said, "Listen. We only can win this as a family. Don't get selfish. We ain't entitled to nothing. Here we go." Then silence and prayer.

Zanen said he did not rehearse his pregame prayers. Back before he left for his mission, he felt crippled by nerves when speaking in public. Then, in Colorado, someone had suggested he let the spirit talk through him, stating, in Zanen's recollection, "God will make sure you say what the people need to hear." So that's what he did. But he always used that line—"Let the refs keep up"—and it sent a current through the room. Like the coach, it was brash and defiant. It was also full of truth. The game as the Arlee boys played it was analogous to the one elsewhere in the state and across America, though guided by its own principles. But the vast majority of Montana's officials were not from reservation communities. In 2012, the Montana High School Associ- ation (MHSA), responding to inquiries from tribal communities, con- ducted a series of listening sessions and cultural-diversity workshops. There had been discussions over the years to ensure a tribal official's presence at every state tournament game, but no such policy had been enacted. Zanen, with his cowboy ethos of self-determination, was re- luctant to blame race for any societal issue. "I get tired of people using it as a crutch and people being ignorant enough to treat people bad because they're a different race," he said. He also firmly believed that most refs had no idea what his team did. Frequently, the officials blew their whistles in anticipation of fouls that didn't materialize.

In this tournament, that was not the case. Before the team took the court, Zanen noted approvingly that the officials had let them play the night before. Today, the defense was even more devastating. By the sec- ond quarter, the Warriors were up 24. Phil took a breather, approaching the end of the bench, where Jennifer Jilot's young son Anthony served as the team's water boy. As Phil approached, Anthony froze. He looked as though he were witnessing a meteor shower over a parting sea. Phil paused and said, "Oh—you getting me water?" Anthony snapped out of it, poured, and they slapped hands.

Will's shot was off, but he seemed to steal the ball whenever he pleased. "Give it to him, give it to him!" said Allen Pierre, in the crowd. "Oh, I just can't wait till he gets hot." Will scored, then raised one hand above his head with two fingers looped. In between munches of popcorn, Allen gestured back, explaining that it was a symbol for his family. He started to sing softly, then said, "I remember when Willie was little and I used to hold him when his dad was playing."

At halftime, Franny said, to the other coaches, "They finally figured it out." HeavyRunner, the assistant coach, advocated keeping the pressure on, to work on the elaborate defenses against a quality team. But things went slack in the second half, partly due to an ankle injury Greg suffered. Phil left the game in the fourth quarter and approached the end of the bench. Before the buzzer sounded, Adam Hiatt, the coach of Montana Tech, a Frontier Conference school in Butte, approached: "We'll chat." Phil nodded and Hiatt left. After the final buzzer sounded, Phil took photos with the fans—"Let's take a picture with Phillip!" giggled some girls. Lane Schall bellowed, "Kings are back, baby!" Then, in the locker room, Phil lit into the team: "That was probably the shittiest half of ball. We got to get better every game. Our defense is good. Our rebounding sucks. Turnovers sucks." Phil blamed himself for that. Zanen blamed himself for not calling time-out so they could regroup and win by 40.

After the game, Becky said Hiatt was ready to sign Phil to a full scholarship. She liked Hiatt and that Tech was a smaller school with good academics. But she knew her son was holding out for the Griz. Phil hoped he might earn a scholarship, or at least some assurance of his place on the roster. He was under the impression that the invitation to walk on meant he'd have to try out for the team, and communication had been scarce. He hadn't heard anything from the university since the summer. "The Griz aren't really making contact," Becky said. "I dunno." The Griz had recently signed a player named Mack Anderson out of Bozeman to a scholarship. He was tall, but did not nearly have Phil's record. A sophomore from Missoula had also, somehow, already committed to the Griz. How could a sophomore commit to the Griz? Becky didn't understand: "It's kind of a tough thing." Maybe Phil needed to win state again. Maybe, she thought, the discrepancy was because he was tribally enrolled and therefore eligible for a tuition waiver. Maybe the Griz coaches assumed he'd get financial assistance, meaning they could save a precious scholarship. That's what Zanen suspected. "He's Indian first off and he's gonna get money." The coach said it was commonly known that Montana schools saved their scholarships for out-of-state kids. "I think he's worth it," Zanen said. "It's degrading in some respects." But, he added, that's just how things went in Division I ball: "It's expected."

12

Why Do You Care What Other People Think?

December 2017

"Y ou got four games to fix your shit or I'm going to turn in my resignation."

Zanen stood in front of the team. It was the Monday following the season's first victories and the coach was in a foul mood. An acquaintance who was friends with a college scout had, after the games, said he found the play sloppy. Zanen did not want to play the way many colleges did. He wanted the other team gasping for air; he wanted what he so often called "magic." Still, he was sensitive about appearances, and the criticism stung. During the second game, he said, the boys had ignored play calls. He mandated fewer turnovers and highlight-reel plays.

"Why do you care what other people think?" Phil asked, eyes forward, brow down.

"Those are the people," said Zanen, "that are going to get you guys a big future." He added, "Critics are important."

"I have critics every day," Phil said. "And I brush it off. And I play my game, and we win."

Franny said, "It's about how far you guys want to go after high school."

Phil hung his head and twisted his hands. "After this weekend, watching you," Zanen said, "frick, dude, there ain't no team within thirty points of us." With a little control, he said, they could blow everyone out. "Do you trust me? Because I trust you guys."

Silence. Zanen asked if the captains had anything to add.

"I said what I had," said Phil.

Will shook his head.

"I take partial blame," said Greg.

"We good?" said Zanen. Everyone nodded. He declared the matter settled: "Squashed, don't ever talk about it again." But Zanen carried other frustrations, too. Bartels, the athletic director, had recently conveyed two unwelcome messages: Anthony was no longer permitted to be water boy, and media were no longer welcome in the locker room. Anthony's presence was a liability concern, she said. The media ban resulted from a series of images, published by the *Missoulian*, of the locker room, which had caused alarm among school board members. Zanen took the news as a personal attack, the latest in a long line. He and certain board members, including the chair, Kris Gardner, a teacher from Connecticut, had clashed for years. Following the 2017 championship, the board had self-reported a potential Title IX violation on account of the boys' victory dinner at Olive Garden. (Zanen had paid for it with team fundraising money, but the girls' team hadn't been treated to a similar dinner.) The MHSA had found no such violation, but the board still disciplined Zanen, ordering him to personally pay back $474.25. He made around $3,500 per year coaching. David Whitesell thought that Gardner and the vice chair had personal gripes with the coach. Gardner disputed that, saying, "It's not like I don't like Zanen." The disputes could seem petty, but they accumulated, and the coach often litigated them to those around him. "I just hate to lose," he said. "I hate haters and I want to prove everybody wrong." He saw the ban of Anthony as an affront. "You take that away from me, you take away everything I believe in."

Superintendent Whitesell didn't understand the animosity toward Zanen. Whitesell acknowledged that the coach could use more humility. During a previous season, Whitesell had chided him for running up the score. But Whitesell tried to imagine bringing in an outsider to coach Arlee: "It would be like bringing a teacher that's from back east. And I'm not talking New York. I'm talking Billings."

Whitesell sometimes attributed the tension to what he called "the crab-bucket effect," the crude analogy for the way people from marginalized communities can treat those who succeed. (When one crab crawls out, the others pull it back in.) Mostly, Whitesell found the board's emphasis on basketball absurd. Where, he wondered, were the discussions of returning to a five-day week? What about foundational literacy? Whitesell was tired of protecting Zanen along with the coach's staunchest defender on the board, Tom Haynes, an uncle of Will's. "The kid's been winning," Whitesell said, of Zanen. "He's a good model. Family kid. Doesn't drink, doesn't smoke."

Zanen stayed up late at night thinking about how to get his players into college. The *Missoulian* wanted to run a feature on Phil, but Zanen tried to divert the reporter, suggesting a story on "the three-headed monster": Will, Greg, and Phil. Zanen hoped that would improve exposure for the other two and squash any intrateam tension. He asked his dad, Terry, who had a good relationship with Les and Inj, to work with Isaac individually. At the gym, Zanen spoke about the kids' overreliance on technology—"You are not the same people," he said, "with your iPhone"—and *Fortnite*, the video game. Only he called it *Fort Knox*, which made the boys crack up. He cajoled the guys about academics and focused on building the program, putting young players into games when the lead inevitably swelled. In early December, Greg floated the idea of getting a tattoo shaped like a cross on his forehead. "Bad idea!" said Zanen. He told Tapit Haynes, following one game, "You made me proud."

Some of the fans who judged his brash exterior didn't see those moments of warmth. But his biggest challenge, in those early days, was star management. He was concerned about the look on Will's face. During the next game, against Seeley-Swan, on December 14, Phil scored 48 points, adding 16 rebounds and 9 assists. He took twenty-six shots, missing just three. A couple of sports reporters remarked on the line with awe. Will scored 16 points, but was displeased. He'd taken just twelve shots. Chasity drove him home afterward, with him venting all the way. Will's game was predicated on moving without the ball to receive passes, and Phil often controlled the ball. Will was not hearing from any colleges. More than that, he was not having fun. Sophie had not been able to attend any games. He told his mom he wanted to quit. Once they got home, Chasity called Zanen, who said he'd resolve it.

Shortly after the game, Montana Tech's coach, Hiatt, asked Phil to sign a letter of commitment. But Phil also heard from the Griz—an assistant coach named Rachi Wortham said he'd like to see Phil at one of the university's upcoming games. "He was dangling the carrot," said Becky. Phil did not sign Tech's letter. He also spoke to Zanen about the growing unease on the team. "I could see it in Will," Phil said later. He asked Zanen if his scoring could cause conflict. The coach hinted that it could, but also deferred to Phil on how to handle the matter.

Phil thought about it all the way to Hot Springs, site of the next game, against the Savage Heat. (The team name had only been changed from the Savages in 2007.) Before the season, he'd dreamed of setting scoring records, and now his individual statistical dominance had sparked interest from two college programs, including the one he'd long aspired to. But he thought about Zanen's words and what he saw in Will. The ball went up, and Arlee quickly took the lead. The Savage Heat crowd jeered at Zanen as the score grew more and more lopsided. Zanen didn't care. Before the game, the board had dictated that his sons were no longer permitted in the locker room. The coach became irate. "They're trying to fire me," he'd said. Kendra and the boys attended every game, no less a part of the team than Franny or HeavyRunner. The ban of his sons from the locker room felt like a personal wound, and he took it out on Hot Springs. Furthermore, two players had misled Zanen about having a low grade, so he had benched them—meaning the starters had to play more minutes.

In the stands, John remarked, "The press hasn't been very good." The score was 61–8. On the court, Phil threw an unnecessary pass, leading to a turnover. "Finish that!" John yelled. Phil turned and nodded at him. John thought his son was overcorrecting following the 48-point performance. But that night, the scoring was equitable. Greg led the team in shots taken, with 17, while Will attempted 16. Phil shot 13 times, while Isaac attempted 12 field goals. The team won 95–19.

After the game, Greg left with Tomi Brazill. She had come to watch on her own, and he said he didn't want her to have to drive all the way back alone. They were both sort of ending things with the people they were seeing. "And," she said, "I *kinda* missed our turn to come home." The night was clear, the roads, too, for the most part, and it turned into one of those long, marvelous teenage drives.

Meanwhile, the team bus rolled across Perma Bridge, rumbling alongside the river and the railroad, stars above and mottled ice on the pavement below. Nate Coulson was listening to music when he felt something bad rush through him. He hadn't been sleeping and stayed up late thinking how life could be different. His father had died years earlier and Nate had struggled ever since. Basketball had taken his mind off it, but tonight he felt adrift. "Just had a weird feeling," he said, "like I didn't belong, and I didn't fit in." He posted something dark on social media. Next thing he knew, Lane Schall was sitting beside him. Nate said he felt that he needed to be alone. Lane said he didn't want Nate to be alone, and that it sounded as if Nate might be suicidal. Lane went up and talked to Zanen. Then Zanen sat with Nate. They spoke for the rest of the ride home, and upon arriving in Arlee, Zanen alerted David Whitesell. When Nate returned to school, he talked to a counselor. He thought it was cool that Lane and Zanen had approached him like that. He couldn't wait to get back to practice. Will often drove him there, and Zanen started paying increased attention, sometimes pulling Nate aside to talk one-on-one and telling him to get it together in school. He also wanted Nate to steer clear of negative influences. "Forever. Not just for the next fifty-two days."

In front of the other boys, Zanen took a more boisterous tack. He shadowboxed Nate—"Finally, somebody knows how to fight!"—and gave him crap when Phil whooped him one-on-one. Nate started looking forward to practice. "These are my brothers, man," he said. "I'd do anything for 'em. I have a lot of family problems, but when I'm here with these guys, I just feel the comfort of having that brotherhood."

The practices were sacrosanct, a venue for humor and a place to work things out. One day Will said, "We don't have enough Native kids on the team." A discussion followed about who was and was not a "rez kid." The Warriors were a diverse crowd—Séliš and Q'lispé, Cree and Norwegian, Filipino and Finnish. Greg was Diné and Lakota and also of white descent. Dar was Séliš and Black. But despite Will's assessment, only a couple of players were not tribal, Lane Schall among them.

"You're not a rez kid," somebody said to Schall one day.

"Yeah, I am! I'm at the window looking in."

"You're looking down."

Schall just laughed as though he couldn't be hurt. Zanen was more gentle about it. He sometimes called Schall Kevin Costner. Zanen often scrimmaged with the boys, talking trash. Isaac blocked him once and bellowed, to everyone's delight, "That's for taking me out last night!" On the Monday following the Hot Springs game, Franny oversaw a circle of junior-varsity players firing around-the-back passes at Sage Nicolai. This was for injury prevention: If the young players got in a varsity game, Franny explained, they had to be ready so a no-look pass wouldn't hit them in the face. On the far end of the floor, the first ten players wanted to scrimmage.

"Phil, Will," said Zanen. "What you wanna play for?"

Quietly Phil said, "Let's just play."

It went unsaid that the seniors would oppose and guard one another. They picked teams and went at it. Will's team won. Phil said, "One more game," and it began again.

Snow fell on St. Regis, a town of about three hundred near the Idaho border. In 2015, the community's largest employer, a lumber mill, laid off ninety people. Mineral County's unemployment rate was 7.4 percent, and it bore symptoms of rural struggle, with youth leaving for cities. During the 2016–17 season, St. Regis' boys had been playing well when, according to the coach, "our boys made some bad choices." They were suspended and the team suffered. This year, the team's best player had transferred to a Class AA school in Missoula. Before the game, the coach said he just wanted to see effort against the Arlee juggernaut. Zanen, meanwhile, asked the Warriors to hold St. Regis under ten points—for the entire game.

The gym was mostly empty, but Bear and Irma Malatare arrived in time for the girls' game. Phil's grandmother wore blue slacks and a loose-fitting jacket, her hair curled high above her head. She had a reserved expression and an angular face, like her grandson's. Bear wore his customary jeans and a tucked-in button-down shirt. Irma did not react much to the game. Bear, on the other hand, grimaced at St. Regis' baskets, grabbed at the air, and exhaled when Arlee scored. Irma smiled. "You missed an awesome thing that happened this summer," she told me. She was referencing the *syulm*. "They chose to honor the boys. It was so awesome. Big thing. It was a Native thing." At that, Bear giggled and wrapped the program up with his great hands. They reminisced about when Phil, Ty, and Al won three-on-threes under the direction of their daughter Cheryl—"They called 'em Cheryl's piranhas," Irma said, "because they could beat anyone. By the time he was two, his auntie Lynette had cancer, and from that time on our lives were devoted to her. We were talking, we missed so much of Phillip's life." Bear's face dropped, his cheeks taking his laugh lines down.

"I don't want him to go to the Griz," said Irma. "I want to be able to travel to watch him."

The big colleges traveled all over, while smaller schools stuck to the region.

"I'd sooner see him go to a small college," said Bear. "Phillip's not a benchwarmer. Not a lot of coaches will let him play his style of ball. It's *set set set set set*. In Indian Country there's no such thing as set." When it came to Phillip's career, they knew that both their grandson and son had ambitions. John was competitive. "That's what drives him," said Irma. But, she added, "That's not for us to decide. That's for Phillip to decide."

They talked about the state championship and all the elders who had joined Phillip for photos. Irma shut her eyes and shook her head, while Bear let out a childlike staccato giggle, a most beautiful thing. "To me," he said, "you just can't ask for anything more. There's a lot that'd be great. But I'm satisfied. I'm not a greedy person."

Earlier in his life, Bear had carried a specific kind of ambition. "It was always one of them deals," he once said, "where I wanted to show 'em because I was an Indian I could work just like the rest of 'em and I could have the best. That's why I've always had the best. The new car, shit like that."

But it had led him nowhere good. For a time, back when he was trying to prove everyone wrong, Bear spent a lot of time in bars. People called him the mayor of Arlee. A rage was in him then. He'd left high school after being declared ineligible for football. When he was eighteen, working in a mill, he punched out his boss's son because the man said he would never take orders from an Indian. Bear kept fighting and drinking. He was not proud of those days. Something had changed him, though. When he turned thirty-nine, he attended an event known as a Cursillo retreat, a multiday encounter with Christ. But that was a story for another time. Now it was time for basketball.

Arlee won 88–10.

The season's next heavily anticipated contest fell just before Christmas break. The Warriors' opponents were the Plains Horsemen, from just west of the reservation. Plains had beaten Arlee one year earlier. They also had a fan, a boisterous parent who once played Elvis Old Bull and who occasionally screamed at Will during the games. During a pre-game meal at the Malatares, Lane Johnson said, "Against some teams you try to work on stuff." Not tonight, though: "We're gonna try to beat 'em as bad as we can."

It was an away game, the Plains gym packed. Jordyn and Tyler were home for Christmas break. Ty and Alex Moran sat together in the front row. (Alex, who studied at Salish Kootenai College, attended many of the games.) College ball was a struggle, Ty said. He wasn't playing enough and didn't like the landscape out east. "When I come west and see the mountains," he said, "I get so happy." He wanted Phil to go to a big school. "He's gotta go D-One. He's a D-One player." Ivory Brien didn't make it back for the game. He was busy with college and pledging a fraternity.

Les sat in the top row, thinking back on the last time he'd been at Plains: "Beat 'em by twenty, enit?" Nearby Dean Nicolai, Sage's dad and the chair of the Native American Studies Department at Salish Kootenai College, talked about how David Thompson, the fur trader, had come through this area. Tom Haynes, the school board member, was here with his wife, Gloria, who wore a jacket in honor of their son David, Will's uncle who had died in a car accident. During the girls' game, Gloria handed a new pair of basketball shoes to David's son Tapit, now a sophomore on the Warriors. Will ate Skittles, wearing a vest given to him by Allen, then went to get his hair done. Chasity, in a shirt that read ANGEL, arched her eyebrows and flicked her comb. Raelena, Greg's mom, sat near Scott and Jennifer Schall. Becky talked to Jordyn about how the Griz weren't offering money to Natives. But, Becky said, "They're dangling that carrot."

Then there were older Warrior fans: Willie and Patty Stevens, Thomas Lyles's parents; Carmen McClure in a cowboy hat; Clark Matt in his flat-brimmed cap over long braids, his brother Bing marking down each basket on a homemade scorecard. James "Bing" Matt had starred for the Warriors in the sixties and aspired to one day be a coach. But when he'd told a white Arlee administrator of his plans, the man had laughed. Bing, who was Séliš, had not gone to college, instead joining the military. He built a career working at a job-training center and later as a facilities manager and a respected Tribal Councilman. He often told kids who were considering college, "Don't try. Go."

The Scarlets played first, as usual, winning by eight. The crowd was rarely completely full during their games. "Everybody undermines the girls," said a player named Laurencia Rose Starblanket, following the victory. The boys, she said, "Just go out and have fun and I feel like us girls, we overthink it. We don't hustle as much as we should." She sighed. "We try to slow it down into a pace that we're comfortable in." She wanted to be a lawyer one day.

Nearby, Big Will sat with Allen. A little higher up, Bear boomed, "Russ! Hot dog! Ketchup, mustard!" Bear told me about the Ursuline Academy, the notorious school. He'd lived an itinerant life as a child, picking berries and haying with his mother. Sometimes they scavenged for scrap metal. When he was young, he was sent to the reeducation academy in St. Ignatius. The school taught him discipline and ambition: "The upbringing I had at the Ursulines made me one of them type of people to work hard and always try to get ahead." But there were downsides. "They wanted to beat the Indian out of us for damn sure. You know, I'm left-handed. And they beat me with a goddang yardstick because I was writing left-handed. Possessed by the devil. The devil's possessed me. So I had to write right-handed. Then I couldn't write that well. Then I'd get beat for that, ya know. It was one of them deals where everything you did was you were really disciplined for it. Then if you got caught talking your language, you got a severe beating for that."

Bear had spoken Cree then. Now, he said, "I know a few words and that's about it. I've got a tape. I've been telling Irma I need to take that tape, put it in the CD, and play it and listen to it and learn how to talk again. But then they turned around and then they taught us Latin. You know, to serve mass for altar boys. Took one religion, one language away from ya, beat it out of ya, and then beat another one in ya. . . . The favorite saying of a nun was, 'I hear somebody sniffling, I'm gonna come and give you something to cry about.' So when I first went there, hell, I wasn't even six years old yet. First time I'd ever been away from my mom. Oh, man, I was heartbroken and crying and everything. And she'd come out and say, 'I hear somebody sniffling, I'm gonna give ya something to cry about!' Pull the covers off ya, pull your little pajama down, had a big-ass club about that big with holes in it, and whack you across the ass about eight or ten times and then tell you, 'Shut up or I'll give you more.' . . . And I still think about them people, them nuns and what they did to us. How the hell could you believe in a God? A Catholic God?"

But he did. He prayed to the Creator and he still went to church. "I believe in a higher power," he said.

The ball went up. *"Get it to him!"* boomed Big Will.

13

It's Not by Accident

Once, when snow was on the ground, I went by the Nk^wusm school to talk to Allen Pierre. He stood outside in a coat. All around him, kids played on sleds and swings. A girl ran up and said the boys wouldn't play with her. He said, "It's 'cause they're boys." He told her to find another group to play with. "Just don't go off alone."

I asked him the question that had been on my mind. It was about the shapes on the mountainside—the powwow dancer and the heart. How had they arrived so perfectly in the mountainside? Then Allen did something curious. He spoke in circles. He never did that. He was always direct in his speech. Eventually he paused. "It's natural and it's not by accident." Then he grinned. "That's all I'm gonna say about that."

Not everything is for everyone.

14

How Can It Be Business?

January 2018

I n November, Big Will went to a social services office, where he ran into a boy whose dad he had arrested for drug possession. In Big Will's recollection, the boy started to talk about how much he liked the Arlee Warriors—and especially Will. Big Will told the boy that Will was his son, and the kid brightened up, calling Will a legend. The policeman said that Will had struggled early in high school, then added, "He's in the gym every day. You can be just like that."

The younger Mesteth heard these stories. He relished his outsize influence and knew his status as a role model would be cemented by his making it to college, something he'd promised his father he'd do. His mother was more ambivalent. When Chasity considered the end of his high school career, her eyes watered: "I'm struggling with it. Because he's my best friend. I do want him to go out to bigger, better things. Better than I've been." The thought of his leaving was painful. "I guess I won't be bored if he goes to college."

Given his early academics, Will's college prospects largely depended on the ferocity of his defense and the accuracy of his three-point shot. But in the early season, his shot was off. Maybe it had to do with the lingering pinkie injury. But Zanen ascribed it to something else: "It's the fight in his head."

Will craved all that leaving signified but seemed ambivalent about actually going. The thought of being away from Saddle Mountain, the Jocko, and all those Valley Cricks caused a longing that was hard to describe. The thought of being away from Sophie was harder still. She was recovering from her elbow injury and had not been able to attend any games. "I don't know how much longer she has on earth," he said. "I know I make her happy."

During the Plains game and an ensuing victory, Will scored 43 points while shooting 57 percent. "It's time," Zanen said. "I'll call Frontier schools." But just days later, on January 6, Sophie slipped and fell again, fracturing a hip. She was rushed to Missoula for surgery. In that evening's game, a lopsided win against the overmatched Noxon Red Devils, Will made only four of sixteen shots and left in a funk.

When I arrived again, later that week, the roads were icy, the snowbanks deep, the parking lot at St. Ignatius High School full of trucks. The gym was sweltering. On the sideline Chasity brushed Will's hair. He wore a black shirt and slacks, his MESTETH medallion, and a somber expression. The *Missoulian*'s story had just come out. It was not about the three-headed monster, but rather squarely focused on Phil, a concern for Zanen. Two men who were not from the valley walked into the gym. One was Hiatt, the Tech coach, trim, with a smiling face and a crew cut; the second was his assistant, Derek Selvig—Robin's nephew—who had played for the Griz. He stood seven feet tall. The coaches walked past John and waved. John returned the gesture and turned back to the girls' game, calling out traps.

Once the boys' game started, Hiatt sat next to Becky. It was hot enough in the stands that the fans were sweating. Phil, on the court, wore long sleeves under his jersey. "He says it keeps him cool," Becky said, "but I think it makes him sweat more. Maybe he doesn't want anyone to see his skinny arms. I dunno."

"We'll take care of that." Hiatt started to tout Tech's weight-lifting facilities. He talked about the school's great academics, small classes, impressive job-placement rate, and its vast salad bar, which would be instrumental in bulking Phil up.

"Phillip doesn't eat salad," said Becky. "He eats chicken. Nothing green."

Hiatt called Phil "the best player in the state." I asked who else was close to his level. "Mack Anderson from Bozeman," Hiatt said, referring to the Griz's recent signee. "Caleb Bellach," the Manhattan Christian star, who was now a junior. Then, as though it were a foregone conclusion: "They'll probably face each other at state." But, Hiatt said, "We just feel like the all-around game, he's special. A lot of players can do one or two things, but Phillip's special."

What about Will? I asked.

"I think he'd probably have an opportunity at a junior college. He could shoot the ball, got good quickness, tough." But tonight Will seemed off, siloed away from the team, his mind elsewhere. Behind us, Big Will boomed, "Gotta give him the ball, Zanen!" Finally, Will drove to the basket in his low, explosive way.

Becky nodded at him and said rather conspicuously, "They grew up together their whole life." The coaches didn't respond, so Becky digressed, talking about John and Phil's annual buffalo hunt. "Usually what happens is they'll go after a game and drive and hunt."

"When?" asked Hiatt.

"After the game."

"Wow. That's crazy."

"My girls go. Whitney, she shot one last year."

"That's a lot of meat," said the coach.

"We have three freezers."

"Good thing Phillip's a carnivore."

"Mmhmmm," said Becky.

Will drove to the basket again.

"Will, number three," Becky said. "There he goes." The ball hung on the rim, then fell off. She continued, "Number three, his grandma is a Malatare. So they're related." She outlined Will's story: that he'd been academically ineligible, but was now a team leader with good grades. She talked about how much Phil loved playing with him. It went on; the implication became less and less subtle. Phil fed Will and he hit a three-pointer.

"Now he's eligible," Becky said.

"And he's sure helping them," said Hiatt.

"Get him the ball!" yelled Big Will. Then Phil grabbed an offensive rebound, and the Tech coaches turned the conversation back to his court vision. Will attempted only seven shots, scoring 12. The Warriors won by 18—their narrowest margin of victory since opening night. Zanen was disgusted by what he saw as selfish play. Everything, he said in the parking lot after the game, needed to change.

The boys screamed and the walls shivered. Will turned, pivoted, and fired a basketball like a baseball. He missed a sophomore but hit the curtain behind the basket. It must have been going seventy miles per hour. Finally, he was smiling.

THUNK!

Whump!

"OOOOOHHHHH!"

Zanen sat calmly on the sidelines, watching as his team played dodgeball in the old gym. "They don't ever get to have any fun," he explained. Will let one rip. The ball crashed into something wooden. Zanen rubbed his chin and said, "This might be a bad idea." Then, as though it had just occurred to him: "This might be a liability." Franny ambled in, unflappable as ever. The aerial assault continued. Franny had crucial information to share: he had heard, through the grapevine, that the Charlo coach had told a newspaper that he planned to put eighty points on the Warriors.

Zanen paused. "Gonna score eighty, huh?"

The balls whizzed and crashed.

"Gonna score eighty on us. That's what he's saying."

"Charlo coach, huh?" A smile crept across Zanen's face.

"Some young guy. He doesn't understand the kind of ball we play."

Zanen rubbed his hands and whistled and looked upward as though manna had tumbled from the ceiling. The coaches agreed to not share the news with the team until the next day. They had to clear the air first. After a few more minutes Zanen stopped the dodgeball and the boys lined up on the baseline. "We need to make sure we're starting to have more fun," he announced. "More fun is not watching each other have their own fun." He was seeing, out there, a move toward individualism rather than the beautiful game. He wanted more crossing motions from wing players to open up the floor—a practice the team called buffalo. He said he had three guards who could score with ease, but he needed someone to assume the role of primary facilitator. He added that it shouldn't be Phillip. He addressed Will: "What do you want? When you play ball, what do you want? Do you want buckets? Do you want to be the point guard? What would be fun?" Zanen wanted the decision to come from them. Will didn't say anything. Nothing was fun right now. He was shooting under 30 percent from the three-point line and wasn't getting the touches he wanted. His *túpye?* was back in the hospital. No colleges had called. He didn't respond. Silence.

"Do you want to be the point guard?" Zanen asked.

Will rubbed at his chin. Finally he spoke: "What am I right now? What am I?"

Zanen shifted the focus onto other players. Isaac, he said, needed to be tougher down low. Lane Johnson was shooting too many three-pointers. Schall needed to be more vigilant about box outs. Greg was missing transition passes to Will, and Will was floating on the three-point line rather than slashing. "There's no malicious intent," the coach said carefully. But the offense looked stagnant: one pass, then dribbling. They were isolating themselves, doing what everyone else did. He said in his most gentle way, "What's nice? Tomorrow everyone will forget."

Then Franny interrupted with a great bellow: "I got one thing to say. If you wanna dribble the ball up, let's play Class AA ball then. If you're gonna dribble the ball up the fucking court, we might as well just run a set every fucking time. Right? You wanna do that? I don't!"

The boys' expressions turned grave. Franny's voice amplified and the criticisms ratcheted up until he said two words that stopped everyone cold: *"Missoula ball."* They were playing Missoula ball. That was about as exciting as watching Flathead Lake freeze. "I don't like it. I want to be *gone*." He added, "If you don't understand that, you don't understand about Indian ball."

The coaches left the gym, taking the junior varsity with them. They wanted the boys to sort this out on their own. Tears welled in Greg's eyes. "You don't know the shit I go through." Being the superintendent's son was tough. He wanted more effort from the reserve players. "We die out there. I'm sure Phil put fuckin' hours and hours in the gym. And Will, too."

Now Nate Coulson spoke out, issuing a charge to the second team to step up in practice to help the senior captains: "This is the last time we're gonna play with these two."

Will addressed younger players who were on the verge of losing their eligibility. "I was in the same boat as you a couple of years ago, end of freshman year, start of sophomore year. I didn't care.... Once Jenn gave me my opportunity to become eligible, I wanted to play with my boys." He added: "That's the way I feel."

Phil spoke next. "We go into gyms, and all these little kids are running around looking for us. They're like, 'The Arlee Warriors are here.' Do you know how inspiring that is? We fricking are touching little kids' hearts around the state." He continued, "Kids would die to be in the position you guys are in. And you guys just take it for granted. I love all you boys. I'll fricking do anything for you guys. But on the court, I need you to come to play. You better start becoming leaders. Not here in this gym, in the classroom. In the fricking hallways. This game we're playing for this little town, it's huge. It's touching a lot of people. And some of you guys, you don't get it." Phil closed by invoking Butte in March: state. "I sit in my room and I just think of the shit that we are about to do."

Lane Johnson said, "All I got is, I'll battle for you guys every night. I'll guard whoever. I'll box out whoever."

Greg confessed that he was thinking of transferring to another school following the season. He didn't get into it all, but said that it had been a hard year—"Just shit." But he wanted another ring. "I'm willing to accept whatever role. I just want to win the title."

"That is what we're trying to do," Phil said. "State championship. Nothin' else. It's business." Then he paused, as if some interior voice had grabbed him by the neck. "But how can it be business when we're all family?" Everyone looked up. "That's what we need to do. We just all need to become family."

The next afternoon, Sage Nicolai and Ardon McDonald, a junior, sat in the bleachers, wearing sharp collared shirts and grave expressions. "You read the paper?" Ardon asked. "They put in the paper they're gonna beat Arlee." The Charlo coach's unfortunate comments had made the rounds. A girl started braiding Ardon's hair. He continued, "Gonna beat us by eighty. Shut down the kings." His expression conveyed some mix of contempt and pity. In the locker room, Zanen sawed off one of Phil's overgrown toenails with his knife, then addressed the team in a slow, methodical voice: "I want you guys to unleash on them." He added, "They don't belong on the court with us."

Franny said, "People don't really like the way they brought you out in the paper."

According to the *Lake County Leader,* Charlo's coach had said, "We are going to have to put up eighty points if we want a chance against Arlee." But he had also made the error of favorably comparing one of his players to Phil. What was said mattered less than what was needed: a common enemy. Zanen allowed that he had been scolded, in the past, for running up the score. But today, he said, he had received a green light from the athletic director: "Amy told us she'll support me." It would be difficult, he said, to set a state scoring record, given a mercy rule that let the clock run during foul shots once the lead swelled to 40. He set more realistic goals: "I want to hold these guys to four points a quarter. That's fair right now." The boys nodded earnestly. Zanen said, "Shut them down." He prayed, then Allen and Big Will hit the drum, and the Warriors pulled hoods over their heads and swooped onto the court. The Charlo Vikings appeared concerned, and with good reason. A couple of minutes into the sublime evisceration, Phil flew down the court on a fast break. Two defenders converged, but with a thump, Dar simply took one out. Then he grabbed two rebounds and hit a three-pointer. Jennifer Jilot took a deep breath and said, "To see these kids do this." The final score was 75–33. Zanen was slightly disappointed, as Will and Greg combined to miss fifteen three-pointers. Had they shot more accurately, the team could have reached 100 points.

The next day, Becky and John took a scouting trip. They drove east on I-90, through the Clark Fork River Valley past Drummond, then Butte.

The land opened into long plains. Their destination was Churchill, home of the Manhattan Christian Eagles, Arlee's opponent at state the previous year, who would that afternoon play Gardiner, another highly touted team. A cloud layer hung over the slushy highway and the Tobacco Root Mountains; John and Becky dropped through Cardwell Gap into Three Forks. In 1855, this area was designated a communal tribal hunting grounds in a treaty organized by Isaac Stevens with the Blackfeet, Gros Ventre, Séliš, and other tribes. That was before gold was discovered at Grasshopper Creek. After that, the government kept breaking treaties to accommodate settlers who poured in on the Bozeman Trail, so named for a man who deserted his family in Georgia in search of riches. Then came the railroad. That was the end of the buffalo hunts.

These days, there is a different sort of boom in Gallatin County. It started in the 1990s, when technology companies moved in, noting the low cost of business and the high quality of life. One arrival was Right-Now Technologies, a customer-relations software firm run by Greg Gianforte, a wealthy entrepreneur and fundamentalist Christian who moved from New Jersey. In 1999, he hired a man named Clair Daines and his son, Steve, to build an office park; Steve Daines later joined the company as an executive. RightNow would eventually sell for around $1.5 billion. Steve Daines became a senator, Gianforte a congressman and then Montana's governor. From 2010 to 2018, Bozeman's population increased by 30 percent. There are few natural features to inhibit growth, and subdivisions fan out. The median home price is nearly $600,000. Of cities its size, Bozeman has for three consecutive years been the nation's fastest growing.

But just a few miles before the edge of all that new development, protected by a fork of the Gallatin River, there is a small farming town. Manhattan, and its neighboring unincorporated communities, Amsterdam and Churchill, were settled by Dutch farmers in the late nineteenth century following the construction of the railroad. The lawns are shorn, the sidewalks clean. The Manhattan Christian School sits next to the Manhattan Christian Reformed Church and across the road from the Bethel Christian Reformed Church. Steve Daines's son attended the school, playing basketball, and Manhattan Christian has received funding for scholarships from a school-choice organization financially supported by Gianforte. The school itself is modest; its gym, less so. The facility is large and impressive, with a windowed walkway overlooking the court. The community funded it with donations following the tragic death, in a car accident, of three students and a teacher in 2003.

The parking lot was full of pickups when John and Becky arrived. They hoped to slip in without anyone noticing, but that didn't happen. Caleb Bellach scored a couple of early baskets, making impressive moves. John took it in quietly, while Becky leaned forward and looked down into her phone. "Oh, I dunno," she said softly. "I don't know." She took a breath. "The big boys were sucking air in the first quarter," noting that a couple of players took rests. She shrugged and smiled sweetly. "My son plays the whole game." And then: "Gardiner might have been overranked. I don't know." Her eyebrows peaked. She smiled, texting Phil and Dar. I asked John what he thought. "No comment."

At the end of the half, Caleb Bellach and his father, the Eagles' coach, argued following a botched play. Caleb clenched his fists and stalked off the court. It remained close throughout the third quarter, but in the fourth Manhattan Christian pulled away, Caleb and another player dunking emphatically. Still, Becky couldn't help but notice that, afterward, the Eagles put their hands on their hips. "All that dunkin' and fancy stuff takes a lot of energy." The buzzer sounded, and some little kids took the floor before the girls' game. The crowd filed out behind them. Soon the gym was nearly empty. Caleb's mother, Carly Danhof-Bellach, emerged, wearing a gold sweater, distressed jeans, and bracelets on one wrist. She sat with Becky and talked, Caleb close behind. In the fall, before the season, the Bellachs and Malatares had run into one another at a showcase for potential recruits at Montana Tech. At the time, Becky wasn't feeling kindly toward Manhattan Christian. She never was able to figure out who called her son that awful slur at state, but she assumed it wasn't an Arlee fan. But at Montana Tech, Phil forgot his shorts and Caleb lent him some. Then, following an ugly on-court collision that left Phil with a concussion, Jeff rushed to his aid. "I saw kindness," she said. "We share a common thread, in that our kids are in the limelight. The boys are young and innocent and they've been thrust in this world of people critiquing them and judging them and animosity and jealousy."

Just sixteen years old, Caleb had a round face and braces and a crew cut and came off as considerate and kind. Like Phil, he wanted to play Division I ball, and like Phil, he found it hard to imagine leaving home. "If I have a chance to go to a really good college, then I would," he told me after the game, "but I'd probably come back here." Like Will, he said, "I drive but I don't have my license." Like both boys, he wanted to one day work in the mountains, hoping to eventually become a hunting out-fitter. His dream was to play for the Montana State University Bobcats, so he could both reach Division I and stay near home. Jeff Bellach once expressed disappointment to me that the state's Division I programs recruited so extensively out of state. He brought up Mack Anderson, the Bozeman kid who had recently signed with the Griz: "Hopefully that'll open some more doors for some Phillips, some Calebs." Caleb had already received an offer from MSU Billings, the Division II school. But when it came to his place among the state's top players, Caleb was exceedingly humble. He cited a recent article in the *Great Falls Tribune* listing twenty top players, which started with Phil. "In today's game it comes down to size," he said. "But it's also heart over height."

We spoke about the previous year's championship. "To play in the state championship game," he said, "I was dreaming about it ever since I could remember." He occasionally thought about the play, in the third quarter, when Will had hit a three to tie the game, starting an eight-point swing. He wondered if he could have done anything differently. The crowd noise had been incredible: the sounds, the eyes. "When it came down to the fans," he said, "the Indians cheered for the Indians, and the non-Indian teams cheered for the non-Indians." He added, "I have nothing against them. Because we're all playing for the same thing and we all respect each other."

Caleb said basketball in Churchill had its own meaning. "We have a basis to why we play," he said. "We're playing for God every night. To go give Him all the glory." Before games, his father prayed that Jesus Christ might reveal himself to the fans. A Manhattan Christian parent named Faith Dyksterhouse, who formerly sat on the school board, said she hoped to see God's hand in everything the players did. "All belongs to God, and that's what we believe. That goes well beyond basketball." But, she said, "Basketball is in it. Basketball is in it."

Manhattan Christian requires that at least one parent of each student be a member of a church, and kids are taught both evolution and creationism. Scott Wolf, the girls' coach that season, who had played basketball at Harvard and lived in Bozeman, characterized the community as cloistered: "Their perception of the world is 'We're farmers and we seek bounty from the land and God protects us.'"

Manhattan Christian's tuition is around $10,000, although financial aid is available, and church members can offset the cost through volunteer programs. When it came to athletics, Wolf said, "We have a distinct advantage. We're private, so kids can transfer in." Three starters from the previous year's runner-up team had transferred into the school. But according to Jeff Bellach, that dynamic led to misconceptions. "People say, 'Oh yeah, they recruit all the Bozeman kids,'" Bellach told me. He objected to that characterization, pointing out the high number of players whose parents attended Manhattan Christian. Furthermore, he said, "Our problems might be different than Arlee's problems, but we do have problems." They, too, faced stigmas. "Certain people think that we're just a bunch of white rich kids." He noted that most of his players came from farming and middle-class families that scraped together the tuition. The school, he said, contained kids from broken homes, kids who struggled with self-worth—kids, in other words, who were kids. Jeff said Caleb occasionally wondered why some players from other teams said negative things on social media. "He would say that: 'I'm so nice to those kids. Why don't they like me?'"

After the game, Caleb apologized to Becky for the dispute with his father before halftime. She didn't think he had any reason to apologize, but he was held to a high standard. "Caleb has a big heart," she told me later. "He's emotional. He wants to be accepted, wants to please his dad, his community, his church. He's maybe more a pleaser child than Phillip is." On the drive home from the game, John and Becky discussed Churchill. They found it curious. Quiet, orderly, just so. Did anyone, John wondered, arrive home not knowing where the next meal would come from? "Caleb and Phillip," said Becky, "are from different worlds."

15

Should We Smile?

January 2018

Traffic slowed on US 93 to accommodate a throng of boys crossing the highway. Most wore shorts and basketball sneakers despite the freezing temperatures. Troy and Trey Tewawina, the team managers, wore grass dance regalia. Will and Phil wore war bonnets made by Allen Pierre. It was team photo day. Zanen was pissed because Phil had said he'd wake up early to shoot one of the elk that had been eating the coach's hay on a lease. But Phil had slept in. Zanen opened a section of barbed-wire fence and the boys slipped through, walking to an aspen draw bordering a meadow. Will dropped his phone in the snow, and Billy Fisher and Nate started jawing at each other. Then, in the meadow, Dar and Lane Schall, both experienced riders, appeared on horseback. One of the boys said it was weird to see Dar on a horse. "That's racist!" yelled Phil. He thought the kid had said that because Dar was Black as well as Séliš.

"Stop!" yelled Zanen. "Somebody define *racist*!"

Billy Fisher spoke up. Billy was kind and optimistic and took a long time gelling his hair and hoped to be an architect one day. He sometimes wore fanny packs that he described as "extremely fly." Billy also knew what racism was and he hadn't been allowed off the bench in one game until he could provide a definition: "It's when you treat someone different because of their race!"

"Good job," said Zanen, and everyone walked out to take the photo. Zanen told them to go through the trees, not the meadow, so they didn't track up the snow. Sage asked, "Should we smile?"

"No, look tough," said the photographer.

Zanen exclaimed that he should have brought the horns he had at home.

"Are they big?" Phil asked.

"They're six-pointers."

It was agreed that they should wait for the antlers, and Zanen was gone, sprinting through the snow. By the time he returned, fifteen or twenty minutes later, laden down with antlers, Dar was trying to get the horse to go backward, Schall was trying to help him, and Greg was complaining about the cold.

"Stinkin' Navajos!" Zanen said.

16

A Perfect World

January 2018

John Malatare sat in the passenger seat, hurtling through the darkness. He and TJ Haynes, Will's uncle, had heard that bison were moving out of Yellowstone National Park, so they had loaded up TJ's trailer with snowmobiles and rolled south at 2:00 A.M. They were layered up in hoodies, vests, and snow pants. TJ, a burly Séliš guy with a mustache and a wool cap with elk teeth on the brim, had come from a shift with the Tribal Police Department. In past years, when the hunt took place earlier in the winter, Phil had joined. But with playoffs looming, he couldn't.

John and TJ whistled and rubbed their hands in anticipation, reminiscing about past hunts: the gutshot calf they'd discovered and dispatched ("We did him a favor," John said), and the time they sent Phillip to scout two huge bulls up a hill. "We brought horses," John said, "but it was pretty steep ground. So we drove around all day, there was really nothing around, so I asked this guy"—meaning TJ—"said, 'How hungry are you?' He said, 'I'm damn hungry.' I said, 'Well, let's go kill 'em.' So we sent Phillip." The boy followed the tracks, light as air, and next thing you knew, he was up on the hill, waving. They had walked up and shot two bulls that weighed two thousand pounds. "Holllly man," said John, "it took us *allll dayyy!*"

At the time of the drive, the Confederated Salish and Kootenai Tribes were one of five Indigenous nations with rights to hunt bison once they left Yellowstone National Park. Sometimes the hunters had to wait for animals to move off roads before shooting; sometimes they competed with other hunters waiting at narrow bottlenecks where the animals moved off park ground; sometimes they fired under the watch of environmental protesters. Frequently, a crew of back-to-the-landers showed up in buckskin to help the hunters pack out meat in exchange for tongues. John and TJ found them amusing, but, John said, "They're nice people."

Any day, John and TJ could hunt elk or deer in solitude within the vast Mission Mountains Tribal Wilderness and the adjacent peaks and valleys. Still, despite the prescribed and chaotic nature of the bison hunt, John preferred it. "I've shot hundreds of elk," he said. "The first time I shot one of these, it was a whole different feeling. It was just the respect out of that guy. Out of that buffalo, and it was something that—that's why we're here. That's why we're still alive."

In the 1870s, a Q'lispé man named Latati moved a small number of calves from the plains east of the mountains onto the Flathead Reservation, fulfilling a vision his father had held. At the time bison populations were falling to the bullets of the US troops and colonizers who slaughtered them. With their territories diminishing due to broken treaties, and people going hungry, nations including the Séliš played a part in that grim chapter, with some tribal hunters furnishing the booming fur trade back east. A Q'lispé man named Lassaw Redhorn was once quoted as saying, "The fur traders with their insatiable demand for robes, and then, more robes, were of course responsible for this wholesale slaughter of the herds. Prior to the appearance of the fur traders, our Indians had always conducted winter hunts to procure the needed robes, but it was a rule among all the Montana tribes, that during no season would there be a needless or excessive slaughter."

The bison moved by Latati built up a herd that grew to number over five hundred. At the time, it was called the largest free-ranging population in the country. Starting in 1907, to make way for the opening of the reservation to white settlement, the herd's owners shipped hundreds of the animals by rail to Canada. A small group remained in private hands. They were later used to both establish the National Bison Range and revive the flagging Yellowstone herd, which at the time numbered only a couple dozen.

Over the next century the Yellowstone herds swelled to number in the thousands, attracting hordes of camera-wielding tourists, who were occasionally gored. The bison also displayed symptoms of brucellosis, a disease affecting large ungulates that can lead to stillbirth. This concerned ranchers, who carry great political sway. For decades, Montana held "brucellosis-free" status, meaning its ranchers didn't have to test for the disease before shipping cattle elsewhere. In the 1980s, the state culled Yellowstone's bison for fear they might pass brucellosis to cattle. But, as John said, "It's never been recorded that a buffalo has given cattle brucellosis."

In the early days of the hunt, state game wardens led sportsmen to idle animals. Images of men shooting bison at point-blank range led to widespread outcry. In the 1990s, the state suspended the hunt, the Department of Livestock took over the cull, and tribes were given the right to take some meat—though not to hunt. It was still not very sportsmanlike. "Man," said John, "they were just slaughtering them." Back then, he and other tribal members waited on snowmobiles, then drove in after the killing to harvest the meat. In the 2000s, Montana opened the hunt to tribal nations that could demonstrate that the treaties they'd signed with Isaac Stevens ensured their hunting rights on "open and unclaimed land." Pressure had since increased. The way

John saw it, not everyone did it right: "There's Indians and there's tribal members. And there's some of these guys go over and hunt these buffalo because they're tribal members. They don't know anything about being an Indian, but they're tribal members, and that's the only part of the Indian they know is they get to hunt now. I grew up Indian. I grew up around traditional grandparents. I grew up around traditional parents. We know what it's like to—" John paused. "We know what it's like to be an Indian." He continued, "We come down here, we shoot a buffalo, we say thanks to the Creator, we say our little prayers, and we take care of that meat and we treat it with respect. Not coming down looking for the biggest bull you can find, bring it home, you're gonna sell the hide, sell the head. We don't do that."

They were headed to West Yellowstone, Montana, one of two access points with open hunting grounds. TJ had heard that a ranger was checking permits on behalf of the Forest Service—"being a dick," as TJ put it. "Dad'll be down there. Tell him to pound sand." Dad was Tom Haynes, the school board member and a tribal game warden. On lands with treaty-conferred rights, his authority was equal to that of any federal ranger. "It's gonna be a little rodeo down here," TJ said, "with all those protesters running around." Since the 1990s a bison-advocacy group called Buffalo Field Campaign had been documenting the hunt with the goal of ending it. "Dad said they all had their camcorders out yesterday," TJ said. John said he'd heard that one of the organizers was from Arlee. He warned me, "Somebody'll flip you off, cuss at you a little bit."

"I'm a reporter," I said. "I'm used to that."

When they were done laughing, TJ said, "We take that kinda personal when they do it to us."

TJ had recently been shot at three times during a car chase, and he said he was quitting policing. He planned to work at the logging company that he and his dad operated and raise the kids he and Roberta had fostered. There were nine of them at home. TJ said he planned to make some vests out of bison hides. John said, "Phillip, he sleeps on his. Got to keep the fan on just 'cause he says he stays so warm!"

Somewhere east of Missoula, TJ showed off a new knife, a gift from a woman he'd started seeing: "It's engraved and everything."

"That a bone handle?" John asked.

"Yeah. Bone handle and turquoise. Handmade."

John said almost tenderly, "Pretty nice, Buzzard."

I sat in the back seat, wearing just about every warm thing I owned. During the five-hour drive, John and TJ talked about their kids, small-town rumors, the new Arlee Warriors State Champions seat covers someone had made, and the coming postseason. John thought Manhattan Christian's guards wouldn't be able to handle Arlee's press. He was thinking of going to scout Melstone, a team six hours out east with a powerful forward named Brody Grebe. But from what John had seen, Arlee's most potent foe was itself. He didn't like the way some boys chirped to the refs—Arlee kids were taught not to do that, he said—and he was worried about what he perceived to be a focus on individual stats. "Hope they get this shit figured out," he said, "before they go against some competition."

John acknowledged that the team was under pressure. But, he said, "I think it sets them up in life to succeed. Their hard work. It doesn't matter what you do, whether it be a marriage, whether it be a job, whether it be a school subject. If you're willing to work at it, you'll succeed."

When John joined the Forest Service back in 1991, he heard talk about how certain bars were full of "drunken Indians." He developed thick skin and outworked his colleagues. He expected the same of his son. "That's why I'm a little harder on him. If he really wants to go play basketball, he has to work hard. He has to prove 'em he has the willpower to stick it out. Don't be another stat." John was referencing the stigma about kids returning home early. "I talked to that coach at Butte about that," John said, referencing Hiatt. "Native kids. He said, 'You're exactly right they are a little gun-shy about recruiting because of that history.'"

John respected Hiatt and wanted Phil to respond to Hiatt's offer. Phil had recently told his dad he and Ty planned to walk onto the Griz together. John was fine with that—he just wanted Phil to make a decision. He had told Phil to talk to those in the valley with connections to the Griz: Don Holst, the former coach, and JR Camel. John also wanted Phil to consider every possibility. "I said, 'If you and Tyler go try to walk on, what happens if one of you make it, one of you don't make it?'" Phil said they had already discussed that scenario. Tyler, Phil said, would continue going to school. "I said, 'So flip that. What happens if Tyler makes it, Son, and you don't?'" Phil hadn't thought of that. "I said, 'So these decisions that you're trying to make, you really need to think about the pros and the cons.'"

But John felt his son had the talent to play for the Griz. John realized he hadn't considered his own life once Phil's career ended. "What are we going to do if he doesn't continue and play through college? I don't know. I don't know if I've thought that far." Should John knock down DeCuire's door and ask what it would take? He thought of a friend who had played college ball. The coach had given him a hard time. "I said, 'They're testing you out,'" John recalled. "'They're seeing how tough your willpower really is.'" His friend quit. John said, "Proven point right there." Native kids got one shot. John considered the older kids who'd taken Phil to the lake, in the summer. In a voice somewhere between reprimand and plea, John said, "Let him get there."

We passed Butte, home of Montana Tech. I asked if there had been any truth to Phil's assessment that basketball was John and Becky's dream. "There was probably a little bit of truth to that," John said. "But I know deep down he wants to play college basketball. I know he wants to go beyond college basketball. He told me that he wants to be the best player that Montana has ever seen." John thought about Dar, and how down he'd been after not receiving the honors he deserved following a terrific football season. John hoped Dar would get a chance to play in college. "These are their days. I done wasted mine." John had been a track star in his youth, a distance runner who could go forever. Terry Pitts thought John had Olympic-level talent and had trained him back then. As an adult, John looked back and wished he'd been more committed. "But now, I can support them. I can give them experiences." And, he said, "That's all I can do."

Dawn revealed a blue, snowed-in landscape, with long stands of timber on the side of the road near the border of Yellowstone National Park. TJ parked at a pull-off and fired up the snowmobiles, backing them off the trailer. A helmet was on the seat of the small one. TJ said to me, "Gas on the right. Brakes on the left." Then, almost in passing: "Brakes don't work."

TJ said, "See that dog?" Across the highway, a wolf had run past. I'd missed it, too worried about the brakes. We crossed the highway and rode down a track abutting it, like a snowy frontage. We crossed back over the road and pulled into the timber on a groomed trail. A low fog hung over everything, the passing conifers deep blue. Up ahead, a group of men were stopped by parked snowmobiles, bundled in heavy jackets. In the trees just off the trail was a dark mound against the snow: a dead bison calf. TJ and John helped the hunters load the carcass onto a plastic sled tailing behind a snowmobile. Then TJ and John disappeared again, steering through the lodgepole. I tried to keep up but couldn't, made a turn, and slowed in the fog, profoundly lost. TJ emerged from nowhere, beckoned, and made a U-turn. The fog lifted as we ascended a long curving track, the Madison River emerging on our left and, beyond it, a ridge turning gold with the sun. A butte overlooked wide plains, craggy peaks, the frozen Madison Arm of Hebgen

Lake, and no bison. John descended toward a draw, looking for tracks, while TJ stayed on the groomed trail. I followed him back through the lodgepole until everything materialized at once: two groomed trails, two roads, and, as TJ later put it, "sixteen Indians and nine hippies." The bison moved slowly through the trees, their hooves crunching softly. Shots rang out. The herd split up, some moving toward private property, some back to the east, toward the park boundary. A FedEx van drove past. One of the campaigners, clad in an orange vest and standing by a parked Subaru, wept.

John stopped his snowmobile and walked onto a trail where a calf shot by one of the other hunters had died. He knelt over the carcass to help the hunter, who sawed through the sternum. Steam rose from the body cavity and John reached in. A group of cross-country skiers rode past on the trail. One asked if the animal was a bear. TJ arrived on foot, as his snowmobile had locked up in deep snow. "Fifteen of 'em hittin' that brush." After a pause, he continued, "You gonna run down there and shoot some of them or what?" At that John was gone, tailing the herd back toward the park boundary. TJ helped the hunter on the trail move his gut pile. TJ asked me if I had any water. I offered some out of my backpack, and he told me to pour it into the coolant reservoir of the snowmobile, which was empty. A red light glared on the dash; the engine was overheating on account of my failure to cool it by driving through deep snow. "We call that the idiot light," said TJ. He started heaving on his own snowmobile, freeing it, then we took off after John. But the herd had made it back into the safety of the park. Back at the truck, John said, "Everyone without sleds killed 'em. Shouldn't have brought sleds."

"Them protesters must have pushed 'em all onto that private property," TJ said.

"If I'd gone the right way," John said, "maybe woulda shot."

TJ drove toward town, looking for a diner, and they thought about the scene. The hunters they'd just helped had been uncomfortably close to private property and the groomed trails. TJ said, "You have to be, what they say, a hundred yards off the road before you start shooting?" He thought about the calf that he and John had helped gut. Because of where it finally died, he said, "It looked like it got shot right on the groomed trail." The treaty right to hunt was newly recognized and precious, and the protesters with cameras represented an ongoing concern.

"That's the shit that gets you in trouble," John said.

At the diner we all ordered burgers, but the waiter informed us they were out. They did, however, have buffalo burgers. I ordered one, not thinking about its agricultural origin. John and TJ looked at me as if I were on some new drug and ordered chicken wings. TJ's face turned sour as he thought about some tribal members who hadn't left any offering after killing bison. "No tobacco. Nothin'." But TJ had helped anyway. He and John discussed the presence of the ranger who was checking tags. "I'm Indian," said John. "Don't need no tags."

The afternoon was warm, and we shed layers as we once again parked and took off through the lodgepole. We drove the same way we had that morning, past the mouth of the river and up to the great butte. We passed gut piles adorned with ravens but no bison. As the sun lowered, we met back at the truck, joined in the parking pull-off by a larger group who cracked jokes and talked about their bad luck. Someone showed up with a trailer equipped with a crane, hauling two animals, skinned and quartered. Someone else pulled in with a sled full of bison heads, tongues lolling. Protesters arrived on skis, their faces drawn. Some of the hunters looked at them askance; somebody suggested sticking a buffalo tail in their windshield wiper. But John approached a dreadlocked campaigner and started to talk in a friendly manner: "You're not from Arlee, are you? How long you been with this?"

On the drive back to town, John took on a serious tone: "Our tribe has ties to these animals. To this herd. Right here. When there was just a few left, our ancestors came over and hunted them, they brought calves home." He narrated the history with specificity. "So if anybody has rights to these buffalo, Abe, it's the Séliš have rights."

I marveled at the beauty of the hides, all those reds and yellows and blacks—a mistake. There was a long pause. John said, "After I read your story, Abe, I might have to give you my hide. Would you appreciate that?"

A longer silence descended. As a writer for *The New York Times Magazine,* I could not, to prevent undue influence, accept gifts from story subjects. But *The New York Times Magazine* also employed no tribal staffers. I could ask my editor's permission, given the cultural sensitivity, but the time to answer was now. Trapped between two ethics, I stammered and lost my voice.

"Would you treat it with respect?" John said. "Out of friendship?"

Something fell in me. "If I were to take a gift, I would lose my job."

TJ said, "Tell 'em it's shaming us."

John said, "For not accepting the gift."

I tried to say that I was sorry. I tried to say what my job, and the story, meant to me. I thought of what TJ had endured, and I thought of my own mother, and what she went through after her brother died by suicide. I said we could talk after the story was out—after I'd had a chance to consult with the *Times.* It did not matter. The only decent answer was yes, and I had said no. John and TJ moved on, trying to find a hotel. Over dinner that night at a sports bar, the men talked basketball and hunting and parenting. One guy tried to imagine life with endless buffalo: "Used to be a perfect world."

"Sure ain't now," TJ said.

The next morning, the temperature gauge in TJ's truck registered −10. As we drove away from the hotel, it dropped further. Soon it was −18. The sun sat low on the horizon, a silver orb obfuscated by clouds at the end of a funnel of pine. We drove down a Forest Service road and crossed fresh bison tracks. John looked at the place and said, "Pretty sure I brought Phillip down here. And he and Al would jump in the snow-banks." And the boys would disappear. We saw more Buffalo Field Campaign protesters on cross-country skis. I asked John what he told his kids about them.

"I'd tell them, shit, to just go talk to them and ask them why they're doing what they're doing. And tell them why you're here."

No one had seen the herd. "Son of a gun," said John. "They're somewhere." The other guys decided to bag it. John and TJ waited to see if it would warm up. It didn't warm up. When they decided to leave, nothing was said. They drove to a log-walled restaurant. Over lunch, John allowed that Phillip had lost his ring while fishing. The guys thought Arlee Schools should get him another one. "Put Arlee on the map," someone said. But John just shook his head. It was the boy's responsibility. After lunch, while driving home, TJ received a text saying buffalo were at Gardiner. He'd have to come back in a couple of days. John considered the state championship in Butte, six weeks away. He had already booked his hotel room: "Stars are going to have to start falling out of the skies for us not to be there." The truck pulled into the Malatares' driveway, the trailer cutting ruts in the mud. "The field of dreams," said John, "that never turned out." Then he looked up and noticed that his wood truck was empty. The boys had finally unloaded it. That was something to be grateful for.

17

As Good as Your Word

January–February 2018

On January 10, David Whitesell announced his resignation from Arlee Schools effective at the end of the year. He was burned out. "Empathy fatigue," he said. "Compassion fatigue, whatever you want to call it. Secondary trauma. I'm in the middle of it. I'm wiped out. Absolutely wiped." Furthermore, he was constantly between the board and Zanen. He wondered how the coach would fare after David had left, given Zanen's defiant tendencies. "I been running herd on this guy for three years," Whitesell said, "trying to protect him from himself. He thinks his accomplishments will be enough to get him his next job. It's not." Whitesell was ready to move on, as he had so often before. He wanted his son to do the same. But that would be Greg's decision.

Jilot was nervous that Whitesell's successor might be less forward-thinking about educational equity. The state was full of administrators—many of them white men—who rotated through reservation schools. "I'm scared," she said.

One day, shortly before tournaments, I walked into her classroom to find her wearing a concerned expression. "I'm sending grades to Zanen," she said. "Not good."

Jilot turned to a girl wearing distressed jeans and said, "You have holes in your pants." She asked another girl, a basketball player named Halle, who was sitting on the couch, if she needed her grades checked. Halle said, "No, I'm okay." She was simultaneously reading a book and typing on her laptop, earbuds in. Jilot turned to the boys. "So just a heads-up. Your practice today might not be fun, because I just turned in grades."

The boys stood on the baseline. An uncle of Will's named Clayton spoke to them, wearing a serious expression: "You bring people here, to give them something to be proud of." But, he said, all that was in jeopardy. Zanen was in danger of losing about half his players before the tournaments due to their grades. He was looking for help wherever he could get it. When Clayton finished speaking, Zanen ordered everyone with a D or an incomplete paper to step off the line. Nine boys moved up, Greg included.

HeavyRunner, the assistant coach, said, "Basketball's the biggest thing going. You guys are rock stars." And, he said, in the long term, it meant little. "Would you rather make sixty thousand dollars a year or ten bucks an hour? It all starts right here." It wasn't about basketball, he said. "You can have a better life. And that's totally up to you guys." Some parents, he said, were calling teachers on their kids' behalf. "That's just enabling you guys. You work hard. That's up to you guys now."

Zanen told everyone to take in the players still on the line: "This could be our team come Monday." Phil confessed that even he had a C-minus. But, he said, "Will's good." The boy who once carried so many Fs now had the best grades on the team. But he wasn't present, as he was attending a wake. Zanen said, "Who has iPhones? Who gets on 'em out during school?" He praised his flip phone. "It makes me a better husband. It makes me a better father. You are not the same people you are with iPhones. I challenge all of you to leave it home for a day." He said, "Not prioritizing the important things—family, school, this team. That stuff you guys look at, it just takes you away."

Franny's speech was brief and less philosophical. Zanen seemed desperate. He said, "Abe. Come here. You got any life lessons for these guys?"

I thought about that. With the vast advantages conferred upon me, I had made the somewhat dubious choice to pursue a career as a writer, often relying on a Subaru and a storage unit. The trade-off was a life lived around the planet, traveling in proximity to many forms of favor and injustice, but not the one that had cleared my endlessly open road. I knew, from firsthand experience, that the clarion purpose offered by sports eventually runs thin, but I understood that, within the walls of this gym, my life experience carried limited relevance. The only thing I knew with certainty was that the amount of time I spent away from family must have appeared truly insane to the Warriors. I stumbled through something about hard work.

Clayton took over again, telling the boys that they were role models whether they liked it or not. Then HeavyRunner took half the team into the cafeteria to work on their homework, a practice he would maintain for the next week. On one such day, a TV crew arrived, hoping to film. Zanen sent them away: he didn't want the boys' academic struggles publicized. Furthermore, police were investigating a nearby shooting. Zanen was worried the reporters might lump that in with the team.

On January 25, in the middle of the season, Plains, the rival from just off the reservation, came to town. Before the game the team gave Jilot a beaded pen, making her cry. Once the ball tipped, the atmosphere was tense, the gym overflowing with spectators. The score was 15–4 when Greg picked a Plains ball handler's pocket near half-court and took off for a layup. As he rose, the kid clobbered him. Greg crashed to the floor and slid in a lump against the wall. Slowly, Lane Johnson, Will, and Phil walked toward the Plains player. Lane diverted away, but Will and Phil kept on with silent intent. Zanen sprinted across the floor after the boys, chastising the referees. Did they think they planned to talk it out? The rest of the game turned heated enough that someone called the police. But law enforcement was already present. Big Will sat courtside, trying to control himself when Will fouled out and a Plains fan bellowed, "Take him out!"

On the court, Arlee dominated. Following the game, on a talk show viewed by a few thousand people, a MontanaSports.com reporter called the Warriors "the team to beat," adding, "If you're a team that hasn't seen them before, you basically start out in a 10–0 hole. . . . There's a little bit of a shell-shock factor." In practice, Will and Phil pulled out blocks, stacking them high and jumping over them in a brutal tandem workout. Will had lost weight since the beginning of the season and was experiencing sharp pains in his side. More concerning, he had recently discovered blood in his urine. Chasity took him to the emergency room, where he tested negative for a kidney infection. He said nothing about it. His college aspirations came down to the next month. He figured there might be scouts at divisionals and state. "Hopefully someone looks at me," he said. The early season, he acknowledged, had been a struggle, but he was happier now. "I don't care about highlights and stats. I just care about making history." If he did that, he figured, he might have a chance to keep playing. "I can hardly make mistakes. Not try to put on a one-man show, because if I try that, probably barely any coaches would want me." Four weeks, he said. "That's all I got left. If I don't make it to college, then it's probably the end of my basketball career, much as I hate to say it. But. Oh, well."

When I asked Phil if he had considered life after sport, he turned pensive. "Definitely will be a lot more time on my hands. Definitely might get fat."

For a week the temperatures rose and the hills began to melt. Phil disappeared in search of horns. This was Zanen's worst fear. "I pray for snow," the coach said. In the first week of February, Phil was headed out to shed hunt when he received a text from Rachi Wortham, the assistant coach at the University of Montana, asking if Phil had a moment. Phil called right back, and Wortham asked him if he wanted to be part of the Griz. The coach clarified that Phil would still be a walk-on, but that his place on the team was guaranteed. Phil said he'd like that very much. Then he pumped his fist and found some horns. When John heard the news, he told Phillip he needed to call Hiatt. Then John went to his recliner, sat down, and exhaled. Phil had one request for his parents: he didn't want word getting out before the end of the season. Nothing could distract from the run to state.

Phil was nervous about calling Hiatt: "I feel pretty bad. He's given me a lotta love to go there. I just feel bad." He hoped the coach wouldn't take it personally. For all the hope she'd carried about the Griz, Becky seemed slightly disappointed. "My dream is for an education," she said. "It's hard to write off that kind of scholarship to a top college." She worried Phil might get lost in the university's lecture halls. Furthermore, Hiatt had won her over with his candor and decency. "You're only as good as your word," she said. Shortly after making his decision, Phil called Jordyn. She had been talking, for a while, about leaving college in Arizona. Now she said she was coming home. She'd decided to go to Tech, to enroll in a nursing program. But she hadn't told him because she didn't want to influence his thinking. "That was a very adult decision," Becky said. "I thanked her for that."

Jilot was concerned about Phil's going to the University of Montana, given her experiences there, but she knew he had a good support system and the breathless attention of the valley. "He has God syndrome," she said. When she asked Will or Nate to do something, they hopped to. When she asked Phil, he stared incredulously. I had grown accustomed to that look, too. Once, when I posed a question, he said matter-of-factly, "You asked me that already."

In Jilot's mind, Will was one of the voiceless. It felt as though she needed him to succeed. His grades in his current classes were strong, but he still had to make up coursework from his freshman and sophomore years, and by February, he had yet to apply for financial aid or college. Jilot said she'd help with the forms, but worried he was waiting for some opportunity to drop from the sky. Will's demeanor about the matter appeared less urgent. He figured maybe he'd get offered a scholarship. One day he rolled into her classroom, Jordans untied, headphones on. Jilot said that Will had outstanding assignments: "This needs to be done."

"It just sucks. It's just boring."

"You just need to get it done. I'm really starting to get worried about you."

"You always stress me out." Will left.

The last game of the regular season fell on February 10, against Two Eagle River, the public school in Pablo, the seat of the CSKT government. Before the game, each member of Arlee's class of 2018 walked onto the court with their families. It took a while for the announcer to talk through all of the girls' extracurricular accolades: class vice president, Reservation Ambassadors, Indian Club, Big Brothers and Big Sisters. The boys' announcements were shorter:

"Phil participated in football for one year, basketball for four years, and Eagle Club for one year." He walked out with John, Becky, and his sisters. The announcer read his statement: "To the next generation of Warriors: You are the future. Follow your dreams and be true to yourselves."

The announcer continued, "Next senior is Will Mesteth Jr. Will Mesteth participated in basketball for three years, football for three years." He walked out with fifteen family members: Chasity; his *yayá* Sharon; his siblings; Kelly and Allen; Kelly's father, Jim; Will's uncle Sean; Big Will and his wife, Ashley; and their kids. Will led the way, pushing Sophie in a wheelchair. She wore an astounding smile. Will's statement was even more to the point: "I want to give special thanks to my *túpye?*, my number one supporter, for being able to be here."

The game started and the cousins played with devastating joy, running two-man fast breaks in which the ball didn't touch the floor. Will scored 37; Phil, 35.

It was tournament time.

18

If It Could Just Be This

February 2018

The season came down to three weekend tournaments: districts (at Salish Kootenai College), divisionals (at Hamilton, in the Bitterroot Valley), and state, in Butte. The week before districts began, the temperatures fell, with lows near zero. On Tuesday, February 13, Zanen arrived at practice with a frozen carcass of a cow under a hay bale on the bed of his Chevy. "You see her on the truck?" he asked cheerily. He focused on the positive—the return of frigid weather, he noted, had ended Phil's horn hunting. He also seemed invigorated by the impending playoffs, and started to hint that maybe he wouldn't depart following the season after all. "I'm not gonna fight for my job." But, he added, "It's my program."

Kendra was also at practice. I asked what she wanted. She said, "I was thinking back on how long he's been coaching." She remembered the moment, years earlier, when someone informed her that Phil, then in middle school, had briefly quit a team after getting kicked in the crotch. "I thought, 'Oh great!'" She laughed. She loved Phil. She loved Will. She loved Lane Schall. She loved Billy Fisher—her favorite player. To her, basketball was family and community. But, she said, "We're getting burned out. Outside this gym, the boys and Zanen, it's politics." She sighed. "If it could just be this all the time."

On Wednesday, news circulated that a pack of wolves had treed a teenager in the area. That afternoon, at practice, Zanen expounded upon his decision. He was thinking about some of the new players: Nate, Tapit, Trey Malatare, and Shadenn Stone, a junior. "Maybe they need me." He paused. "And I need them. Every one of us is connected." He said, "Phil's dad lived with my parents. Schall's my cousin. Shadenn's my wife's cousin. Lane"—Johnson—"is like a fifth cousin. Cody's dad played with my brother." He remembered when Chasity was pregnant with Will. Zanen had met Greg later, but the point guard now considered his coach like family. Greg had recently aced an exam, raising his grades at the last minute, as was his habit. He'd also put on weight and seemed happier now that he and Tomi were steadily dating. He said he would consider staying in Arlee if Zanen did. "If Zanen's strong enough to stay through everything he's been through," Greg said, "then I feel like I should probably stay, too."

But all that was moot if the team didn't win. "If I don't win," Zanen said, "I'm done." One day he said it wasn't about victory, but rather teaching life lessons; today, he needed a championship to keep his job. "Who wants a coach that loses? I've never been taught that losing was okay." He elaborated: "If you don't win, yes, they will fire you. But if you teach them principles like discipline, getting up on time, being here at time, and holding them accountable, and they're talented, you're doing two things. You're teaching them. But you're probably going to win."

The district tournament included the teams that Arlee had played during the regular season. The top two would advance to divisionals, and the Warriors' progression seemed a foregone conclusion. But Will's health was concerning. Strange pains traveled through him. Sometimes his back and sides felt as if they'd been knifed; sometimes he had a splitting headache; sometimes it hurt to sit down. "Just miserable," he said at practice, an elastic bandage wrapped around his torso. He had tested negative for a kidney infection, but the discomfort seemed to radiate from that part of his body. He wasn't sure. He'd lost twenty-five pounds since the start of the season. Early that week, he emerged from class and walked into the school parking lot to find one of the team's superfans, Clark Matt, waiting with a bag of Indian medicine: muscle rubs made from plants. "The med kit," Will called it. So he figured he'd be fine. No doctors, he said, a point of tension between him and his mother. Chasity wished he'd take a day off. But, she said, "He won't."

As the top-seeded team, the Warriors did not compete in the first round of the district playoffs. Still, they left school in the morning on Thursday to watch the games. On the drive up, Zanen thought about Phil playing for the Griz. Kendra was already setting money aside for season tickets. "It's beyond what you could ever imagine," Zanen said. He thought Phil had been touched by God, and sometimes found himself pleading with the boy to thrive in college. "All those little kids behind you on the rez," he said, "coaches need to know that they're worth taking shots at. Because they are that good kids. They are that talented." He said he'd told Phil, "Do not forget: you're doing this for every kid in the world that's ever looked up to a basketball player coming off the rez."

The assistant coaches had a less dramatic view about the matter. HeavyRunner liked what Tech offered education-wise. Franny just said, "It's ultimately up to him. Even if he stays in the tribe. There's nothing bad about living in your community and raising a family." Franny would be proud of Phil if he worked on the Tanner ranch.

Zanen veered toward glory and gravitas, Franny toward home and humor. But they complemented each other. That afternoon, while the coaches ate lunch, Zanen sought sensitive advice: "Will and his mom are fighting. She wants to take him to a doctor. Should I make him go?"

Franny shook his head. "No. Let them work it out."

Then the team went to the gym to shoot, to refamiliarize themselves

with the rims at Salish Kootenai College. Meanwhile, forty-five min-
utes south, class was in session. Jilot thought ballplayers missing class
for a special shootaround was "a bunch of crap." When I asked David
Whitesell about it, he just chuckled. It wasn't an Arlee thing, he said. St.
Regis, Hot Springs, Plains—they were all missing school. He smiled.
"We love our tournaments in Montana."

On Friday, February 16, Arlee's first night of districts, Alex Moran,
Phil's cousin who'd graduated the previous year, took in the game with
a displeased expression as the Warriors allowed Noxon to play them
tight. "If they play like that," he said later, "they'll get beat."

The next day brought fast snow and a rematch against Plains for
the district championship. Beforehand, Chasity said Will felt better.
"And if not, I got a bag full of whatever he wants." Overlooking the
court, one of Plains' fans said he just wanted the Horsemen to make
it competitive, and that Phil was one of the best guards he'd ever seen.
He talked about his own playing days; he had faced Elvis Old Bull, and
claimed to own one of his jerseys: "I should put it in a glass case."

The ball went up and Plains hung tough. A pressure filled the building; it felt as though the unthinkable might occur. On the bench, Phil
told the team to be mentally strong: "Play these fuckers like they're the
number one team in the state and we got something to prove." Then
Will stole the ball and nearly dunked it; Lane Johnson ripped down a
missed shot, scoring and drawing a foul; Dar hit a three-pointer; and
Zanen called for an alley-oop to Isaac. Phil pulled down a rebound and
took off in a dead sprint, tossing the ball in front of him in a high, fast
dribble. He beat a couple of defenders down the court and caught up
with Will, who slowed just enough to wait for the pass. As Phil reached
the free-throw line, he crossed over with his left hand, caught the ball
with his right, and wrapped it around his waist, slinging a blinding pass
between two defenders. Will was already elevating, both hands cupped
in front of his neck. The ball arrived precisely there, and Will cradled

it off the backboard into the net. He scored 26; Phil, 25, along with 9 assists. The final score was 95–59. Arlee had twenty wins and not a single loss. Outside, a blizzard filled the roads.

Deep snow, drifted in great mounds. Phil and Cody Tanner got stuck checking cows at the Tanner ranch, and John had to tow them out with the wood truck. By Tuesday, Phil had a hacking cough. Dar also fell sick. More concerning, Will had rediscovered blood in his urine. At the insistence of Chasity, Zanen, and Kendra—an emergency medical technician—Will had finally relented, going to a doctor. But he first laid down some rules of engagement: "Before we start with anything," he recalled telling the doctor, "if you tell me I can't play, I'm still going to play." He left with a prescription for antibiotics for a potential kidney infection. But at least Greg was healthy. "I don't get sick," he said. "I just get mentally hurt."

The Malatare house was tense: laundry piled in the kitchen, a newspaper story featuring Phil and the headline UNSTOPPABLE on the fridge. Becky suspected, based on online chatter, that a scout for Manhattan Christian had attended Arlee's district games. It seemed likely that the Warriors and Eagles would meet once again, this time in the divisional semifinal. "I'm sure Bellach has it all figured out," she said. For his part, Zanen called a rodeo buddy to get a scouting report on the Eagles. When I went into David Whitesell's office, I discovered a different side of the philosopher-superintendent. He anxiously tapped his foot as he discussed the necessity of the shootaround at Salish Kootenai College, which had taken the boys out of school: "Those baskets are independent of the wall. So for shooters, you don't have that back reference." He contemplated the possibility of the team falling behind: "What happens if we get into adversity? Who's gonna step up?" Holst, the elementary school principal and former Griz coach, entered, and the two educators analyzed Manhattan

Christian's shooters, Greg's lateral quickness ("that's our off-season," said David), and the tendency of certain officials to change their calls during the postseason. "Pisses me off," said the superintendent.

The only place that wasn't tense, it seemed, was the gym. There, Greg brought levity to the team. As a result of a bet he'd recently lost with a girl, he dyed his hair silver. But because of the gold coloring he'd put in earlier in the year, it took on a curious greenish sheen. It wasn't his best look, but Zanen, optimistic as ever, said it was badass and started calling him Silverback. Zanen tried to get the boys to focus on their first opponent, Darby, a team from a struggling timber town in the Bitterroot Valley. But everyone's attention was trained beyond that, on Manhattan Christian on Friday night.

"Has Manhattan changed?" Greg asked.

"They're exactly the same," Zanen said. "Caleb's kind of gonna be the issue." He turned to Phil: "You know him better than anybody."

"He's a good player," Phil said. "But put a little pressure on him . . ."

Throughout the week, one topic of conversation loomed above the rest. Phil instructed the boys on how to steal the ball from the Eagles' guards, putting his hand in the space where he knew a crossover dribble would come. Franny said, "I love when their coach gets pissed off." Zanen said that, if Jeff and Caleb started arguing, "It's over." During the two district games, Isaac had amassed just 8 points and 7 rebounds. Shortly before the divisional tournament, Franny and Phil approached Zanen with a bold proposal: they should start Lane Schall, who was boxing out well. But Zanen believed in Isaac. He simply said, "As long as I'm coach, he's gonna stay there."

After shootaround on Monday the team headed to Missoula so the boys could practice at Dahlberg Arena, the Griz's gym. Zanen wanted them to taste the big time. On the way down, he talked about Will's recruitment. People didn't know how hard it was to get a kid recruited out of Class C, he said. Never mind two kids. "Phil will do everything in his power to set you up, but it doesn't matter," Zanen said. "They only want him. They just want him."

But, Zanen said of Will, "I *know* this kid can play. He's got heart, he's got desire, he loves it. He's got the backup, he's got the support." Zanen grabbed his phone and called a Frontier Conference coach. The man inquired about Phil. "I can't say," said Zanen, "but he's going somewhere. He said he doesn't want it getting to anybody because then it'll focus on him and not the team."

Zanen transitioned to the sales pitch: "Will Mesteth. Lefty. That sucker that, I mean, he's tough, man. He's really tough." Zanen said Will had excellent passing ability and that his ball handling needed to tighten up. "But he can stretch any defense out to thirty-five feet. He's got the green light." Zanen added, "Now he's got the highest GPA of all my boys."

Zanen listened as the coach asked a question.

"The kid's solid. His dad's a cop for the Tribe. Married, got a nice family going. Stable. And his mom is one hundred percent in his life. He's honestly, out of the kids that people are afraid to give a chance to, I'd give this kid a chance. I know it sounds biased, but I *know* he would make it." Zanen said that if the coach gave Will a chance, Chasity would have him there "tomorrow." Then Zanen said, "I know, I've had other schools say, 'Well, what's the story?' What you've just asked. This is one kid I definitely— I'd stick my job on the line for him."

The call ended. Zanen shook his head. "Oh, fuzz," he said—the interjection he used instead of another four-letter word. "There's that whole issue I told you about. They are so scared to drop the money on these kids." According to Zanen, the coach had said, "You're really wanting to put your job on this kid?"

Later, I would run into another Frontier Conference coach, Steve Keller, of the University of Providence. He told me, "You can't just win in the Frontier anymore with just straight Montana kids." He had, however, offered scholarships to Brody Grebe, out of Melstone, and Caleb Bellach. Of Caleb, Keller said, "He's six-six, he's athletic, shoots the three." Then he said something that stuck with me: "Great family."

The day after the Warriors practiced at Dahlberg Arena, on February 21, Phil slept in with a cough and a splitting headache. Word spread within the community that a boy had died by suicide. He had played for the Two Eagle River School in Pablo. He was a friend of some of the Warriors. "It's fricking unreal," Zanen said. "It really is."

19

It Can Also Break Your Heart

February 2018

The boys gathered in a hallway at Hamilton High School on the east side of the Bitterroot River. The gym was full, Arlee red on one side, Manhattan Christian maroon on the other, Arlee's band playing a sweet rendition of Metallica's "Enter Sandman." It was Friday, February 23. As expected, the Warriors and Eagles had advanced to a divisional semifinal game with larger implications. Ten minutes remained before warm-ups. Today, there was none of the usual pregame joking. Jordan Lefler, the camera-man, lined the players up. They were silent. The light on the camera blinked, and Phil spoke:

"We, the Arlee Warriors, are dedicating this divisional tournament to all the families that have lost a loved one due to—um—"

Lefler asked for another take.

"We, the Arlee Warriors, are dedicating this divisional tournament to all the families that have lost a loved one due to the pro—due to the pressures—"

Phil tried again: "We, the Arlee Warriors, are dedicating this divisional tournament to all the families that have fallen victim to the loss of a loved one due to the pressures of life."

"We want you all to know," said Greg, "that you will be in our hearts and in our prayers as we step onto the floor to represent our school, community, and our reservation." His eyes and voice were steady.

Lane Johnson spoke next, in his soft tenor, the consonants and vowels blurring together: "As a team, we rely on each other to get through the challenges on the court or in life."

Then Isaac said, "To all the youth on the Flathead Reservation, we want you to know that we stand together with you." It was his eighteenth birthday.

Dar spoke next: "Remember, you are the future."

Will closed it: "Please help us share this message and join our team as we battle against suicide."

Lefler turned off his camera and the Warriors retreated into the locker room.

The idea was hatched the previous morning. After everyone loaded up on breakfast sandwiches at the Malatares', the boys had gathered on the bus. Zanen had asked the team if they wanted to make a statement following the suicide. The boys thought it was a good idea, with Will and Phil both voicing support. Zanen proposed that they make a video, but talking about suicide was hard. The boys weren't going to write the script. That fell to Zanen and Lefler, the videographer. A CSKT descendant, he was known in Arlee as a thoughtful and humble presence. While he aspired to produce sports films, he also wanted to make a positive impact—he loved the reactions on kids' faces when they saw their own highlight videos. Zanen sought input from a number of people, trying to strike a balance between acknowledging what had happened while being respectful and not glorifying the act.

On Thursday, before Arlee's first game, Greg, wearing a stony expression, watched Manhattan Christian play. He didn't seem impressed: "Nothing special. If they press us, they lose." Will, sitting nearby, said, "They're good. I don't think they move fast enough to play against us." He rarely criticized anyone without adding a caveat about what they did well. In the closing minutes of the girls' game, a close contest, Zanen texted the boys, instructing them to stand and cheer. Soon most of the team was underneath the scoreboard, roaring as the Scarlets pulled out a close victory. Then, in the divisional quarterfinal game, the Warriors put 101 points on Darby as Manhattan Christian watched. Billy Fisher led the scoring with 23, not missing a shot; Isaac scored 16, including a dunk. Afterward, Inj, Isaac and Billy's auntie, beamed. She invited Zanen to Isaac's birthday party: "Stop by in your work clothes, with hay in your hair and shit on your shoes. We don't care."

Friday's rematch with Manhattan Christian represented the Warriors' first real test since Rocky Boy. If they won, they would go on to the state tournament. If they lost, their season could effectively be over, on account of Montana's complex challenge rules. The boys woke and gathered once again at the Malatares', this time for breakfast burritos. Then they drove to a shootaround at a gym outside Hamilton. Zanen carried himself with a strange calm. He had stayed up watching tapes of Manhattan Christian until eleven thirty the night before. Then he'd risen at two fifteen to feed and calve. But now, he said, "Just another game. There's other things in life to worry about." As a younger man, he had struggled with nerves, to the point that he was occasionally overwhelmed before games and rodeos. His father helped with that, teaching him to slow down and control what was in him, separating thought and action. Now Zanen spoke about the need to defend Sam

Leep, a terrific shooter, and to guard against backdoor cuts. He offered Lane Schall a steak dinner if the boy could pick up two charges. Phil interjected, asking who was guarding Caleb. It was Lane Johnson.

"You limit him to ten points," said Phil, "you'll get all-state." He took the floor, outlining in minute detail the moves Caleb liked to make. Phil wore a white T-shirt, his shoulder blades cutting through, and a pair of Will's new shoes with the laces untied. Phil's hair was messed up, his cough hacking and dry. He illustrated precisely where Caleb liked to post up, and how he swam with one arm: "He wants it here. Front him." Phil turned to Isaac, whose job was to rotate if a pass to Caleb floated over Lane's head. "You played a hell of a game yesterday. 'K? But it don't matter now. I don't really care. Tonight is bigger. I want you to do what you did yesterday, but do it better tonight. 'K? Rotations, you have to drop to here." Phil walked the route. He provided a forensic analysis of the way Manhattan Christian's center shot layups: not straight up, but with a slight turn. He told Isaac not to swat at the ball, but rather to tip it. Phil oversaw a drill in which the second team mimicked Manhattan Christian's press; he offered instructions on where he wanted Greg and Will and Dar, the shooters, to position themselves if Manhattan Christian ran a zone. Phil said, "Once you set me a screen, look for the ball. I guarantee you they're gonna come"—meaning they would double-team him, creating a mismatch. "They don't talk well and they're kind of . . . weird."

"They're pretty selfish as a team," Franny said.

Phil hollered, "Yeah!" That was it.

To reach Hamilton High School from Arlee, you drive ninety minutes south on US 93, through Missoula's commercial sprawl, then along the railroad tracks and the Bitterroot River, down into the ancestral homeland of the Séliš. These days, the Bitterroot Valley is known for its political conservatism and resistance to regulation such as zoning.

Ammunition shops, subdivisions, trailers, and exclusive communities for multimillionaires sit together in strange juxtapositions, as though coughed up in a historical hiccup.

The roads were icy and Arlee evacuated by noon, everyone leaving early to secure seats. Bear wore pins bearing both Phil's and Dar's faces. He was in his seat by 2:28 P.M., even though the game didn't start until six. Inj and Les arrived earlier still. John wore a special shirt saved for big games, red and white, with a Séliš phrase that translated, depending on whom you asked, as "I'm proud of my Warriors" or "Big feelings for my Warriors." On one wall, Manhattan Christian had hung two banners. One was covered in Bible verses; the other, the girls' and boys' teams sitting on Chevy pickups. Both read UNFINISHED.

Becky paced the halls. She discussed a friend who planned to arrive at six ("I said, 'You'll be in the nosebleeds'"), the school board's decision not to pay for a hotel the previous evening, forcing the teams to commute (she was displeased), and the date. It was the deadline for coaches to file applications for Gatorade Player of the Year, a coveted statewide honor. Zanen hadn't yet sent in Phil's. "Phil don't give a shit," Becky said. But she did: "As his mother, you better get that damn thing in." Also, Phil's flu-like symptoms had worsened. Her eyes flashed, her polished demeanor gone. "My son's coughing and it's the game of the year."

The boys sat, heads in phones, looking at photos of bucks and waiting on lunch. Will had ordered pancakes, Phil a French dip sandwich. Both had hot chocolate. Phil also had an orange juice, mandated by Zanen, who opted for the all-meat omelette. They talked about a bull elk at Ravalli Hill with a horn already hanging off, and the wolf that Phil's cousin had recently trapped. Will pulled up photos of a mule deer he'd shot. "Fuzz, man, his brow tines are wicked," said Zanen.

Phil said, "I bet you my dad has a bigger mule deer than both of you."

Zanen said, "I know he does."

Will replied, "But you don't."

The conversation turned to the news. It was just over a week since the school shooting in Parkland, Florida. A student from Darby had recently been arrested for making threatening posts on social media. Phil said, "Big Sky got shut down, too," referring to a Missoula high school.

"It's just like suicide," said Zanen. "It's freaking contagious." He expressed enthusiasm at President Trump's recent suggestion, in response to school shootings, that teachers should be armed. The boys didn't say anything about that. Zanen grabbed his flip phone. He'd received a text from Jordan Lefler with the proposed script for the video. He recited it. Phil looked down and played with his utensils. Will looked directly forward. Phil said, "Tell 'em, like, you're the future of this team." He thought for a moment, then added an edit: "You're the future of your team."

"Okay." Zanen proposed further simplifying it: "Remember, you are the future—leave it at that?"

"Mmhm." Phil turned back to his utensils.

Will pulled up another photo of a buck, and Zanen asked about their ACT scores. Will's mind was on the recent school shootings: "You know it's coming. Be at our school sometime."

"Better not," said Phil.

"You never know," said Will.

"You never know," said Phil. "But I hope not." The food arrived. Phil carefully removed the onions, lettuce, and tomato from his French dip.

Bear told a friend to join him in the parking lot: "Come on." He walked out of the heat of the gym and into the cold of the late afternoon. His friend, a beloved community member who'd been having a tough time, followed. The sun hung over the Bitterroots as Bear lit a cigarette. When he was a boy, he used to come down here in summers, doing farmwork: haying, picking berries. The man asked Bear how, given the history, he could visit the area without experiencing blinding rage. "Because," said Bear, "you can't live holding on to that." Then he told the man to wait. He went into his van and emerged with his state championship jacket, the red-and-black one from the previous season upon which he'd hoped to put his grandkids' names. He told the man to try it on. It fit perfectly. Bear said, "That's yours." And the man could not speak.

Back in the gym, I sat with Big Will, Clayton Malatare, and Allen Pierre, who wore a red-and-black ball cap with pins bearing the faces of Will and Clayton's son Trey. On the court, the girls played a terrific Twin Bridges team. Big Will warmed up his vocal cords, yelling at the refs. Allen had by his side two large, bulky pillowcases. In the fourth quarter of the Scarlets game, Will approached and took the two items from Allen, carrying them carefully to the locker room. Then Allen, Big Will, Sean, and Clayton took the court to sing. At the first note, Phil and Will sprinted out in war bonnets. A great sound rippled through the place as Arlee's crowd rose. John, who hadn't always thought that Phil fully embraced Séliš culture, felt as though something in his chest might burst. A few rows away, Irma wasn't sure a basketball court was the proper venue. "I don't know," she said. "Just like that whole attitude, token Indian kind of thing." She and Bear were also concerned that a feather might fall out of one. They were original war bonnets, not replicas, so if a feather fell, someone would have to do a ceremony on the court.

But Allen had already contemplated those concerns. Originally, Zanen had wondered if the whole team could wear bonnets. Allen talked it over with his father, Patlik, and they concluded that it would only be appropriate for the two seniors. "I could have come up with a dozen war bonnets," Allen said, "but it would have took the significance away. That's the role that these boys took was leaders of that team. So I believed that the two leaders should be the only ones." And, he added, "Phillip is a part of our family." Will wore Patlik's bonnet; Phil's belonged to Jim Malatare, Allen's father-in-law and Bear's nephew. Will had also been concerned that a feather might fall out, but Allen told him not to worry about that. Allen had made them both by hand. The feathers stayed on.

Manhattan Christian scored first, on a transition play in which Phil was uncharacteristically beaten down the floor. On the next play, Phil drove and spun, drawing a double-team. He dropped the ball to Isaac, who rose for a basket. Arlee fell into a half-court matchup zone, and Greg made an aggressive move, trying to pick the pocket of the point guard, who hurried a bounce pass toward Parker Dyksterhouse, which Will intercepted. He tore off for a layup, kicking his feet with a flourish as the ball fell through the hoop. Back on defense, Phil's hands were on his knees—the first time I'd seen that. Manhattan Christian executed a terrific play, the ball whipping to Parker without touching the ground. Will's rotation was a half-step late, Parker's shot good. Phil brought the ball up and isolated on Caleb, driving past him with a crossover. Parker helped; Phil dumped the ball to LJ for a layup. Three possessions later, Phil left the floor, running past the team to the locker room. Whispers echoed through the crowd. Was he hurt? Sick? In his absence, Dar checked in.

The boys revealed something when they took the court. For some, it wasn't hard to find. Phil was an artist: always stunning, occasionally reckless, never compromising. Within the crowd, a rising feeling took hold whenever he surveyed the court and decided what astonishment to produce next. As he accelerated, shifted, took to the air, or spun through hopeless defenders, everyone's heart rate rose, because you had the distinct feeling that each play might be his last. You also suspected that he knew that, too, and was mildly amused at the possibility. Allen Pierre once told me, "Every time he grabs that ball, Phillip, it's like he's telling a story." Will was tough, explosive, capable of anything, including out-bursts that could go sideways. To watch him play was to become accus-tomed to surprise. For years people had bet against him. For years they had been wrong. Franny once said that, if he had to have one player take one shot to win a game, it would be Will. Will played until he passed out; Will was unending. Greg was skilled and ambidextrous, a pure point guard, smooth and precise, able to accommodate different scenarios, capable of seeing space and shooting from great distances. Zanen some-times said Greg's game would translate most easily to the college level. Greg sought attention and was not afraid of complaining at injustices, barking at the refs, talking trash. But when a teammate hit the floor, Greg always arrived, pulling the boy up. Lane Johnson was a superb athlete, long and fast, willing to do the unglamorous things to win. He guarded the toughest opponents and fought for rebounds and shook his head side to side when he was frustrated and moved in a straight line at all times on the court, no matter who was in his way. Isaac was full of skill, kind and eager to please, and often hesitant. But sometimes a more aggressive side took over and he produced sudden and spectacular runs. With his athleticism and size, he clearly had college potential. Lane Schall was all try, tough as anything, utterly unconcerned with himself, his body merely an afterthought should it require sacrifice. He preferred coming off the bench so he could choreograph an elaborate pregame routine, with him greeting each starter. Dar was a little bit hard to find. He was extremely fast and had a sweet shot but rarely used it. He was a protector with a football star's strength—against Charlo, he'd taken out the defender who attacked Phil—but Dar did not always show it. Now, with Phil in the locker room, Dar took his place. Here is what happened:

Will isolated and passed to Greg, who missed a three-pointer. Dar fought for the offensive rebound, then passed it to Lane Johnson. Back in the locker room, Phil vomited repeatedly, whatever illness he'd been incubating now fully on him. On the other end of the floor, Will committed a foul, and the Eagles narrowed the lead. Arlee set up in a full-court man-to-man press, and Manhattan Christian broke it. Dar saw something and darted into a passing lane and stole the ball. Back in the locker room, Phil caught his breath. On the court, Dar took off the other way. He passed the ball up and it swung to Isaac, who tossed it in the basket. And on defense, Dar held fast, deflecting another pass.

With the score 9–7, Arlee, Phil checked back in. He held his arms across his chest, signaling the onset of the press. Manhattan Christian responded in kind, and the game turned frenetic, a series of press breaks and fast transitions. With the score 31–23, Arlee, Caleb stripped Greg and went for a breakaway but Will fouled him hard. Arlee was pulling away, Caleb doing everything in his power to keep his team close. When Phil attempted a three-pointer, Caleb contested and released, the way Arlee's players often did. Parker Dyksterhouse pulled down the rebound, turned, and threw a full-court pass that landed in Caleb's hands. He took two dribbles and planted his legs, preparing to rise for a dunk. But Will arrived from nowhere, ripping the ball away. It bounced to the Eagles but Greg stole it, drove the length of the court, and wrapped a pass to LJ for a layup; back on defense, Isaac rose for yet another block.

Then Zanen called for an isolation: Phil against Caleb. Everyone cleared out save Isaac, who set a screen. Phil dribbled between his legs three times as he approached Caleb, like a jazz soloist playing a brief first note, then letting a silence hover. He decided. He feinted a hard crossover to the left but brought the ball back to the right and was gone, Caleb reeling. Another defender came to meet him, but he spun and jumped to his left, rising toward the rim with two hands, then pulled the ball down and scooped it to the right. His body moved one way but the ball went the other. The defender followed his body, and Phil laid the ball in softly. At halftime, Arlee was up 39–30, and Phil threw up again. So did Will. In the third quarter, Manhattan Christian closed the gap. Then, in the span of a minute, Will hit a three-pointer, made a layup, stole the ball, and threw an around-the-back pass to Greg for two points. The announcer from Hamilton marveled at the noise. "You think this many people lived in Arlee?" he chuckled, out of range of the microphone. "Nobody's guarding the stores tonight." He did not say that about Churchill, although Manhattan Christian's attendance was similarly robust. The final score was 69–60, Arlee. LJ did not hold Caleb Bellach to 10 points. The all-state forward scored 11, with Lane matching his output. Will, meanwhile, scored 25; Greg, 16; Phil, 12. After the game, Phil told a *Missoulian* reporter, of Will, "If I have him, we won't be beat." John pulled the two boys close, whispering in their ears. Chasity and Becky debated buying extra hotel rooms so the boys could get good sleep before the divisional final, but Becky decided that Phil should go home. She and Phil's sisters, Whitney and Morgan, converged, outlining a plan to get Phil home and hire a nurse to provide him with a bag of intravenous fluids to replenish all he'd lost. He'd stopped sweating and looked almost green.

"I think you need an IV," Becky said, touching his neck.

Morgan and Whitney chimed in, agreeing.

"Okay, okay," Phil said. "I got three moms!"

Then he went to meet his family, starting with Irma and Bear. Outside the Manhattan Christian locker room, Carly Danhof-Bellach, Caleb's mother, was near tears. "He's still not out of the locker room," she said of her son. "He wants to beat them so bad." Arlee, she said, was a great team. "They get in our head. We can't make any mistakes against them." In her account, her husband had left the court and told her, "I don't want to see your tears." The Eagles still had a chance to make the state tournament: they had to win three successive games.

On Saturday, Phil received intravaneous fluids from the nurse Becky knew. Jordan Lefler released the boys' suicide-prevention video. It quickly circulated, accumulating tens of thousands of views. There was just something about the message—boys in a hallway, simple and to the point. As the team warmed up for the divisional final, against Plains, Anna Whiting Sorrell (Séliš), who helped oversee the Tribes' response to the suicide cluster, sat near Allen and Kelly. She considered the video. She paused and gathered herself. "It broke my heart," she said. "Every other team gets to come celebrate, have the time of their lives. These boys feel a real intense responsibility. It made me sad. Proud, of course. It all has to matter. I know it's much more complicated than that. We all have to do our part." She referenced the kids from Marjory Stoneman Douglas High, in Parkland, who had started advocating for gun control, attracting a fervent national audience. "Maybe," she said, "that's what happens here. Maybe it's those kids saying, 'enough.' Maybe these kids can. I want them to just be happy and enjoy their lives." But, she said, "They chose to engage. They've all been there. They say, 'enough.'"

Near the court, before the Plains game, Zanen took a call: it was a coach from a junior college in Washington, inquiring about Will. Zanen smiled and pumped his fist. Not far away, a Plains fan predicted a one-point upset victory. He was wrong. At the end of the third quarter, with Arlee up by about 40, Zanen instructed the starters to spread the court. He ran a full minute off the clock, then, in a dismissive flourish, removed his star players. A Plains fan yelled at me, "Why don't you write the real story, about how disrespectful they are?" Phil gathered the boys at the end of the bench. Between hacking coughs, he said, "One more weekend. That's all I ask of you."

On Sunday, Phil received more fluids by IV. There would be just two days of practice that week before the team left for state. On Monday afternoon, in the old gym, Zanen briefly ran through what the team should expect from its first opponent, Belt. Then he turned his attention to directing another video. Buoyed by the success of the first, he had stayed up late choreographing a more involved routine. It started with Phil dribbling two balls at once while wearing a war bonnet and saying that warriors protect their people. He drop-kicked the ball to Greg, who talked about how social media could make you feel down. Greg tossed an alley-oop to Isaac, who dunked and hung off the rim and talked about bullying. Dar flew across the floor, suggesting that viewers "dive into someone's life." He rolled the ball to Lane Schall, who bricked a free throw. Lane Johnson rebounded it and passed it to Will, clad in a war bonnet. He shot a three from about forty feet and asked everyone to join the fight against suicide. When Will drained the shot on his first take, the boys all started screaming, "*Ooooohhhh!*" But that ruined the tape, so Lefler asked for another. Will calmly fired, turned, and recited his line as the ball again ripped the net. Still, it took about ninety minutes to get the thing right because the boys occasionally lost focus. "This isn't funny," Zanen snapped. "It's not clicking." The first video, he said, had reached a couple hundred thousand people. But in his estimation, it should have been "freakin' five million." He said, "Hopefully by adding a twist to it, somebody will actually step up and share this."

"Hey," said Phil, "shouldn't we be getting ready for a state tournament?" Zanen said this was more important. A sophomore started messing around and Zanen yelled at him, making the boy cry. Toward the end of the production, a man in a black suit and cowboy boots arrived. It was Camas McClure, formerly an assistant coach on Arlee's staff and now a coach at Two Eagle River School. He had a thick build and a buzz cut and, often, a wide smile. But not today. He had come from the wake of the player who passed. "I just wanted to say thank you, guys," he said in halting breaths. "I just love every single one of you guys to death." His chest heaved, and his voice broke. "I've coached pretty much every one of you guys. You are really doing something special." He told the Warriors to bring home the trophy. A long silence followed.

"Can we hug him?" someone asked. Phil embraced him, and everyone followed.

Will helped Phil put the war bonnet back in the pillowcase and the Warriors piled onto the bus and went to the movies to see *Black Panther*. Before they left, Zanen stood outside, wondering about the suicide video. "Think it will look cheesy?" He regretted having made the sophomore cry. He needed to get back to ball, he said. He looked almost cornered.

The boys had only one more practice before leaving for state. Most of the town planned to follow. People painted trucks with the boys' names and arranged carpools. One fan said he'd walk if he had to. Scott Schall, Lane's dad, asked Zanen who would monitor his cattle during the tournament, given that pretty much everyone planned to be in Butte. "God," the coach said.

On Tuesday, Will and Phil both slept in, feeling ill. While the other boys worked on rotations at practice, the captains shot free throws. Will rubbed his forehead. Phil coughed, looking wan, wearing open-toed sandals and socks. I closed my eyes and heard the balls bouncing, spinning against hands, snapping nets. Why basketball? I asked.

"No clue." Phil looked down at the ball in his hands. "It's hard. It takes learning. You gotta work for everything you put into that basketball."

Will said, "I dunno, man. Just something I grew up with. It either runs in your family or it don't." He paused. "And it's pretty fun, too." The ball spun off his fingertips. "But it can also break your heart."

20

"Love You" on Three

March 2018

THURSDAY, MARCH 1

The boys woke up groggy at the Butte Comfort Inn. Phil and Will shared a room with Troy and Trey Tewawina, the managers. It smelled like a hospital, and not on account of the twins. Phil had been on cough syrup with codeine, antibiotics, and albuterol; Will, antibiotics. "They got their binkies and blankies," Zanen said, rolling his eyes. The first game of the three-day tournament was that afternoon. Their opponent was Belt, a former coal town near Great Falls, and the team against whom Phil had thrown that bad pass in the state semifinals three years earlier, when he was a freshman. Belt was also housed in the Comfort Inn, making for a slightly tense scene at the breakfast buffet. Zanen was energized, as he and Lefler had arranged to release the next video at 10:00 A.M. David Whitesell wanted to keep the prevention efforts going following the season. "I think people are ready to talk about it," he said. "I love that we have a coach using that platform to make a statement that's relevant." Zanen said he envisioned community trash pickups and kids reading to younger students.

"I love it," said Whitesell. He paused, as this raised a question about the coach's future in Arlee. "Do you want to come back next year?"

"Yeah. If Greg's back."

The superintendent nodded.

Belt's girls' coach entered the buffet line. He was influential, Zanen said, helping decide who attended a postseason all-star event that Zanen thought might help Will's college prospects.

"Go talk to him," said Zanen.

"I don't wanna go talk to him," said Will.

"Quit being a pussy!"

"I'm not."

At 10:00 A.M., the boys huddled over their phones in the hotel hall-way. "Pretty sweet," Greg said, peering into the screen. "It's already got a lot of views. This one a lot more kids can relate to." Shadenn Stone had a wide-eyed look. "It feels better to get it out than to hold it in," he said. "It just feels great to get word out there." Nate Coulson strutted with his shirt off and said, "It's pretty badass. I feel like it's going to affect a lot of people."

The others were busy with video games: Dar and Chase Gardner played *NBA 2K*, while in his room, Phil blasted avatars in *Fortnite*. Will said, of the suicide-prevention video, "It makes us feel good for the fact that it makes others open their eyes and maybe go to people." Phil launched some large rocket and said, "Boys can't fricking hide their feelings forever. Everybody has something wrong." Then the captains started bragging about how many kills they averaged in *Fortnite*. Their bed was piled with fleece Pendleton blankets; after a while, they rose to brush their teeth, and Phil splashed water on his cowlick, pushing it to one side as Will arranged his medallion. I asked how many deaths by suicide they'd known. "A few," said Phil. I asked what a few was. "Twenty or thirty."

A couple of hours later, both seniors stood stooped over trash cans, hurling up everything inside them in front of a few thousand people.

They were not the only ones. Isaac had vomited just a few minutes earlier. It was the second quarter of their first game. The score was tight, Arlee holding a two-point lead.

I sat with Don Wetzel Jr., the cofounder of the Montana Indian Athletic Hall of Fame, who was here to award trophies as a board member of the MHSA. He asked, "What do you think about the pressure we put on our boys?" He nodded. "The mental and physical strength they need." Chasity ran around the court, headed for her ill son bearing cough drops. Wetzel Jr. talked about the videos: "Our youth are bringing such a powerful message." He first started working on suicide prevention in Indian Country in 2006. Back then, he said, "You couldn't even mention the word 'suicide.'" People often weren't willing to name it, out of pride or shame. The video, he said, was "where we need to go."

After just a couple of minutes, Will and Phil checked back in. Wetzel Jr. said, "They're carrying a lot." I asked what he thought of the kids' college prospects. He said Phil had Division I talent and that Will was a "fiery warrior." But Wetzel Jr. wanted to put a lens up to my question, and the implications it carried—that success meant migration, validation, ego, fame. "You get people wondering, college this and that. How many student-athletes get to go play a state championship?" He felt that those who desired to continue playing needed a chance, and that those who got the chance needed to finish what they started. But he knew, from firsthand experience, that college could never offer the same meaning. "Is this the pinnacle of Native athletes? The state tournament? I don't know. We need to look at that. And accept it. I don't hear that enough." What did it mean, to make it? The phrase itself implied something strange and static—an end point.

The game remained close until halftime, when Phil admonished everyone: "Did we leave our heart back at home?" Zanen and Greg interjected with strategic adustments to the defense, then Phil bellowed: "We rely on each other. That's how we beat these teams. We rely on each other." The boys went on a 22–7 run. Will led the team in scoring, with 15, Greg adding 12. Everyone who dressed played, including Tapit Haynes and Trey Malatare, and Nate scored 6 points. But Will and Phil did not look well. "That was pretty rough," said Will as he left the court.

Back at the Comfort Inn, Becky hustled around, asking what kind of fruit the boys liked. "Capri Suns," said Tapit. Will and Phil rested. Will also made a disturbing discovery: the blood in his urine had returned. Greg, meanwhile, was fixated on the overwhelming online reaction to the latest suicide-prevention video: "Damn." Tens of thousands of people had viewed and shared it, and Zanen's phone had been ringing all day, with calls from people on reservations across the country, media, and a local chapter of a national suicide-prevention organization. Following a nap, the team returned to the Civic Center to watch Manhattan Christian play Heart Butte, a Blackfeet team. Heart Butte had been staying in hotels for weeks due to overwhelming snowstorms on the Blackfeet Reservation. Some hoped that the team would make a stunning and inspiring run to state. But the Eagles won easily. Afterward, a Manhattan Christian parent said he felt bad for Heart Butte, and that he just wanted the kids to have fun. "It's not life," he said.

FRIDAY, MARCH 2

Overnight, the views of the video mounted, and Zanen's phone rang off the hook. Phil and Will slept in while Greg woke early to do an interview with NBC Montana. A reporter started with a pro forma question about the game, and Greg replied with an explanation of the slow defensive start. Then the topic turned to the video. "Do you know people who have been affected by this?" the reporter asked.

Greg paused. "Um. Yes. Both—I've been affected by it. I've known some people. Definitely know a lot of people been affected around our community." He seemed to be moving toward something. That afternoon, Zanen played the boys a recording of the interview, as an example of how to speak to the media. About half a million people had seen the most recent video. Zanen saw an added potential benefit, as well. "If they try to fire me now," he had said, of the school board, "they're messing with a whole other thing."

I met Jennifer Jilot in the Walmart parking lot along with, in her words, "the rest of Arlee." She was decked out in red and white. She thought the videos were a strong idea. "It started conversations between people," she said. Most of the Scarlets were in Butte. The girls' team had not made it to state this year. Ashley Tanner, a senior guard, said, of the video, "Some people understand it needs to be talked about. Some think we don't need to talk about it. I think it's an issue that should be talked about. It'd be cool to be part of that." She added: "Be part of a movement."

Before Arlee took the court in the semifinal, one of Phil's cousins, a rancher named Leon Wieder, arrived with a box of black T-shirts he'd designed and printed. They were simple and clean, reading ARLEE WARRIORS #WARRIORMOVEMENT #TOGETHERWERISE. They were delivered to the student section. Today Zanen was not calm. He said the team didn't need to win the title game. But, he'd told me, "We have to get there."

That meant beating, in the semifinals, Scobey, a fast team from way up north near the Canadian border. The town, 550 miles from Arlee, took its name from an Indian agent who, at the turn of the twentieth century, had remarked on the difficulty of assimilating Native kids. In 2011, Scobey had beaten Arlee in the state championship after the Warriors blew a seventeen-point lead; this year, Scobey's team ran and pressed. Greg would later call them "some white Indian ballers."

"These suckers are coming for blood," said Zanen in the locker room. The boys pulled the Warrior Movement T-shirts over their jerseys and took the court. Then they got knocked down. Scobey pressed like Arlee. At halftime, the Warriors were down by six. In the locker room, Phil screamed, "I need a play from everybody, all right?" He hacked—*eehuhhh*—then said, "I'm not scared one bit! This shit's fun when we're down. I like it when we're down! When we come back and beat their ass, that's gonna be better!"

HeavyRunner talked about communication, Greg about rotation, and Zanen said that they were playing the team that most closely resembled them. They had to be patient on offense and run even harder on defense, to get back. "You'll know when there's blood in the water," he said. "Trust in yourselves." All the while, the sounds from Phil's throat got louder, great heaving, dry, guttural noises. "They're tough," said Phil between coughs, "but they are not tougher than us."

Zanen said, "Get out there and shoot. Ready, go. One, two, three."

"Brothers!" came the reply.

Then Will's voice cut through: "Four, five, six."

Everyone boomed, *"Family."*

As the team warmed up, Phil stayed behind, Zanen lingering with him.

"It's coming up," said Phil. "It's gonna come up."

"Then go ahead. Try it."

Phil threw up yet again and took the court. Out of the half, Greg missed a three-pointer and Scobey threw a full-court baseball pass—the Arlee play—for a layup. The Warriors didn't get back; the score was 41–33, Scobey. The crowd quieted. Big Will and his brother Sean, Terry and Crystal Pitts, Jordyn, Chasity, Becky, Jennifer Schall, Raelena, Dave, Tomi, TJ, Clark, and Bing—they all looked nervous. John's jaw rotated. With 4:28 remaining in the third quarter, Scobey led by four. Phil rebounded an air ball and heaved a full-court pass to Greg for a layup. The crowd boomed:

Ar-LEE

War-RIORS

With less than three minutes to go in the third quarter, Arlee was still down four. Zanen hopped up and down and screamed on the sideline, and the boys were everywhere. The next sixty seconds passed in a vicious ballet of steals and turnovers. Greg and Will each hit a long three-pointer, the second giving Arlee its first lead. A few possessions later, Scobey brought the ball down and Greg smacked the floor with both hands. The other players followed. Phil took off in a straight line for the ball handler, who looked terrified. Phil ripped it out of the kid's hands and flew off for a layup, then sprinted back down the court, beckoning to the crowd. The noise sounded like the inside of a breaking wave.

In the fourth quarter, the team huddled on the court and someone brought out a trash can so Phil could throw up. The Warriors gathered close to obscure the cameras. Then Phil took over, scoring basket after basket. With a couple of minutes left, Greg sprinted out of bounds after a loose ball, skidded into the stands, and crashed into a metal gate. He staggered back on the court. With 1:24 remaining, Phil drove, met a defender, and spun around him like a drill bit, laying the ball in. The final score was 76–71. After the victory, Zanen teared up. "Freaking Greg," he said. "Going out of bounds and coming back and separating from your mind."

The coach thanked each boy individually, even those who had not played: "You don't know what you do. It takes sixteen cats to win a championship." A weeping Lane Schall embraced Phil, whose body heaved. Phil's voice broke: "All glory to the man upstairs."

Afterward, all the boys greeted their families. Then Phil joined me to watch Manhattan Christian play for the right to face Arlee once again in the title game. He was breathing heavily and his face was drawn, but he appeared at ease. "This is the atmosphere I love," he said. "If I could play every weekend in something like this, that'd be awesome." He wanted to face the Eagles: "They deserve to be in the championship." He looked at all the red shirts. "Arlee's empty." I wondered what that was like—all that energy coming into you. "I mean it's kind of pressuring. But they come to watch basketball. I mean, they're proud of us for what we're doing. Win or lose, they just come to watch us play. And battle. And that's what we know how to do. That's what makes it fun. They'll stand behind us the whole time. Win or lose, they are proud. But as of, like, coming out and performing every night for them? Yeah, I feel a little bit of pressure right there. But I'd do everything I can. I think I can perform every night for them. And I will. I'll give my heart for them." He looked at me, paused, and asked a two-word question about the season:

"Change you?"

"Yes."

"You think you'll ever see something like this again?"

We both knew the answer to that. Manhattan Christian won, setting up one more rematch.

SATURDAY, MARCH 3

Becky and John Malatare staked out their seats for the final by 11:00 A.M., nine hours before tip-off. The boys went to warm up at Montana Tech's gym with the blessing of the coach, Hiatt. Greg and Will shot with TJ Haynes rebounding. TJ was nervous and wanted to be around the team. He'd offered to help pay for a hotel in the event the board wanted the boys to return home that night after the game. He said, "These kids with their video they made. Shows a lot. A lot of respect."

A moment earlier, Zanen approached Hiatt and started talking about how much work Greg and Will put in. Zanen also mentioned that they were both tribally enrolled. The implication was clear: they were eligible for tuition waivers. "Oh, he's always selling," Hiatt once said. "I respect it. That's the number one responsibility of a coach. It's all about the players. At the same time my job's to find what's best for our team."

Terry Pitts entered the gym. He had an update on the referees in the tournament—two were Native, one of whom would work the championship. "They'll let you play some," Terry said, meaning the boys could likely defend aggressively without fear of punitive calls. Zanen nodded and gathered the team. "It will be the loudest gym any of us have ever been in," he said. The Civic Center seats about six thousand people. "And four thousand will be Arlee fans." The players, he said, would not be able to hear the coaches. "Tonight you're on your own. Go over hand signals for offense." Zanen had one thing to add: "Phillip Malatare. I do not wanna see a pass like . . ." Then the coach mimicked a full-court Hail Mary.

On the sideline, Hiatt said, "I don't wanna see that pass, either."

Phil hollered, "I'm gonna launch one of 'em!" Then he did, the ball sailing into Greg's hands.

Shortly before tip-off, Chasity did Will's hair by center court while Senator Daines took a seat across the gym. Manhattan Christian's cheering contingent also included a lively student section and a group of people from a retirement home. Chasity's eyebrows were raised, her motions tender and confident. She said nothing when Will was ready. He hugged her and went to Sophie, nearby, who wore Will's face on a pin. Chasity said, "We're gonna go back to the doctor Monday. He's been urinating blood." The illness was yet undiagnosed, but she suspected his kidneys. "We're trying to prevent basically kidney failure." She also added that in previous weeks, he'd been going to the center on his own after practice, late at night, to correct his shot. She had tried to stop him from practicing once, she said. "Second time he told me, 'Mom, no doctor's gonna tell me I can't play.'" She had come around on college. She wanted him to experience it. She was thinking about the postseason tournaments, all-star events where he might catch a coach's attention. But that could wait. "I hope he will give one hundred percent tonight," she said. "I know there's a over-overdrive in there."

Fifteen minutes before warm-ups, the boys gathered in the Civic Center's practice gym. Phil had received yet another IV of fluids. Zanen, in his pregame remarks, was once again calm. He asked them to be strategic and avoid fouling Manhattan Christian players who tried to dunk: "If I can end the game with my five starters on the floor, we will win." He told them to enjoy the moment. "You're ready."

HeavyRunner spoke next: "We have pushed you all year for this one moment. Big moment. But it's just another basketball game. That's all it is. Another basketball game. You're still gonna wake up tomorrow. Win or lose, you're still gonna be the Warriors. Win or lose. Nobody will ever take that from you."

"Who are they?" Franny's voice boomed, the words echoing. "Don't give them no opportunity to dunk. Fuck that." He put his hands on his knees and said, "I want to see them like this: *hehhh hehhh* . . . We need to prove a point. Of who we are. And who they are to us."

Zanen gathered the team one last time. He prayed for their families, for Arlee, for the reservation, for Manhattan Christian, for the refs, for those struggling with depression. He closed by saying:

> And most of all, let us just have fun and enjoy this game
> And every moment that we have in it.
> It's the last one you boys are going to have together.
> In Jesus Christ's name, the Creator, amen.

He turned to Phil and Will. "I love you and I love you."

Phil gathered everyone and spoke in a dry voice. "It's already over. It's already over. It was a pretty short year, wasn't it? We're gonna make mistakes tonight. But it's how we react to 'em. It's how we counter 'em." He turned to Lane Johnson, who would be guarding Caleb: "Hound that guy!" He turned to Isaac. "Dunk it. Rip that rim off! Will, Greg, fricking rip that net off! Let's go get history." He told them, "Don't get down if we go down by two points. We've been down. All right, boys? Come out, battle for me. Battle for Will. Battle for each other. Let's make that crowd happy."

The long, slow cadence of Phil's voice changed. It got small and rushed. He started to cry. "There's a bigger picture for all of us." Rather than the customary sign-off, he said, "'Love you' on three. One, two, three."

And the boys said, "Love you."

Big Will and Allen and Sean and Clayton hit the drum. Phil and Will sprinted onto the floor in war bonnets, Greg trailing in a Diné headband Raelena had made. On the east side of the Civic Center, the town of Arlee rose as one.

Manhattan Christian won the opening tip-off, but Caleb missed a long shot. Then Will missed a three, but Isaac stole the ball and dropped it to Phil. They took off together up the court and Phil spun through a trap, throwing a no-look pass off Isaac's hands. Caleb made a three-pointer; Phil missed his first five shots and had two turnovers, while Will made just one of four. But Lane Johnson scored four tough points, battling down low. For Manhattan Christian, Caleb kept firing, scoring six of his team's first eight points. On the quarter's final possession, with the game tied, Phil spun and tried a one-handed shot, but Caleb rose, emphatically blocking it.

In the second quarter, Will missed two more three-pointers, and Manhattan Christian's boys began to nod their heads. Bear sat in the second deck, hands on the rails in front of him, jaw protruding. Isaac scored, then pulled down a rebound. For all his inconsistency during the season, he now flew around, hustling, contesting shots; he scored six points in the quarter. With the score tied 17–17, Phil finally made a shot, and Bear threw a fist pump with his whole body. "Take him, Phillip!"

With one minute remaining in the half, Phil tossed a lob to Lane

Johnson, who leaped, kicked his legs, caught the ball, and flipped it in off the backboard for his eighth point of the game. With forty seconds remaining in the half, Phil dribbled slowly upcourt. He, Greg, and Will spread the floor, running time off. Fifteen seconds, ten, five. With three seconds remaining, Phil dropped the ball to Will about ten feet behind the three-point line. Will eyeballed the waning clock and fired an immense, arcing shot. The ball hung near the rafters for a moment as though suspended. As the buzzer sounded, it plummeted through the net. Will pumped his fists and screamed. Bear exhaled with a great sound, his hands unclasping.

On the first possession of the third quarter, Manhattan Christian hit a three-pointer, narrowing the margin to four. On the way down the court Will bodychecked an Eagles guard named Josiah Amunrud, then shoved him, resulting in a technical foul. Caleb made one of the two free throws for a four-point swing in seconds. Greg and Will trapped, forcing a travel, then Lane Johnson missed a shot in traffic. For all the beauty of the season, the game turned ugly. Lane traveled, the crowd letting out a long, sighing boo at the call. On the far end of the court, Caleb rifled a pass for a layup. Greg and Will missed threes, a pass went through Caleb's hands, and Greg overshot Lane Johnson. John shook his head.

The Eagles played as a team, whittling the lead. Manhattan Christian pressed in a full-court zone. Zanen took Isaac out and put Dar in the game. Midway through the quarter, Phil missed yet again, and Caleb rebounded the ball and pushed up court. Rather than force a shot he whipped it to Parker Dyksterhouse, who immediately passed for a three-pointer. Manhattan Christian had the lead. Two Eagles players beckoned to the crowd, urging it on. Arlee broke the Manhattan Christian press, the ball skipping through the air from Lane to Dar to Phil to Lane to Greg, who faked a shot, then passed to the corner. Will caught it, crouched, jumped, and snapped his wrist, reclaiming the lead. He carried the Warriors to the end of the quarter, scoring five more successive points, trading off in a duel with Caleb. Going into the final period, Arlee held a four-point lead.

It's sometimes said that truth outs in the fourth quarter of close games. On the period's first possession, Will drove and passed to Phil, who dropped the ball to Isaac for a one-handed basket. On the next two Eagles possessions, Phil boxed out Caleb. The first time he was successful; the second time Caleb jumped over him, rebounded an errant three-pointer, and scored. On the subsequent play, Greg passed to Will in the corner. This time, his shot missed. The ball caromed downward; Phil, bodied up against Caleb, grabbed the rebound with one hand, then bullied into the bigger boy and scored. On the far end of the court, Phil guarded Caleb. As Caleb cut from the three-point line toward the basket, Phil slid laterally, saw a pass coming, and stuck his hand up. The ball arrived just there. Phil deflected it away, secured it, spun, and lit out down the court, passing ahead to Lane Johnson, who scored and was fouled. He made his free throw for his twelfth point. The Eagles kept pressing, but Phil split a double-team with a flashing move, leaving his defenders visibly bewildered and the television announcer laughing out loud. Caleb hit a three, pulling the Eagles to within five. But it was as though he were playing alone. Will missed a jumper and Caleb missed a three, but a possession later Caleb hauled in a rebound and drew a foul on Lane Johnson, his fourth. Two more free throws made it a three-point game. The gym shook:

AR-LEE
WAR-RIORS

M-H-C-S

Phil isolated against Caleb, drove, and drew a foul. He made both free throws. On the far end of the court, another Manhattan Christian player finally shot, a guard named Matthew Amunrud (Josiah's brother). He moved the net from a distance, making it a two-point margin. Just over three minutes remained. Zanen told Phil and Will to win the game. Greg and Will broke the press and delivered the ball to Phil. Parker Dyksterhouse now guarded him, giving Caleb a break; Phil's crossover came hard and vicious, leaving Parker two steps behind. Phil took two dribbles, rose, scored, and was fouled, then made the free throw. On the far end of the court, he picked up Caleb again, and again Caleb drove. Phil fouled him. But Caleb missed the free throw, and Phil rebounded it. He drove and flipped up a layup. It hung on the rim and fell off, but Isaac sailed in and tipped the ball through, for his tenth point without a miss. It was as though something had come over him. His gentleness gone, Isaac now played with an edge of desperation. The Eagles made two free throws, and Greg and Will once again broke their press. From near the half-court line, Phil slashed, pulling up his dribble when the double-team came, then bouncing a no-look pass to Isaac, who did not hesitate. His shot snapped off his fingertips, high above his head, and fell through. Caleb's next shot bounced off the rim and Will tore down the rebound; he was fouled, and as he walked to the far side of the court for free throws, the crowd rose, the gym reverberating.

AR-LEE
WAR-RIORS

In the second deck, Big Will said, "Gotta have 'em." Twice the ball fell through the net. Caleb scored on a hard drive, then stole the ball. Manhattan Christian hit a three, making it a four-point game. Fifty-eight seconds remained.

M-H-C-S

Manhattan Christian changed its press to a full-court man-to-man denial. Greg broke it and passed to Phil, near the sideline, who spun away from a defender, dribbled, and fired the ball from half-court to Isaac, streaking toward the basket. The pass moved as though suspended on a wire. Isaac caught it and rose with both hands for something between a layup and a dunk, something that looked a lot like prayer.

AR-LEE
WAR-RIORS

Caleb drove, but missed, Isaac defending and smacking the backboard with fury, then grabbing the rebound. On the next Arlee possession, Manhattan Christian double-teamed Phil, trying to foul him to stop the clock, but he danced through the defense, precious seconds ticking off. With thirty-three seconds remaining the margin was six. Caleb fouled Phil, who made both free throws. Manhattan Christian scored quickly, Arlee allowing the point guard, Matthew Amunrud, to get to the basket. Twenty-five seconds remained. Greg inbounded to Phil, who was fouled again, then again made both free throws. Amunrud scored again, on a putback; with twelve seconds remaining, the margin was still six. One basket would seal the game. This time, the inbound pass went to Will. Three defenders converged on him; he lowered his shoulder, hugged the ball to his body, and drew the foul. Slowly he walked to the end of the court as the crowd rose. He and Phil grabbed hands and bowed their heads, speaking so no one could hear. Will spun the ball off his fingertips at the free-throw line. Jilot, toward the back of the lower section, said, "Just breathe." Twice the ball rolled through the net, and Jilot wept. The final seconds ticked off. Caleb missed a three-pointer, and Phil rebounded the ball and hurled it in the air, just as Ty had done one year earlier. He ran to Zanen. The boys flooded off the bench, the community following, and Phil and Will held each other in a long embrace.

For all the electricity of the season, the postgame celebration felt quiet. There were photos and hugs, a few tears, too, but the feeling was one of calm. "It's good," David Whitesell said. "It just makes sense. It was right." He and John Malatare, who didn't often see eye to eye, shared a congratulatory moment. "Hell of a kid you got," said Whitesell. John thanked him and said, "They're warriors. They're not done."

TJ Haynes said, "It's good. Felt really good. I was a nervous wreck. But glad it's over with. It's good."

A coach from Carroll College approached Will, asking if he had plans the following season. Will asked for a moment to greet his family before speaking with the man. Caleb walked onto the floor to congratulate Arlee's players. He moved with his head up, with dignity and grace. Allen sang and peace descended. The team bounded to the locker room, Phil screaming, "Hey, boys!" Their laughter echoed off the walls. "Hey, boys!"

On Sunday, the Warriors returned to Arlee led by a fire-truck and police escort. Afterward, the team gathered on the bus to listen to an elder named Frances Vanderburg: "You're preparing for a life when you aren't connected to these facilities." She said that life would soon change: "Some things are gonna be good. Some not so good." She said they would crash, and that the harmony would at some point break, and that they might get mad at one another. And she asked them to forgive themselves: "Keep in mind, it's temporary. It's like the breeze. It'll be gone. Be nice to yourself. Sometimes you want to be nice to yourself."

Attendance at school was sparse on Monday. Will soon went to the doctor, where he discovered he'd been playing with walking pneumonia and a kidney stone so large it would require an operation. Greg decided to stay in Arlee. Phil had talked to him following the victory, revealing his own deliberations about whether to leave. Now, Greg said, "Arlee is home."

Zanen received congratulations from all three members of Montana's congressional delegation. Senator Jon Tester secured a grant to support mental health services at Two Eagle River School. Governor Bullock planned to visit Arlee Schools and meet the Warriors. Zanen started arranging for the boys to speak to other schools and hoped they might get the opportunity to go on a national television show. Over lunch we discussed the possibility of a book on the team. "This is kind of a fairy tale," he said. I said there was no such thing. I arranged to stay a while longer.

Before I left, Greg approached and said he wanted to share the story of his hospitalization. I cautioned him about the level of exposure the revelation would bring. He started to cry, and I asked him to think more about it. I talked with David and Raelena; David said they would confer with Greg's therapist. Greg eventually reached out again, saying he was ready to tell his story. He thought it might help someone. We spoke and spoke. I sought counsel from an outside mental health expert. I wondered if Greg was there yet; I wondered who I was to silence him. In accordance with Raelena's wishes, I asked Greg on three occasions whether he wanted to share the story. He sounded more sure each time, finally saying, "I'd like to have it in there." So I wrote it down. "It feels like relief to talk," Greg said. The videos, he said, made him think, "What if I was watching that four or five months ago?"

On Wednesday Phil got his spotting scope and took me to look at some elk. We met at the pizza place in town. He got chicken pasta and asked me to drive. He navigated as I steered his red Chevy sedan toward one of his horn-hunting spots. As we drove, I asked if he was ready for the academics at college. "Better be!" he chirped. He didn't know what he was going to take or when he had to register. He told me to pull over by a river and fastened his scope to the open passenger window. The snow was still deep up high in the hills. He scoped until he found a herd of about one hundred elk. "Can't hide forever!" he said. "I'll walk all this even if it don't melt. If I know they're dropping, I'll go in there." But the herd was all cows. He was looking for the big tawny bulls.

As he scanned the hills, Phil thought about the coming summer. He figured it would be his last as a kid. He planned to be starting for the Griz by the time he was a sophomore. He wondered about the temptations of Missoula. "After a big win in college, am I going to want to go be dumb?" he asked, as if it were a question he couldn't possibly answer. He was excited to leave high school. He felt that some of the teachers from outside the community didn't understand the kids: "I mean, there are some of them kids, you don't know what goes on after school. They come to school and try their hardest. I mean, some days they might slack, but I feel like there's some kids that don't have nothin' at home and they come to school hoping to have, like, to have a good time there. Not to, like, just see friends and goof off. But to have a *good time*. And some of them teachers . . ."

He was glad to be leaving. I asked about Jordyn—were they good for each other?

"I think she's a lot like me. Cares for other people before herself. I mean, in a way also she's better. Sometimes I'm an asshole, but rarely I'll catch her ever being an asshole." He talked about his father and TJ, who could walk the hills all day without eating. Phil couldn't do that. He had recently seen his *túpye?*, a fluent Séliš speaker, die. He said he planned to learn the language. "I'm sure I'll try to learn. I hope I do."

Phil's story about his *túpye?* stuck in my head. I was thirty-six and had reported in disaster zones. But I had never seen a dead body. I blurted that out now.

"Really?" said Phil.

"Yeah. Like even my relatives." It seemed ridiculous, that amount of shelter from fear. I felt ashamed.

Phil paused and took it in. Then he said, "When some family member passes away, they have a funeral. Being Native American. They'll have a rosary. They'll sing for you at night. They'll sing for hours. All through the night. Then they'll have the funeral. . . . It's just praying and singing all through this. And the casket's open." He paused. "Really? That's odd that you haven't seen." Phil had first experienced it at Bearhead Swaney's. "He was, like, my elder." Phil wasn't sure how old he was then. "Minors in baseball," he said with authority. Then: "All righty, well, should we try to find some more?"

He found them now, three bulls bedded down in the snow, all still packing their antlers. "They'll shed right now." The animals dropped their antlers, Phil said, from "end of February to middle of April." By then, he said, "majority of the bulls all shedded." They regrew their antlers in just a few months. "Then after summer's over, comes August, then end of August they start scraping off all that velvet. That's when they're hard, they have their solid horn. Rut starts. That goes till end of October, maybe November. Then that's over, then winter comes. Then—fricking get ready for them to shed their horns. These big guys are standing up." He said you didn't want to go in too early and push the elk when they were on their winter range. He talked about the superiority of brown antlers—which are fresh with blood—to white ones. "White's old, brown's new," he said. "Put it this way: You rather have a Lamborghini or a Subaru?"

A Subaru, I said.

"But if you lived in California?" Phil didn't want to live in California. "Everyone's like, 'Oh, you need to get out of here.' Which I believe. But if you love where you live, why not live there? No use movin'."

Once, I asked him about the pressure of making it with the Griz.

He said, "To be a Native American and going into a college program? You should be honored, man. You're representing all Native Americans." But, he said, "It's my life. I could call it quits after this. And just go to college and get a degree. But I want to go—I *love* basketball. Until I can't run up and down the court like I can at a young age, I mean, I'm gonna play until I can't." But Phil didn't want a jersey entombed in glass. He couldn't take that with him when he died. He was going to play ball as long as he could, but when it ended, he wanted to be a game warden, like Tom Haynes, so he could work in the mountains.

As chance would have it, Tom drove by just then. Maybe he was out busting someone for illegal firewood cutting. "Shoulda stopped," Phil said. "Sucker." He went back to scoping. He was hoping to see a bull drop its antlers right there. "That's my dream"—to see one shed through the lens of his scope. "Come on, guy," he said to the elk. "Lose your horns." His right eye affixed to the scope, the boy in constant motion was absolutely still. Only his left eyelid fluttered. "I wish I could sit here all day." He stared out at the land.

On Sunday, March 11, Arlee held a final event for the team: a second *syulm*. About 350 people showed up to the community center. Chasity wore a headdress; Tom Haynes arrived with his sidearm on his hip; Jilot wore regalia. The gym smelled of turkey, fry bread, spaghetti and meatballs. It was the anniversary of Thomas Lyles's passing. "It's good," said Patty, his mother, with a smile. Irma and Bear Malatare arrived early. Irma was thinking of buying a fifteen-passenger van so she could take the whole family to Phil's college games. She went inside while Bear stood out front, long arms dangling at his sides. He had been reading a history of the Cree. He didn't normally dwell on the past. He never told Phil about his time at the boarding school, when teachers beat him for speaking his language. "We can't constantly sit and cry about what they done to us," he once said. "We need to move forward." But the book made him think about his grandparents' migration from Canada, and his own father, for whom Phillip was named, and Bear's time with the nuns; the constant efforts at assimilation and extermination.

"All the things they done to us," he said, his face turning momentarily dark, immense hands clenching. "We're not supposed to be here." Then a great smile worked its way across his face, and his hands unclenched. "We're still here. And we will be for a long time." He walked inside, where dancing mothers pushed the laughing boys down to the floor.

Part Four

What you decide is where we're gonna be.

—BEAR MALATARE

21

The Cracks

March–April 2018

Will decided to delay his surgery until after the postseason tournaments in hopes of getting into college. Along with Phil, he went to the Hi-Line Invitational Tournament, on the team representing Class C, where they played with Caleb Bellach. The team won the championship, beating the best players from both Class A and AA. Together, the cousins forced four consecutive turnovers in the fourth quarter of the championship game, a victory against the Class AA team. Will led all scorers in the final with 31 points while playing with a kidney stone. He also amassed the most steals in the tournament. Phil was the tournament leader in both rebounds and assists.

Will waited for a college opportunity within Montana. It did not come. Zanen suspected his braid had something to do with that. But, he allowed, Will was an undersized shooting guard who needed to work on his right-handed dribbling, an area of relative weakness that was acknowledged even in Haynesville. "That's his dad," said Chasity. "He dribbles that ball like his dad."

But Zanen also found himself confronting an uncomfortable possibility: that the philosophies driving his team's singular, thrilling play might be incongruous with college recruitment in Montana. "We don't really promote a single-man college prospect," he said. "We promote winning a title." Class B and C schools are small and rural, often in rugged, remote parts of the state. The roads to reservations may run both ways, but many college coaches seemed to travel them only when lured by thunderous individual stat lines. "They're like, well, if the kid can't even score twenty a night in Class C," Zanen said, "he ain't going to play college for me." During the season, Will had averaged 16 points per contest, Greg 15; they had not lost a game and they had, between them, not one college offer.

Phil did not win the Gatorade Player of the Year award. The honor went to a Class AA player from Missoula who had averaged 22.8 points, 7.3 rebounds, 2.9 assists, and 1.6 steals per game. (Phil averaged 22.3 points, 9.3 rebounds, 7 assists, and 5.8 steals.) Hundreds of miles to the east, Ty Tanner was tiring of Dawson. He'd cracked his team's rotation by the end of the season, earning significant playing time, but he didn't love the style of ball. "He was a good player who could have helped us," his coach, Joe Peterson, later wrote me, "if he could have just accepted his role." Ty considered transferring somewhere closer to home. Maybe, he thought, he'd join Phil at the University of Montana.

The University of Montana, despite its proximity to Arlee, presented its own challenges. The university has long had a Native American student population above 5 percent. But in 2011, the university published data showing that just 7 of 504 tenured and tenure-track faculty members—1.4 percent—identified as Native American. In July 2018, the *Missoulian* covered the university's struggles to retain Indigenous students, writing that, in the fall of 2017, the university "only retained 51.6 percent of its American Indian freshman [*sic*]."

Ivory Brien, the tall, thoughtful Arlee graduate, was one of those who would leave. At the university, he had lost himself among decadent hungers and mediocre classes. He lived in a hall where partying was the norm. Around him, people got high for fun, then got high to study, then got high to unwind. His floor contained multiple drug dealers. Ivory drank and smoked pot, then started experimenting with harder drugs. "When I was in it, you can't see it," he said. "It's like a brand-new car—like I got this hot new Ferrari and I was taking it around the curves of the lake and it was superfast and I was trying to learn how to drive it and didn't know how to drive it. And I ran into a wall."

On the Monday night after Arlee's championship, he'd gone out with friends. One kid led the way, a boy from the Bitterroot Valley named Chase Munson. Along with two other guys, Chase and Ivory went car hopping—attempting petty thefts. Three of them later approached a gas station to steal beer. According to the account Ivory later gave to police, he didn't know what was going to happen. "Munson asked Brien something to the effect of, 'Want to do this' and Brien replied, 'I don't know,'" read a pretrial affidavit. "Munson showed Brien his gun and gave him [Brien] the pepper spray." Munson entered the store and shot two people, both of them military veterans. Ivory sprayed the bear spray from inside the doorway before running out. According to court documents, he was crying.

But none of that made the papers. Rather, what graced the home page of the *Missoulian*, on Thursday, March 8, was a glaring mug shot of Ivory in an orange jumpsuit next to the bold-font words ARRESTED IN CONVENIENCE STORE SHOOTING. Jilot cautioned against quick judgment. "The newspapers make it look like it's mainly him. It's the big Indian kid." She was in her classroom alongside Will, going over the work he needed to make up. Will said that, when he heard the news, "I was speechless." He and Ivory had been close. But in the immediate aftermath, details were scarce. All Will knew was that his dad had picked

Ivory up. On Wednesday, Big Will had been corresponding with Aaron Brien. Big Will knew that police in Missoula wanted to talk to Ivory. But, Big Will thought, people's identities got mixed up all the time. Maybe they had the wrong kid. On Wednesday, the seventh, the Briens asked Big Will to come over. Big Will sat with them as Ivory cried. Before leaving, the policeman repeatedly apologized to the Briens. Then Big Will drove Ivory to turn himself in.

If he had not seen the photo, Zanen said, he would have fought anyone who asserted that Ivory was involved. "He's by far the best student athlete I ever coached," Zanen said. But Ivory's mug shot had been blasted over the state—over the next four days, it appeared in newspapers in Missoula, Helena, and Billings, near where Ivory's extended family lived on the Crow Reservation. The story in the *Billings Gazette* featured Ivory's mug shot but not that of the shooter.

When it came to Ivory's day in court, his family had cause for concern. According to the nonprofit Prison Policy Initiative, in 2010 whites, despite making up 88 percent of Montana's population, comprised just 69 percent of its prisoners. That same year, Native Americans represented 22 percent of the state's incarcerated, despite making up 6.7 percent of the population. In April, Ivory was granted supervised release from Missoula County jail in advance of his trial. He returned home, where he saw a therapist and a drug-treatment counselor. Greg reached out in private to see if he was okay. One day, Ivory was surprised to find Lane Schall at his door. *Whoa!* thought Ivory. *The heck are you doin' here?* They talked for an hour, something Ivory would always remember. He spent long hours in his own mind. The time alone, he said, was a period of "reevaluating life. It made me comfortable to be inside my own head and deal with the mental warfare that I had."

In mid-April, Greg, Will, Phil, and Isaac flew to Denver, for a Native all-star tournament. Their parents made the fourteen-hour-plus drive. John and Becky drove Raelena; Chasity went with her kids; the

Fishers decided to go after Isaac promised he'd assert himself by scoring. In Denver, John planned to buy Broncos paraphernalia and a pile of *New York Times*, as the article I'd written had just been published, and they were hard to come by in Missoula. The Arlee Warriors were on the cover of *The New York Times Magazine*. It was to be a weekend of relaxation. As John and Becky sat in the stands, watching their son play, Becky's phone rang: Zanen was on the line. Becky hung up with a wan expression. It was Phil, she said. Something was wrong with his credits. He was apparently not eligible for NCAA basketball. John's first reaction was "We're just finding out about this now?" A bubble of pressure emerged. "I'm thinking, 'What the hell are you doing, Zanen? What was you doing, Dave Whitesell?'" Becky called Amy Bartels, the athletic director, and it sounded serious. Out on the court, Phillip spun through defenders. Becky held out hope they might be able to figure it out, but John had a feeling about these things. He bought *The New York Times*. There, in its pages, he was speaking about how a system turned Native boys into statistics. "Here now," he said, "my son is one of those stats. And I mean, it was just, it was heartbreaking."

Chasity's car broke down outside Billings on the return trip with Will's siblings. "I walked into the grocery store to get the kids snacks," she said, "and I'm just like popping in there. I'm not thinking anything, and then all of a sudden I felt, like, the entire place staring at me." She did not feel threatened. But she did not feel welcome, either. She arranged for a tow and called Will. He was already headed back to Missoula on a flight. The next morning he drove across the state to pick her and the kids up.

After returning from Denver, John met the Arlee administration. Somehow, Phil was not registered with the National Collegiate Athletic Association and, despite his solid grades, did not have enough core credits to qualify for Division I sports. Zanen thought he remembered someone from the University of Montana telling Phil to register with the NCAA during a previous Griz camp; Becky thought she remembered Don Holst mentioning it in February. Phil still had time to register, but the larger issue was his core credits. He did not have enough time to make them up. Inexplicably, during Phil's earth-shattering senior season, no one had looked into what classes he needed to be eligible for the Griz. John's fury radiated throughout the school. "Those school people are professionals," he said. What, he wondered, had happened? "I was under the assumption that that's what the school does. That's what the coach does."

But John also looked inward. In his mind, he and Becky had failed. Had he known, he would never had let Phil take a work-study on the Tanner ranch. John could not bear to deliver the news, so Zanen did. The coach met Phil at the Store, where he got right to it, telling him the school had failed him. He told him to stay positive; to not be a statistic. "I know," said Phil, in Zanen's recollection. Upon returning home, Phil told his dad it was not the end of the world. His chin started to move, and then his chest. John hugged his boy and told him, "I'm sorry. I'm sorry I failed you."

Phil went horn hunting. For a couple of days he didn't even tell Jordyn, who was still in Arizona. He did not blame others. He thought it was his fault. Greg came to check on Phil. That was nice. Some of the other sympathy he didn't want. Rumor and blame swirled. "We all took the hit," Arlee's principal, Jim Taylor, said. Amy Bartels, the athletic director, said it was a "joint responsibility for everyone involved." Zanen, despite his constant talk about accountability, did not accept responsibility during our conversations, instead deflecting to the school. But Don Holst, the former Griz coach, put it this way: "Everybody is culpable. Your parents, the player, the school, the school recruiting you. I mean, everybody should be all on the same line, but that wasn't the case."

The lack of communication from the University of Montana during the season raised a question among some in Arlee: Had the Griz really wanted Phil, or was his walk-on invitation largely symbolic? TJ Haynes said, "I just ain't very impressed with the Griz." The Griz would not comment on Phil at the time, citing NCAA rules prohibiting them from discussing prospects who had not signed letters of intent. But I did meet with Rachi Wortham, the assistant coach, at a breakfast joint in Missoula. My breakfast was bought as soon as I walked in the door. Wortham said he had a story for me—something about awesome coaches. Later, he said he was raised in a tough neighborhood full of gang violence. "Everyone deserves an opportunity," he said. But, he added, you had to seize your chance when it came. Thousands of kids were vying for these spots. During another conversation, when I raised the historical issues surrounding recruitment from Indigenous communities in the state, he said, "I don't understand that. I'm two years in and I don't know, and I'm not from Montana."

Zanen tried to turn a negative into a positive. "Phil's going to make it," Zanen told me. "I ain't done." Wortham had a friend who coached at a junior college in Idaho, North Idaho College (NIC), with a reputation for producing Division I players. Other Griz recruits had gone there, including RayQuan Evans, the Crow star out of Billings. The Griz reached out to the North Idaho staff about Phil, and soon Zanen was on the phone with North Idaho's coach, Corey Symons. "That coach told me, full ride, starting point guard position," Zanen said. Zanen told Symons that Phil had a friend, Tyler Tanner, who was looking for a new home. Zanen made it clear that getting Ty would assure Phil's signing. Zanen wondered if he could get Will a shot there, too. North Idaho, Zanen said, was "a gold mine." Becky wanted him to slow down. "Zanen's peddling," she said, "trying to make it up." He was under pressure, too—Phil's ineligibility did not look good for his program. "He's trying to process this himself," she said.

In mid-April, North Idaho invited Phil to work out with its players. Becky made him throw his gym bag in a car. They drove west, past St.

Regis and over the state line. Coeur d'Alene is a picturesque town on a lake. In the 1970s, the area was known for white supremacism. The town has since tried to shake that reputation, but its demographics are still homogeneous—nearly 94 percent white. Becky took Phil right to the gym, where tall kids hung off rims in front of Division I coaches. North Idaho's staff asked Phil if he wanted to suit up. He said his ankle was kind of hurting. Becky made him get his shoes, and he shot her his angry look. The college trainers taped his ankle and Phil took the court. Becky noted that he was the second-smallest player out there. But he held his own and played well with RayQuan Evans, who was receiving national interest. Furthermore, Zachary Camel Jr., the Arlee graduate who had walked on with the Griz, was joining North Idaho's coaching staff, the next step on a path he hoped would one day lead to his heading a Division I program. He saw the highest levels of ball, notably the Golden State Warriors, moving in the direction of the philosophies he'd grown up with—quick, positionless play. "Once we break through," Camel Jr. said, "it's gonna be crazy. We've played this style our whole lives." Symons, the North Idaho coach, wanted Phil. Phil wondered if Symons had a spot for Ty. Another incoming recruit, Emmit Taylor III, was Yakama and Nez Perce. Symons also acknowledged what went unsaid publicly in Montana. He referred to a "stigma that has happened in the past, where Native kids tend to not like to be far from home. And when things don't go exactly how they want, sometimes they just go home." He saw his program as an antidote: "Having three or four kids"—not to mention a coach—"they can help each other."

Later that week, Phil and Becky walked into the Griz's handsome offices, with the flat-screen TV and plush carpeting. They had been summoned by DeCuire, the head coach. In Becky's account, DeCuire was direct. He said he respected Phil because he'd grown up with adversity. He said he wanted Phil because he could play, not because he'd fill the stands. DeCuire allowed that things had fallen through the cracks and said it was time to move forward. Phil asked what it would take to get back to the Griz. DeCuire said Phil had three options. He could enroll at the university for a year without playing or being affiliated with the team. He could go to North Idaho, then look DeCuire up in two years. The other option was Tech, but that, DeCuire said, would likely preclude a reunion. Phil asked if DeCuire would be at the Griz in two years, when Phil returned. DeCuire said that, in his business, nothing was guaranteed. But he told Phil that, should he go to North Idaho, the Griz staff would watch him there. And, Becky recalled, "That kid hung on every word he said." Phil knew himself well enough to dismiss the idea of a year of school without so much as basketball practice. Becky saw Coeur d'Alene as a gamble. But the connection to North Idaho had come directly from the Griz. Phil left believing that if he proved his commitment to the Griz, he'd return in two years to the only program he'd ever wanted to play for.

Will's options had dried up. Carroll's interest vanished. Their coaching staff had changed, the men who had approached him moving out of state, and the college's anemic record of Native American athletic recruitment continued. The junior college in Washington also disappeared. Will worked feverishly to make up three classes in one semester with Jilot's aid. Then she was accused, by a colleague, of inflating his grades. Big Will and Chasity each called Jilot, furious. Big Will wondered, "Are you teaching Will how to succeed in life? He needs to learn the hard facts of life. You're going to fail when you deserve to fail." She explained her philosophy and that the support she offered to Will was available to other kids. An inquiry by the school also determined the accusation to be without merit. Afterward, everyone calmed down. Still, Jilot said, "I feel like I'm on a freaking island by myself sometimes."

Will's kidney stone was removed on April 13. Then Will was back at the gym: lifting, shooting, working on his right-hand dribbling, waiting for opportunity to fall from the sky. He was, he said, "hoping for anything at this point."

Zanen continued to court attention for the boys' suicide-prevention advocacy efforts, which he now called "the Warrior Movement." He arranged for the team to talk at other schools, with the boys missing class to do so. The owner of the art gallery in town said the videos constituted "the most effective suicide-prevention effort" she'd seen in decades because it "closed the gap" between the cool kids and those who felt left out. Many in the community were shocked at Greg's revelation in the article I'd written, Jilot among them. She had no idea, and she knew everything. One day, at school, he told her he thought a classmate was struggling with depression. She looked into it and Greg was right. Bear Malatare could barely speak, he was so proud of the boys. He had not gotten sober until he was thirty-nine, and it had taken him years to unburden himself. Afterward, he had thrown himself into sobriety advocacy. But he had never talked much about the deaths by suicide he'd known. Greg's revelation, in the *Times,* Bear found particularly moving. Now, he said, "We need to talk about this."

But something started to happen, too, something that I was a part of: the boys were flooded with attention. Their efforts to close the gap between the cool kids and those left out made them even more cool. Before my article was published, CNN reached out, Senator Tester made a video along with Senator Cory Booker honoring the Warriors' prevention efforts, and Governor Bullock visited Arlee to meet with the boys. Both Becky and David Whitesell were wary of the politicians' affinity for the videos. They didn't want to see the boys politicized. Whitesell had another concern, too: "What happens when the next kid who they know who saw the video decides to go ahead and do it anyway? Do they [think], 'Man we didn't do enough?'" Whitesell arranged to have the boys trained in basic prevention techniques. He was in favor of their continuing to speak if they wished to. "It's what we're supposed to be doing as educators," he said. "Give kids opportunities to be successful on and off the court, outside the classroom."

After my story ran, the opportunities and attention only increased. Nike reached out, wondering if there might be a way to assist the boys' efforts through N7, its division dedicated to Native American athletics. For Zanen, Nike was larger than *The New York Times*. Nike was LeBron and Jordan; Nike was an express lane to American greatness. "I want to leave something powerful," he said. "Bigger than ball."

22

The Singing

April–August 2018

C an you hear it?" asked Sophie. "The singing." She was in the hospital again. In late March, she had suffered another stroke. Now it was April, and most of the family was there, but not Will. She started to sing in Séliš. "My aunts know her songs," Chasity said later. "This was different." No one recognized it. One of Chasity's aunts recorded it and sent a version to Patlik Pierre. He said it was a family song to alert her ancestors so they would be waiting.

Chasity broke down. Will was not ready yet, she thought. He would not be able to take it. He would not graduate. She called him and he rushed to the hospital. "If she gets in the state of mind she's gonna give up," Chasity said, "he's the guy we call." When he heard what had happened, Will put his head down and got quiet. Then he went in alone. When he emerged, he announced that Sophie was going to recover: "My gramma's gonna make it." She recovered.

Everything turned green, the mornings stinging and the evening air dusty and sweet with the smell of aspen. Irrigation lines spun water into the air, creating small rainbows. Kestrels chased mayflies, songbirds chased magpies, and eagles descended into pastures, cleaning up after birth and death. One day, Terry Pitts drove a horse trailer up to Perma Bridge and then toward Hot Springs. He had to check on a mare with a foal. He had recently sold some horses, so he took an older one that was "kind of sour." On the way up a hill, the horse blew up. As it approached a fence, Terry tried to dismount but ended up dangling. His head met a rock at full speed. Drenched in blood, he descended the hill and started to load the horse back in his trailer. A law-enforcement officer passed. Terry insisted on driving home; the officer called an ambulance. Soon Terry was on an emergency flight to a hospital, where he underwent emergency brain surgery. He had a collapsed skull, a swollen brain, a shattered nasal cavity, a broken jaw, two broken vertebrae. The following day, he demanded to go home. His request was unsuccessful.

Every morning, at 6:43, Allen Pierre's phone rang. It was his father, Patlik. "He'd tell me the same thing every day." He wanted to be picked up by 7:40. "And—'I know. I know, Dad, what time I got to be there. I know.' But every morning he called me." And then they would go to school. At the end of the day, Allen drove his dad home, then returned to his own house. At 10:00 P.M., his phone rang again. It was Patlik. "When the news would start, he'd say, 'Are you watching the news?'" And Allen said yes.

In the spring, their drives took on added significance as Patlik started to tell Allen stories or discuss serious tribal issues he'd worked on—for example, the ongoing negotiations over the CSKT water compact. An effort to quantify the Tribes' water rights in the state, the compact was crucial and fraught, and the nation's claim went all the way back to the Hellgate Treaty. Patlik kept a copy of the treaty at home. As the old man spoke, Allen tried to surreptitiously turn on his iPhone's recorder. And Patlik stopped talking. "We'd be driving down the road and he'd be telling me a story, and I sneak over and try to hit that record button. He seen me fiddling with my phone. Silent. Nothing." After a few times, Allen said, "He pointed to his head, to his brain. He pointed to

his chest, where his *spu?us*, his heart. And he said, 'These are the com-
puters that the Creator gave us. That's how come when I tell you these
stories, you're not to record 'em.' He said, 'Because through modern
technology you push the wrong button. You could lose that story. But if
you wholeheartedly listen to me, have got a contact with me, and really
know that we have that connection of the stories going on, then when
you need the story, it'll be right there for you.'"

On May 1, the phone did not ring at 6:43. Allen drove to his father's
house. "I found him when I got there." Patlik Pierre had died. Allen
sank into grief and turned to art, staying up until four in the morning
making bustles and ribbon skirts. He thought about his grandkids, who
needed role models, and the future. So much depended on Will. Allen's
own sorrow engulfed him; he imagined facing that at seventeen. Sophie
had been released from the hospital, as Will had predicted. But, Allen
said, "I tell him, you know, Grandpa gives you these talks, it ain't to
waste your time. It ain't to see, you know, where you're at in life. It's to
tell you that there's going to be a time when your *túpye?*'s gonna go and
it's gonna hurt. But that you can't bottle that up. You can't hold all them
tears in because that'll bring sickness to yourself." And when the time
came, and Sophie passed, Allen told Will, "I can take your grief."

In early May, Phil signed a letter of intent to play for North Idaho
College. Soon after that, he and Ty went back to Coeur d'Alene to play
together, Phil taking it upon himself to guard RayQuan Evans. Symons,
the coach, said, "They wowed us with how hard they played, how well
they played together." Symons offered Ty a walk-on position. Ty decided to redshirt—meaning he'd practice with the team but not play
games. Because he'd already played a year of college ball, that meant he
and Phil could live together for two years. He hoped he'd get a chance
to go somewhere bigger after North Idaho. "Or," he said, "get two years
and be happy. Otherwise I'll have regrets like everyone else."

Symons did not extend an invitation to Will. But in May, one opportunity finally presented itself. The University of Montana Western had hired a new coach, Mike Larsen, who invited Will to work out with the team. "He played well," Larsen said. But, he added, Will's height was a challenge and he wasn't yet academically eligible. Once that happened, Larsen said, "he'd be more than welcome to walk on."

Big Will thought it was a good idea, an open door. But in Will's eyes, he was being offered the role of a manager. He said, "I didn't want that." Furthermore, he didn't get the feeling the coach really wanted him. "Nothing against them. It's not me. I just want to play. I know I can play." But he realized it might not happen. "The most important thing is to get an education."

I asked what he planned to tell the Western coach.

"I just listened to what he had to say. I said, 'Oh, aight.' I ended it. Said, 'See ya later.' He doesn't know if I'm going or not. I'll probably let him know after a while." Will paused. "Or not say anything. *Huh-heh*."

There was something else, too. The school was located in a white ranch town. Will said he hadn't felt "unwelcome." But he was "not totally comfortable." Chasity was less circumspect: "He felt like an outcast." When I asked why, she said, "His hair."

Because of the old credits Will had to make up, whether he would graduate came down to the final week. He had to write a paper on a Louise Erdrich novel. He asked for Jilot's help. She said, in her recollection, "I'm sorry, you're a senior, I've held your hand for a while. I can't this time."

He wrote the paper, and his high grades in his senior classes qualified him for the academic all-state team. Chasity had come around on Jilot's philosophy: "It proved it. He's keeping his grades up, he understands what he's doing." On May 27, in the old gym, Phil and Will sat onstage in caps and gowns. Greg skipped a tryout for an AAU team to attend, to his father's consternation. After their names were called, Phil and Will walked into the crowd with roses for friends and family.

That night, everyone gathered at a party where kids and parents cel-
ebrated together, a country band playing and boys and girls sneaking
into the shadows. Phil stuck to Ty's side, near an outdoor basketball
court, at one point bouncing a long shot off the concrete. He threw
his hands in the air, as though astonished, when it went in. In the days
that followed, he disappeared to the Tanner ranch, avoiding Warrior
Movement events. "I'm out of high school now," he said.

In June, Zanen took the boys' and girls' teams to Nike's Beaver-
ton, Oregon, headquarters at the invitation of N7, the division started
in 2000 by Sam McCracken, a citizen of the Assiniboine and Sioux
Tribes of the Fort Peck Indian Reservation. N7 had given away roughly
$5 million over the previous decade with the aim of bringing "sport
and all its benefits" to Indigenous communities. As a large bus carried
the Warriors and the Scarlets toward Nike's campus, a gleaming, manicured place the size of a town, Zanen sat up front in a sleek Warrior
Movement hoodie, the kind now being sold for $70. As chaperones
he had invited his brother, Zachary; Shannon Patton; Franny; a friend
from Charlo named Devon Cox; and Doug Lefler, Jordan's father.
With the exception of Patton, all were board members of a fledgling
nonprofit organization called the Warrior Movement. Zanen and Jordan Lefler had produced a new video to air, heavily produced with
drone shots. Today, Zanen was going to speak alongside Nike's chief
operating officer, Eric Sprunk, and the NBA star DeMar DeRozan. A
high school team from a Class C school in Montana had reached the
pinnacle of the commodification of sport, with its cobbled walkways,
Astroturf fields, fountain pouring over a staircase, and its shrines: the
Tiger Woods building and the Mia Hamm building and the Michael
Jordan building. "It feels right," Zanen said. In the back of the bus,
Will and Tapit discussed how to tune Sophie's hand drum, which Will
had brought to sing alongside Taboo, the hip-hop artist, an N7 am-
bassador. Nearby, Lane Schall peered out a window and saw the silver

frame of a new building reaching into the heavens. "God bless America!" he hollered.

"This ain't America," said Will. "This is Native America."

The teams' tour started in the Michael Krzyzewski Fitness Center, where Lane Schall and Dar flexed in Nike shirts and Will took approximately three thousand photos of Coach K's trophies. After a workout in a gym with floor-to-ceiling windows, the kids retired to a room full of wraparound leather chairs where a hill of breakfast burritos sat in warming trays. Bellies full, they moved to a design studio full of mannequins and a 3D printer. A designer said, "If you have a dream, keep going," adding, "I grew up on the rez, I was a basketball player."

The kids split into groups. Some tie-dyed socks, some sketched jersey designs, and some sat at a large table in an open-floor-plan room, using laptops to customize basketball sneakers. Will went for the shoe station, where another designer, a tattooed guy in a flat-brimmed cap, sat with him. The man asked if Will liked any players on the Golden State Warriors.

"Nope." Will's eyes were intent on the screen.

A moment later, the man asked, "What's the team everyone follows in Montana?"

"Arlee Warriors."

The arrival of a special guest was announced, and a man with a fedora-style hat entered: Tinker Hatfield, the designer of many of Michael Jordan's iconic shoes. Hatfield said he was deeply moved by Arlee's story and that, when Nike did things right, "We can be helpful. We can make things better for people." He added, "I am part Chinook Indian by the way." A couple of kids nodded off. They perked up once he started to talk about what it was like to design Jordan's shoes. Then it was off to lunch, in an expansive cafeteria. Zanen sidled up to Nike's chief operating officer, Sprunk, who had grown up in Missoula. DeRozan, the NBA star, entered. I ate with Franny. "It's good," he said. Some of the kids, he said, might want to work here someday. "Home will always be there." Then he said, "I respect those guys in the kitchen."

After lunch, the kids went to a large, airy space with great windows to present to Nike staff. A crowd of a few hundred filed in, and Zanen, Will, Greg, and LJ took seats alongside Sprunk and DeRozan, who had recently revealed his own struggle with depression. He played wing—Will's position. He looked to be roughly the size of Will and Greg combined. Jordan Lefler was nervous, as Nike planned to air the new video he and Zanen had produced. After an honor song, Sprunk introduced everyone and asked Zanen, "What was the moment as the coach when you realized, 'Wow, this is something bigger than just Arlee High School?'"

Zanen spoke, first thanking the Creator and Kendra: "Without her the Warrior Movement wouldn't be what it is. So thank you." Then he said, "It's already emotional. When you get to practice and you're missing half your team because their auntie or uncle just killed themself, reality really starts to hit."

It felt like a performance; I felt sad.

Zanen continued, "This isn't an issue of mental health. We've been taught that there's dark and there's light. Without this sadness that we face, which is called depression, how would you ever know what happiness was? That's not a medical issue. That's life." It's been demonstrated in numerous recent studies that certain effects of trauma appear to be genetically inherited, but Zanen saw the issue in a more spiritual light. He said he wished those affected by suicide "could feel the true happiness that the light can give you, whether through Christ or Son or Spirit." He said he wasn't sure precisely what the Warrior Movement was, just yet, but that somehow it might "get people to speak that they're struggling and to stop killing themselves."

DeRozan talked directly to the boys, saying he had taken strength from their story, and Zanen once again pivoted between a discomfiting performative mode and his kind, easy grace. One moment he said,

"You wanna coach struggles, man, come coach where I coach." In the next breath he said, "These boys, they're boys. These girls, they're girls. They're gonna screw up. I challenge all of you to be all right with that."

On a large screen, the teams unveiled the latest video. It opened with a sweeping drone shot of Arlee and the surrounding natural splendor; the kids stood on a hilltop in Warrior Movement shirts while a pop singer crooned, "Help me." It was slick, lacking the raw immediacy of the earlier efforts. The kids read from a script, some of them robotically. They also shared their personal stories, Greg saying that, without his best friends, he wouldn't be here. At the end, LJ cried as he talked about his uncle, and Dar came to him in a slow-motion embrace as the music reached a screaming wail. As he sat and watched the video, Greg cried for his friend. The crowd erupted. Following the presentation of gifts, a Scarlets player said a closing prayer in Séliš, and everyone retired to a lawn for the Taboo concert. The boys ate rainbow ices and shot on minihoops and a few people approached to thank LJ. Nate said he wanted to go to college so he could work at Nike. Taboo took the stage, chanting, "Stand with Standing Rock!" The boys approached, pumping their fists. Following Taboo's performance, Will and Troy and Trey Tewawina, the team managers, walked onstage. Will carried Sophie's hand drum. The three of them sang a song that had been written by the twins' father. It sent a shudder across the lawn; it sounded like the truth. It went like this:

> Don't you feel alone.
> Don't you ever feel by yourself. Ya hey ya.
> Don't you ever give up on me.
> I will never give up on you.

At the end of the day, on the bus, the teams watched Sprunk pull away in a luxury car, and some kids debated how many hundreds of thousands of dollars they thought it cost. Back at the hotel, Zanen gathered everyone for another viewing of the video. LJ did not join, and Dar stayed with him to make sure he was okay. Zanen wanted to clarify what the Warrior Movement was—"so," he said, "you can give a better answer." There needed to be an answer. That's what the world asked of them. The Warrior Movement, said Zanen, was "about getting people to stop killing themselves." He also said the movement needed funds. "A movement has a starting point and then a finish. And you pray you never reach the finish line."

Back in the Jocko Valley, under a strawberry moon, Phil and Ty fixed a busted tractor.

Zanen drove along the Flathead River, fast clouds casting shadows on the hills. With Terry recuperating from his injuries, Zanen had to fix some fence by Hot Springs. He passed a lease where he and his dad grazed horses. "Forty thousand dollars' worth of horses," as Zanen put it. His mind turned to land and grass. He had just looked at a ranch that was beautiful, expensive, and already in demand. "That's Californians for you." He caught himself and corrected his assumption: "Or out-of-staters."

He crossed Perma Bridge and rose through a slot. This, he said, would be his last year coaching. "I'm done. One hundred percent done. It's time to close my chapter, man." Camas Prairie opened up, crested wheatgrass and foxtail shuddering against the wind. He smiled. "We'll win state. You can remember I told you the day we were driving," he said, "and it was blowing wind and the trees were flighting." It was a promise. "You don't often get a team like this," he said, with seven seniors. Only five boys' teams in Montana history had won three consecutive state titles, with one of them reigning above the rest in state lore: Lodge Grass. He would join that company, then ride into the sunset.

I thought he would make a great college coach, but Zanen said he wasn't interested—too much travel, too much time away from family, too much ladder climbing. "I want to keep doing this," he said meaning ranching and the Warrior Movement. He said, "Basketball was just a platform to make a difference." He had been communicating with a documentary filmmaker who had previously worked on the reality television show *Big Brother*. Zanen also corresponded with a young filmmaker who envisioned branded content for Dick's Sporting Goods. NBA TV wanted to come, and Zanen had invited them out. He wanted to write his own book, and he wanted me to write a book, and another author wished to write a book about the season. Once, when I met Zanen in town, two filmmakers approached, pitching a movie based off my work. Zanen sometimes acted as though the flood of attention was beyond his control, but he courted it. He said I was his "media agent." I said I was not. In his eyes, more was better. He was a terrific coach, creative and seeing, driven and compassionate, fiercely dedicated to the boys, and I couldn't help but wonder, How had a man so focused on glory become an emissary for a community that so valued humility? It felt as though some internal restraint button had malfunctioned. "I worry about the coach," said Anna Whiting Sorrell. During a tense conversation about NBA TV or *Big Brother* or whomever, I asked Zanen what he wanted. He said he hoped to become a motivational speaker. He wanted to provide an answer.

During the drive to Hot Springs, Zanen noted with disappointment that, at Nike, one Arlee girl had asked what the Warrior Movement actually did. I pointed out that she had every right to air her views. "You can," said the coach, "but you signed a thing saying what you were going there for. To stay positive, to not be negative."

At Hot Springs, he parked near the pasture and tromped past old cars, checking fence line for a place where cows were getting loose. In the field was a massive red-and-white bull named Warrior. Zanen said he'd recently had a dream in which Lane Johnson was thrown out of a game. Zanen had woken up and called LJ and Greg, saying they needed to play as a team. "Gotta remember, man, don't let this thing get bigger than your heads." He smiled. "Anyways, crazy dream, huh?" He thought about Phil and Ty. They were in a good spot, and he knew Ty would take care of Phil. Ty had always been like that. Maybe something would click in Coeur d'Alene. Zanen thought Phil belonged on Oregon State or Gonzaga. He said he didn't understand why those schools hadn't looked at Phil: "Can't answer it."

This represented a return to safe ground for us. Our conversations had occasionally turned strained as I listened to concerns about the Warrior Movement raised by respected community members. But the college prospects of the boys was a point of unwavering agreement. The coach and I could always return to a common grievance, of all that the boys were up against and all they deserved. But maybe that was also about us. Maybe Phil earning a spot on the Griz or Gonzaga or whomever represented some easy redemption, like a trophy in a case, a symbolic express lane past the harder work that all the boys faced—the larger project of figuring out how they wished to live. If you had to win one game, I asked, would you want Phil or RayQuan Evans, the North Idaho star, drawing the attention of top-25 schools? Zanen smiled: "My brother." Sports are easy like that. A refreshing tonic.

The fence fixed, Zanen drove back toward his recuperating father. I asked if he ever struggled with depression. "All the time," he said. "That's what a lot of this is about." He planned to release the new video publicly on September 11 to commemorate the attacks on the World Trade Center. He envisioned a future in which the community could "give every kid the opportunity to do anything they ever dreamed of. They want to go to fly-fishing camp—they write an essay, boom. Send a check. Go!" It would come to fruition, he said, "If God wants it."

In Arlee, people had started to raise questions. Multiple mental health experts were concerned about the pressure on the boys. Others worried that the advocacy efforts had been commodified, and that the Warrior Movement now seemed geared more toward the outer world than the reservation. When I relayed the thrust of the criticisms I'd heard, Zanen didn't flinch. He ascribed the friction to jealousy, a common diagnosis, and made a fair point when he said, of struggling kids his team might reach, "You'll never know the ones you do save." Once, during a long meeting, I asked him to listen to the voices around him. "I'm going to prove them wrong," he said. "This is for them and they're going to love it."

He could veer into binaries: with and against, victory and defeat. But perhaps the Warrior Movement was something more complex, something that would evolve and reveal with time. What was not up for debate was that the Warriors' videos had brought light to a previously hushed topic. "To kind of normalize that conversation would be nice," said Big Will, who was on the front lines as a first responder. Dar said, "When it's for real it means a lot more." Lane Johnson pointed out that the number of reported deaths by suicide had decreased, and said that speaking had helped him: "Not being so shy, being better with my words." He'd written his own lines for the latest video. Doug Lefler, the father of Jordan, the videographer, became the nonprofit's board president and talked about the strength of vulnerability. Greg, whose voice had been so instrumental, had an idea for the broader community, including nearby schools, to take part. He said, "To me it'd be cool if, in our district, say, Mission did, like, missing Indigenous women"—a national scourge that had recently hit home. He continued: "Charlo could do, like drug abuse." And, he said, "It shouldn't just be championship teams." It was, he said, not just for the winners. But he didn't want to be an organizer. He was burned out, and he had a team to run.

In previous years, Raelena had told Greg, "Your day will come." Now it had arrived. Summer league started, with Greg directing the Warriors. Freed from professional obligations, David Whitesell filmed everything, marveling at Greg's dribbling skill. Raelena put her son's old hoop up for sale and someone drove an hour to see it, asking if it was in fact Greg Whitesell's. Raelena booked hotel rooms for state the following March. She and David now occasionally sat together at games. Greg's hospitalization and recovery, she said, had changed their relationship. "Of course I was angry. Since we've been divorced I've been angry. I can say that now." She added, "When this happened, it was—for me, I don't know about him, but for me, it just changed everything for me. I thought, *Life is too short. Life is too short to feel anger, to feel anything like this.* And I think Greg, for me, really opened my eyes and I thought, *I gotta move forward.*"

Greg said he was trying to make it—"whether it's NBA or overseas." He was excited for AAU. Caleb Bellach had told him what to pack, as the two had become pretty close. "Off court you wouldn't think he's the same dude," Greg once told me. "He's funny, he's caring. He's like—pure. He's a good person. On the court it's different." During the Warriors' summer games, Lane Johnson tore through defenses, Isaac dunked, and his uncle Les discussed his hopes: another championship and more Isaac and Billy. At Spokane Hoopfest, Billy dislocated a finger in a game against boys who were playing rough. Les looked at it askance and said, "Long way from your heart." Billy reentered the game and won it with a bank shot. Isaac said he would have had nothing but net. Lane Schall broke his hand trying to make a Shetland pony buck on asphalt. Becky attended the Warriors' summer games to watch Dar. John did not. "I have a bitter taste," he said. When it came to Phil and the Griz, John held a grudge against Zanen. This was difficult, as he and the Pittses had been close, with him living at Terry and Crystal's one summer during high school, when Terry coached him in track. The families would continue to live in proximity; that's the strength and challenge of close-knit communities. But John felt that the coach had been too focused on marketing rather than the details of his players' recruitment. John said, "I'm not like my wife. My wife can forgive and forget pretty easy, you know. She's paved her way to heaven. I'm gonna have to fight my way into heaven." He was increasingly frustrated with the Warrior Movement. "I bought into it at first." But John had taught the boys, from an early age, the importance of humility, and he found Zanen's bravado grating. John felt that the coach had trademarked something that the community had developed over decades. "He's a seller, and right now he's selling."

In June, during an exhibition game, the Warriors played Manhattan Christian and won without Phil and Will. "We handled them easily," Greg messaged me. Sage Nicolai analyzed Manhattan Christian's play: "Not Indian ball. That's for sure. It just doesn't look professional."

Earlier in the spring, Montana State University Billings had announced the hiring of Mick Durham, the coach who once made disparaging comments about reservations to *The Times*. Phil had never really harbored dreams of playing for the school. But following Durham's hire, he dismissed the possibility. In May, 406 MT Sports published a list of Montana high school athletes recruited for college. It did not list those bound for the state's tribal institutions. It also accounted for the same Arlee football player twice, with different spellings. But it seemed useful as a starting reference for athletic representation. By June, the list contained 427 names, 260 of them attending in-state schools. Of those, according to 406 MT Sports, fifty had been recruited to play basketball. Of those, according to Don Wetzel Jr., who oversaw youth initiatives in Indian Country for the state's Office of Public Instruction, four were tribal, and of those, just one was male, a young man who had also been recruited as a record-setting javelin thrower. "There's this undercurrent of, 'This is how it is and this is how it's always gonna be,'" Wetzel Jr. told me. But in June, the Griz signed an Indigenous player from Washington, a Makah guard named Freddy Brown III who was family friends with Travis DeCuire. "If you don't take an opportunity," Brown told 406 MT Sports, "someone else will."

The snow melted and flushed downward, to the Jocko, the Flathead, the Clark Fork, the Columbia. Fires started in Oregon and Washington and John shipped out. Greg and Tomi were off and on, off and on. "Be respectful towards each other," Raelena said. Will moved bodies at the funeral home. July 4 rolled around. Phil and Ty stayed up at the ranch. Ty couldn't wait to get to college. "Me and Phil got this great opportunity," he said. Also, there would be girls there. Phil, for his part, was committed to Jordyn, but they hadn't been able to see much of each other. "When I'm here for the summer, we hope to see each other a lot," she said. "But this summer it's been really hard just because he's been working every day." She and Ty sometimes butted heads: "Me and him say that we're in a three-way relationship." But someone had to be there for Phil. In preparation for going to North Idaho, Ty had done his taxes and applied for a grant and was dipping into savings to pay his last fees from Dawson Community College. Phil had done nothing. "He's pretty mature but he just does his own thing," said Ty. "I don't know how to explain it. He's just like a kid but not a kid. He still needs somebody there to take care of him."

On the first evening of powwow, a blue Dodge Ram covered in mud and bugs pulled up on the grass near the pavilion: Will, eating a cheeseburger in a Warrior Movement hoodie. Two basketballs sat in the back seat. He had recently suffered a heartbreak and was trying to understand. "She doesn't know what she wants," he said of the young woman. How could girls change their minds so fast? He knew what he wanted. When he was a kid, shooting at the Lyles courts, he envisioned one day being a role model. He had done that. There were billboards of the team on US 93 including the number for a suicide-prevention hotline. But Will needed to go out into the world. He wanted to have kids one day and for them to know new possibilities, to have good grades. "They're gonna be eligible," he said. He was leaning toward going to Salish Kootenai College for a year, to solidify his academics, a plan he would soon finalize. After one season, he now said, he'd transfer elsewhere—somewhere out there. It would be hard: "Something makes me want to come back home. I don't know why. But it happens every time." Fireworks shattered on the horizon, the smoke low and beckoning. "I feel like I could handle it if it was for ball." He walked to the pavilion, where Allen danced for his own father.

The next day President Trump held a rally in Great Falls, where he called Elizabeth Warren "Pocahontas." Bear said that Trump had pulled a crowd comparable to that at a good Arlee Warriors tournament game. Bear grinned and said maybe it was a little smaller. The smile fell away. "That goddamn Trump Pocahontas thing. That's the kind of thing makes Indians feel like we need to keep up with the Joneses. Prove everyone wrong." He knew where that led—nowhere good. "Asshole." He sat by the stick game, tapping one hand to the drums and holding the other out, gambling cash he set aside from cutting firewood. He'd won a couple hundred bucks the night before. "Easy as taking candy from a baby!" He laughed. "Money is the root of all evil." Once he got over that, he was happier. "I don't have to fake my life. I just am who I am." That was his problem with the Warrior Movement. It was smelling too much like money. "It came from them boys' hearts. Let it be done." Summer was almost over. Soon it would be basketball season. He lit a cigarette. Someone called Phil "NBA material" and asked if the North Idaho schedule was out. It wasn't. Bear wished they would play the Griz. "Phillip would put it on that Griz point guard." But Bear was excited for what was to come: Phil playing with Tyler and two other Natives, including RayQuan Evans. Bear grinned: "Hope them boys at North Idaho are planning to build a bigger gym."

The Flathead Lake three-on-three tournament took place in Polson the week before Phil and Ty were to leave for school. Everyone was there: Lane Johnson, Isaac, Dar, Alex Moran, Morgan, Whitney, Will, Zanen. Past state champions from Indian Country were also present, including a star of Hardin's 2018 Class A championship team, David Evans, an athletic player who could jump through the gym. He was headed to Montana State University–Northern on a football scholarship. He told me he'd received basketball calls from out of state, where he didn't want to go, but no interest from Montana programs. Greg limped around in a walking boot. He'd hurt his calf during AAU; some pop that felt like burning. Afterward, he'd flown home with a Montana Tech assistant coach, but had received no offer. "Which is bullshit," he said, "because I'm better than all the guards." He had just learned that Caleb Bellach had signed on a full scholarship with the Montana State University Bobcats. "Caleb's my guy," Greg said. And he wondered where his offer was.

Becky saw Phil walk by in basketball shorts. She did a double take, then called her son. John had instructed Phil and Ty to avoid three-on-threes, due to the possibility of injury. Coming to watch some ball? she asked. Phil explained that Will just needed some guys on his team— *Gosh, Mom.* He hadn't played in months. They won their first game, lost their second, and then it got so hot the blacktop underneath the floppy backboard seemed to bubble. Before the third game Phil did not warm up. He and Ty took turns orchestrating the offense. Phil tried an over-the-shoulder pass to Will that bounced down the street. "He's a little rusty," said Becky. Phil's expression turned hard. He dribbled, darted toward the middle, pulled the ball back and drove. Lacking enough court, he tried to simply jump over the defender. He came down in a long arc and caught the outside of his right foot on the blacktop. His foot stuck, then his leg came down on it, pushing everything over his ankle. He hit the ground and rolled. Silence descended. His sisters ran. "That's why he's not supposed to be here," said Becky. Phil rose. He tried to walk it off. He slowed, paused, and slumped. He sank to the ground. Zanen sprinted to his side. Jordyn left to get a car. Someone asked if Phil was okay. "No," he said, his breath pushing his ribs through his shirt.

23

Home

August 2018

A few days later, Bear and I met at the Huckleberry Patch. Phil had avoided devastating injury, but it was a bad high-ankle sprain. Becky was out of her mind when he continued to change pipe at the Tanner ranch with a lower leg that looked like bruised plums. But Bear seemed cheery as ever: clean-shaven, plaid shirt tucked in, brisk walk. He was disappointed that Phil had played. "But, you can't tell kids anything!" He laughed and let it go. He'd just finished praying. "We pray every day, we pray every night, we thank the Creator that we're here. I just got done praying before I come out, you know. You're thankful for everything, whether it's good or bad. I'm waiting for a call from Missoula on my motor home. Now that's probably gonna hurt, you know, when I find out what they're gonna charge me to fix my cockeyed motor home. It's too challenging for me to drive because my generator was goin' to hell on my motor home. So I know it's gonna be bad news. It's not death news or anything. But it's gonna be bad news when they say, you know, it's gonna cost you a grand to get this fixed. So you're thankful. You're just thankful for everything. That whether it's good or it's kinda bad, that you can accept it and move on."

I'd been thinking about the Warrior Movement, and concerns that smart people had raised about the potential unforeseen consequences of kids who were still unsure of themselves airing deep trauma. I told Bear about my mother. Her brother—my uncle—died by suicide when I was in my twenties. My mom's form of healing was writing a book of poetry. Finding the words took painful years. How do you know, I asked Bear, when someone is ready?

"I really don't know when that would be. You know it's just something that one day they just start talking about it." Bear's best friend was Bearhead Swaney. Together, they used to go on long drives in the mountains, where they argued about logging (Bear was in favor, Bearhead opposed) and tried to think up good activities for youth—rafting trips, hunting camps. Sometimes they tried to get kids to talk at campfires. The kids wouldn't say anything until the adults left. Then they talked. "And it was amazing what they talked about," Bear once told me. "But they're in a safe environment talking, just the younger generation there with no adults."

So sometimes it happened. And sometimes it didn't. "There's some kids or some people that I don't know that they'll ever talk about it. Just because of the way it happens," Bear now said. He had also been a first responder for the fire department. He told me about cleaning up after one suicide. The story unwound me. "You've been through tough stuff," I said.

"Not really. Not anymore. At one time I was, thought I was the toughest thing that walked the earth." That was when he carried the rage. But he no longer did. Something had changed him. I had been wondering about this for a while—how he had gone from being a drinker and a fighter, carrying a rage handed to him by a history of betrayal, to the kind of man who told a friend you can't live like that. I asked him now, and Bear told me a story. It was about his thirty-ninth birthday, just after he'd returned from the Cursillo retreat, the multiday encounter with Christ:

"You know how you gotta party on your birthday. So I went and we go to the bar, and it's hard for me to drink. I mean I was—I'm a recovering alcoholic, I was a drunk. So gettin' drunk was my thing. And anyhow, I go to the bar. Next thing I know I'm crying. I'm thirty-nine years old. Today's my birthday." Then bowling league started. "You know the bowling alley was where Nkʷusm is now. So I and my wife was bowling. I noticed that as I was having two, three beers during bowling, I'm kinda on the same trend again. Starting to get a little high and whatnot. We're sitting there at the table like this, I and my wife. Watching all our friends out there. You see the shit they're pulling." Bear said, "And how they think, like I would think when I was drinking, no one can see me. We sat there for probably an hour, hour and a half. I happen to look over, and my wife's beer was plumb full. She hadn't even taken a drink yet. And so I asked her. I said, 'Hey, what's the matter? You not feeling good?' 'No.' I said, 'Well, you haven't touched your beer.' She looked at me. She said, 'Look at yours, you haven't drank yours.' And I had probably drank that much out of my bottle of beer. And I said, 'Well, why do you drink?' And she said, 'Because I love you.'"

I gasped.

"I said, 'Let's go home.' She said, 'What?' I said, 'Let's just go home.'"

24

Must Be the New Shoes

August 2018–March 2019

Will stood outside Allen and Kelly's, looking past Patlik's old truck and the art studio. When Will slept here in the fall, he said, he'd wake to the bugling of elk: "In September when they're ruttin', you'll hear 'em bugling." That was just weeks away. September meant college, a new team and new classes. Will said he was thinking of studying wildlife and fisheries. "I'm not gonna be in the NBA. Gotta face reality sometime." He paused. "Some dreams don't work out all the time."

Will turned eighteen the next week and bought a Dodge Charger. "Fast as hell. Pretty fast, man; 2006. Everything leather inside." He moved into a place owned by an auntie. The Salish Kootenai College team didn't run as much press in practice. Will registered for class: Native American Studies, English, and math. The teachers were fine, he said, but, "Ain't nobody like Jenn." He wrote a paper on the use of stereotypes in a film about a Native kid attending an all-white school. "I knew what to write about." He started to think more about religion. He wondered about Buddhism. He said he knew who he was, that he had changed. "I was a little-shit kid." He had different dreams now. "I just want to be successful. I want my own house, have a good job. Survive in life." He added, "I'll probably live in Arlee." He imagined himself as an older man, like Allen. "I feel like I'm going to be a pretty cultural guy." Now, when he and Brad drove around, looking for bucks, Will drank chocolate milk. He claimed he could dunk. He earned a starting spot. In his first college game he made four three-pointers and scored 22 points. He messaged me afterward, talking about how fun it was. Then it got less fun. His team, though talented, suffered a couple of blowout losses. Will wore his frustration on his face. The crowds at the games were minute compared to those in high school. On social media, Will posted that he was a "hasbeen." He missed Arlee's system—the spacing, the rotations, the connection. He thought about how he and Phil and the boys used to run. "If you think about it, our fast breaks are pretty deadly." He used the present tense. Around graduation, he and Phil had discussed one day coaching the Warriors. It had been Phil's idea. "I was, like, aight, I'm down. I'm only doing it if you are, though."

Over in Idaho, Phil's life was his team: weights, practice, class. He ran four miles every other day as his ankle recovered. He wanted to study wildlife biology or range management, but his coaches registered him for classes. He was in a humanities program. He had to take sociology and philosophy. "What's philosophy got to do with me?" he asked. His teammates borrowed his car. John and Becky maintained that he'd grown, to six foot one.

"That legit?" I asked.

"That's legit," John said.

"Legit," said Becky. Still, next to his teammates, he appeared diminutive. Once, I showed my wife photos of the North Idaho team. "Where's Phil?" she asked.

"Look down!"

In October, North Idaho played its first preseason games at a junior-college tournament in a sprawling gym in Windsor, Colorado. John and Becky planned to attend until they realized the schedule conflicted with one of Dar's big football games. "Dar needs us," Becky said.

The gym was set between the interstate and a sprawl of subdivisions, a monochrome of freeway-view domesticity as far as the eye could see. Coaches in tracksuits watched tall boys throw down elaborate warm-up dunks. Phil sat toward the end of the bench. Tyler, as a redshirt, did not attend. Phil entered a game and made his first college basket: a jumper off a set play. On defense he tried to dart into the passing lanes. Sometimes he got beat, and when he tried to recover, as he always had been able to, he committed fouls. He still appeared quicker than the rest, but only by one step. It felt deeply strange until on a fast break Phil leaped, near half-court, and threw a no-look pass that sliced between everyone and hit a teammate for a layup. His teammates ran to him, laughing in amazement. In the next game, he jumped for a rebound and got smashed in the ear.

The following weekend, John and Becky drove to Salt Lake City, for another tournament. The coaches from Utah and Utah State were there, scouting, and one coach talked to Phil. Since the games were exhibitions, Ty suited up and played well. For a minute, Becky and John caught a glimpse of what could be: Phil running point with confidence, both Ty and Emmit Taylor III, the Yakama and Nez Perce kid, shooting three-pointers. Then Phil came down wrong on his bad foot. He was done for the tournament. He drove home with John and Becky. He remembered how Whitney had tried to play through an ankle injury before having surgery that effectively ended her career. "Polson Hoopfest is haunting him," Becky said. In Idaho, Becky and John bought lottery tickets. The pot had swelled to $1 billion. John said that if he won, he'd go fishing. Becky asked Phil if he wanted a ticket. He said no. He was having fun at college. If he won, he'd just go right back to North Idaho. They rolled north: Fort Hall, Idaho Falls, and eventually past Dillon, Montana, home of the University of Montana Western. Phil said, "Will's playing there."

That night, Salish Kootenai College faced off against Western. Phil mused about going to watch, but he had been ordered to stay in his team's caravan, so he missed it when Will scored 18 points against the team that had offered him a walk-on redshirt spot. Later on, the Salish Kootenai bus passed. Phil said, "Holy shit, that's Will!" Phil wanted to return to Arlee for the night. No, his parents said. He had to stick it out.

John and Becky drove to Wyoming, where Phil barely played. They drove to North Idaho, where, over two games, Phil played thirteen minutes and scored 1 point. Bear said, "He's gotta have a coach that can allow him a few minutes of mistakes to get comfortable with what he's doing. Once he gets comfortable with what he's doing, he can blow circles around anyone." Irma said, "What's really sad I think about this college ball is they don't let him do what he's good at." She sighed. "It's like he's out there not knowing where his spot is." Bear just saw individual players trying to score as much as possible. "It's pitiful," he said.

Becky wondered if they were the weird parents, as they attended every game. But Phil said he needed them there. They flew to California for a series on the outskirts of Silicon Valley. John was struck by how many people drove BMWs; Phil noticed the surrounding poverty. But Phil finally got to play substantial minutes, scoring 11 points and stealing the ball four times in each of two successive games.

Will's games took him from Dillon to Idaho to Oregon. Chasity drove all over, tailing the team. Some in the family expressed concern at all that travel and occasionally posted warnings related to missing and murdered Indigenous women on social media. But Chasity kept driving. Watching Will play was important. "It's more—I guess pride," she told me. "It's just me seeing all the work, time, effort that we've put into it."

She no longer did his hair. He wore it pulled back in a ponytail, like Allen Pierre. At every contest, she sat down, her children around her, and took out her iPhone to film for those back in Haynesville. The reception in the gyms did not always make for clear viewing. I, too, watched those games, from New Mexico, screaming at the screens, celebrating the baskets, keeping detailed statistics, and feeling empty afterward because it was not and could never be the same.

But in November, in an empty gym in Coeur d'Alene, there was a moment. North Idaho's team wore silver and red, Salish Kootenai's black and silver. The Malatares sat on one side of the bleachers, Chasity and her kids on the other. Will started, while Phil did not. With the score 7–0 North Idaho, a whistle stopped play. Phil rose and walked onto the court with one ankle heavily taped, bouncing in his elastic gait. He pointed at Will, indicating his defensive assignment. They leaned into each other, and it started. They went at each other over and over, bumping, diving, whipping passes ahead for dunks. Phil made spin moves, threw no-look passes, and floated in for swooping layups, driving his bench into convulsions; Will hit three-point shots in bunches and stole the ball from his cousin and almost faked him out of his shoes during a fast break by throwing his hand over the top of the ball, in an imitation of a pass. Phil sliced past Will for a layup, his scoring total and assists mounting as the scoreboard turned lopsided in North Idaho's favor. Still Will did not quit. They guarded each other the full length of the court until the game's final seconds, when Phil dribbled out the clock as Will looked into his eyes, crouched and ready.

In the coming months, when I watched Chasity's live feeds of Will's games, I'd often see a small icon pop up in the screen. It read, "Phillip Malatare is watching with you."

In August 2018, Ivory reached a plea agreement. He apologized to the victims and asked for a second chance, hoping to serve as an example to his younger siblings. His parents solicited character references. In short order, the judge overseeing Ivory's case, Gregory Pinski, received eighty-seven letters of support—from teachers, from Zanen, from the Malatares, from the Whitesells, from Earl Old Person, Chief of Blackfeet Nation.

At home, Ivory got his feet under him, working at a pizza shop, enrolling at Salish Kootenai College, and going to counseling. His sentencing was held on September 26. Judge Pinski wrote, "In the Native American justice system, restoration principles are paramount." And Ivory, according to Pinski, had "engaged in these restorative principles. He has provided meaningful, remorseful apologies. Unlike many criminal defendants, the Defendant truly understands the impact of his crime on the victims and the community." Pinski also cited the letters he'd received: "This is unprecedented. The Court has probably sentenced 1,000 defendants in nearly six years and has never observed such an outpouring of community support." He sentenced Ivory to ten years deferred, plus restitution fees, and five hundred hours of community service. In effect, Ivory received a decade of probation with the opportunity to expunge the charges from his record. Aaron Brien said, "His culture saved him."

Meanwhile, the case of the shooter, Chase Munson, began to wind its way through the courts. The Briens wanted to separate Ivory from Munson in all ways and were frustrated when the *Missoulian* kept covering Ivory in stories about the shooter's case. Twice in three months, the *Missoulian* put Ivory's image in a leering monthly mug-shots feature. "That image is powerful," said Aaron. The *Missoulian*, he said, "has done a good job in appearing to be a liberal source of news. But it's not. Anytime a crime is committed on the rez it's front-page news." He always wondered why it didn't devote a section to the reservation. "It's one and a half million acres just north. It's a tribal government. It's a major coverage spot. How come there isn't a reporter there doing that? Because guess what—they'll find positive things. Tribal people will support what supports them. They'll buy that paper. You hear that tribal people don't buy it. Well, that's a result of what they see reflected in them."

Ivory didn't pay attention to the press. He was more interested in analyzing himself. Therapy, he said, "helped me a lot. It's helped me realize stuff I didn't even know was a problem." He added, "It's nice to know why this happens so I can work on it and become a bettter human." He enrolled in a psychology program. "The way the human brain works, it's fascinating to me. I was into psychology before I even knew I wanted to do psychology for a living." He wrote a paper related to the scant empathy that those in government felt for tribes in Washington, which made him reflect on his experience at the University of Montana. At the university, he said, "I think they don't have an understanding of who we are as people and what some of us stand for." At work, he served Big Will pizza and felt good when the policeman said he was proud of him. After that, whenever Big Will entered the shop, Ivory tried to take the order. And he threw himself into his studies. One night, at home, Aaron woke in the predawn. A light was on in the kitchen. It was Ivory, studying over a pot of coffee.

Ivory told me, "Getting humiliated in that way and getting knocked on my ass like that, it definitely made me reevaluate things. I see life as a privilege and I don't take it for granted." He thought about the victims of the robbery. "I feel bad for them every day." He said he wanted to "live for the better story." He thought about the eighty-seven letters written in his support—"the whole community to get me through," he said—and the responsibility that conveyed. He wanted to be there for Greg and Lane Schall, as they had been for him. He could eventually talk about his journey without his legs shaking. In the late fall, he did so in front of a new crowd: the 2018–19 Arlee Warriors. He did not mince words. Ivory talked to Greg about leadership and to the entire team about academics. He told everyone to listen to their parents and coaches. He talked about his own choices. Franny said, "It was about his path and the choices we have to make; they're hard ones. I was glad he was saying it. And I'm glad kids reflected." Ivory was relieved to find his friends listening closely: "They respected my word."

Early in the basketball season, Zanen was in a defiant mood. The tension with the administration had only increased. The board wanted to be sure that the Warrior Movement and the Arlee Warriors remained separate entities. "They continue to make it harder," Zanen said. Kris Gardner, the board chair, maintained she was simply following rules. Whitesell's successor as superintendent was James Baldwin, a career administrator close to retirement. Baldwin, a short man with sculpted hair, had coached at Wolf Point and lost to Lodge Grass. "I look back now," he said. "If we slowed it down . . . Old Bull hit two or three long threes . . ."

Baldwin's tenure at Arlee began on a rocky note. At the end of October, as though fulfilling Will's prediction from the previous spring, a boy brought a gun to school. Another kid informed a teacher, but Baldwin was slow in reporting the incident to parents. The episode resulted in a tense community meeting and unflattering press coverage. Tom Haynes, Will's uncle on the school board, said that, for his faults, "Whitesell was knowledgeable of the people here. He made himself available to the people. When there's a death, he shows. With Baldwin there's no association with people."

Baldwin seemed wary of scrutiny, and few entities were more scrutinized than the Warriors. According to Zanen, Baldwin told the coach, "You're under a bigger microscope than the president of the United States around here." Baldwin acknowledged saying "something like that."

The *Missoulian* kept covering the Warrior Movement, portraying Arlee's kids—including the girls, who were now involved—positively. Warrior Movement shirts popped up around the reservation and beyond its borders. A group of kids on a reservation in South Dakota had been inspired and reached out to share ideas. A smart Arlee student who had previously been skeptical of the Warrior Movement now said she thought it was a good thing. The kids talked at Nkʷusm; Allen Pierre said he'd been approached by others hoping the boys would speak. "I think it'll be good for kids to hear what they have to say," he said. "Long as them boys are sincere and in touch with what they're doing." It just had to be done with care. "It opened a door that you could take them boys anywhere. But you could burn a child out easy. Is it helping those boys heal? Or are you opening an old wound?" He concluded, "I hope they continue but have that vision of what they're doing it for."

At one talk, in a church, Nate Coulson revealed his struggles to a group of middle-school-age boys, saying, "I do it alone. I cry. But I *say* I cry." And after crying, he said, "You feel fresh." He spoke with command and care; his audience was rapt. Isaac found a real voice in talking about bullying, he and Billy thinking up new ways to address the issue. When speaking to high school students in Missoula, he once said, "You have to stand up for each other and say, 'Hey, quit picking on them,' and bring them into your circle of people." Les Fisher was no great Zanen Pitts fan, but he said, "I think the Warrior Movement is a positive thing, man. If they can reach out and touch someone's life, someone that says, 'Hey, you know, I was thinking of committing suicide and thought of you'—that right there is worth everything." Bear Malatare's feelings had evolved. At first, he'd been hugely in favor. Then, when it started smelling like money, he'd been opposed. After more time passed, his thoughts changed. Everyone sought an answer, some simple truth. "I still have mixed feelings about it," he said. "But that's just the way the world is. That's a good thing."

On the court, Zanen calculated that Arlee could break the state record for consecutive victories by winning every game through January 8, an away contest at St. Ignatius. That would put his program in historic territory. He decided that the latest prevention video should be released publicly on the day of that game, rather than on September 11.

He also invited a delegation from Nike, as well as NBA TV. Soon cameras were everywhere at practice. But the mood was occasionally tense. Greg, frustrated by the slow development of some younger players, declared that he, Lane Johnson, and Lane Schall would win on their own. Greg and Zanen got into an argument that ended with the coach telling him to leave the gym. Afterward, Bartels and Baldwin demanded a meeting, scolding Zanen. He said the team dynamics were none of their business and railed about "their agenda of micromanaging."

The coach's frustration was palpable. At practice, Zanen uttered three profanities in one morning—something I'd never previously seen. I asked if he still wanted to be a motivational speaker. He paused. "I don't think everyone can handle my bluntness. They like to live in fantasies, not reality. But when we live in reality, we win championships."

"He was trying to do something really good," said Jilot, "and there's all the politics in it, and it really pisses him off. And he's young. He's really young, sees things in black and white. And he's burned out."

Before the season's first game, Greg, Chase Gardner, and Lane Johnson got in a car accident, Greg nearly going through the windshield. They miraculously suffered only bumps and bruises, but it wasn't the most auspicious sign. During the next game, against Rocky Boy, Lane Johnson suffered a badly sprained ankle and the team lost, meaning it could no longer set the state record for consecutive victories in NBA TV's presence. Franny didn't much care—he moved his hand in a flat plane, wearing a smile. But Zanen's eyes were glassy. "It was taken from him," he said. I wondered if he was referring to Lane or himself. The coach said, "We're going to win state. Obviously."

Greg said the loss humbled the team "in a good way." He tried to be a better leader. In private, he was caring. On the court it was different. "Off the court, I try to be a good person. On the court, I don't care what anybody thinks of me. On the court I'm a dick. I try to be as real a person as I can be. In ball, if I hit a big shot in your face, Imma let you know. If they do the same thing—" He shrugged. "If you're going to dish it out, gotta be able to take it." Greg said these days he was happy, win or lose. The key was not to get too high or too low. "I've still got a great life, a great family." He had no college offers, despite averaging 22 points per game. His top choice was Carroll, where his sister had gone, but they hadn't reached out. Lane Johnson also had no offers. Following a terrific football season, LJ had received interest on the gridiron, but basketball was for him, according to his father, the moon and stars. LJ had reached out to the University of Montana Western but received little interest. Isaac's phone lines were quiet, too. "You can't tell me if Isaac was white, playing in a white school, he wouldn't have offers," said David White-sell. "You can't tell me that. You cannot tell me that. He's six-nine."

In December, the Warriors played Hot Springs. Phil and Ty were home on Christmas break. Earlier that week, Phil had earned his first college start, putting up 10 points, 7 steals, 8 rebounds, and 8 assists. Will, nursing a badly sprained ankle, stood near the floor at half-court. Phil was too nervous to enter the gym until halftime. He and Ty had brought a college teammate to the game, a kid from the Bronx whom the Malatares welcomed and hosted over break. At halftime, Phil walked into the gym and his face opened into a huge smile when he saw Will. They both boomed, *"Oooooohhhhhh!"*—then embraced. Phil sat in the bleachers. He was disappointed that the boys weren't whipping the ball in that beautiful way. Still, he said, "Proud of 'em. Love 'em."

I asked what he missed most.

"This."

I asked why he'd disappeared in the summer.

"Too many cameras."

On January 8, a camera and a mic on a boom tailed the boys as they entered the St. Ignatius gymnasium. Greg wore distressed jeans and headphones; Isaac a tie; Schall's state rings sparkled on his hand. Zanen led the way, dressed in all black. Lane Johnson was finally healthy. As the NBA TV crew swept their cameras across, one dedicated Arlee fan put his hand over his face. Will snuck in unnoticed. The Nike contingent arrived, among them McCracken, Sprunk, and Hatfield.

Before the game, the boys gathered in the locker room, where Zanen opened box after box of Nike apparel. He presented two sets of new uniforms, one red, one turquoise, both incorporating designs the kids had made back at Nike headquarters. "Whooo!" the boys yelled. A Nike designer spoke about how the Warriors were his role models. Greg quieted the team and said, "Eyeyey! Bro! You put these on, bro. Think of all the people that are here watching you. Think about everything they're giving. We gotta play, bro. This has gotta be the hardest game you ever played. We have so many eyes on us."

Franny interjected, "You're getting this nice shit, but it's mainly about that name right there." He ran his hand over his chest, where the Warriors logo sat. "That's who you are. Prove it. Show it. Who you are." He didn't care if the jersey had a Swoosh on it.

Zanen told the boys to play with pride, to represent their families. "Arlee. And the name that you carry that your parents gave you. You freaking— you respect the refs. You respect the other team. You treat them with class. You do not disrespect anything about this game." Then he opened one more box and the room exploded. Inside were new Nike basketball shoes, custom-made for the Warriors. Zanen told someone to find the NBA TV crew. Then he prayed.

Our Father in heaven,
We are grateful for everything this game of basketball has given us
Most importantly the friendships that it's given
The family that it's developed

And how it's forced us to become supportive of one another and have
   each other's backs.
We're grateful for all the people
And all the companies
And people that have taken care of us
And given us this opportunity
And joined this ride with us.
We pray that, Father, we can be humble and we can remember what
   we represent. . . .

When the team took the court, Billy, Isaac, Dar, and Lane Schall played with class. But some players taunted, Greg included, and their complaints to the refs almost took on an entitled air. "It's hard to watch that," Alex Moran said. One boy cursed in front of the elders. Another slipped and fell, fouling out. On the sidelines, Irma whispered, "Must be the new shoes."

The next weeks were difficult. Zanen and Camas McClure, the Two Eagle River coach who had previously told the Warriors how much their video meant, got in a confrontation. At the district playoffs, the Warriors and Charlo nearly fought following a hard foul; Zanen threw a towel on the court to show a ref the blood that had come from a player's lip and gestured to the crowd. He did not receive the reaction he hoped for. An unnamed Arlee Schools board member reported Zanen to the MHSA for a violation of rules around liability, for having his sons on the bench, and Baldwin, the superintendent, suggested Zanen look for other jobs. Zanen felt attacked; some of the Warriors, meanwhile, carried themselves in a way that disappointed fans. John called Zanen to suggest the boys act with humility, and the coach thanked him for the call. But something was loose. Bing Matt considered staying home: "Sometimes it's just hard to believe they act like that." The displays of ego, he said, were "not the Arlee way."

I even sensed, for the first time, space between Franny and Zanen.

They were fiercely loyal to each other, and Franny blamed the season's strife on the administration: "They're the ones that are trying to put a roadblock between our basketball program and the community." But when it came to the off-court drama, Franny said, "You gotta separate me and Zanen. We've got two different ideologies. I don't give a shit about that. . . . I'm not here about that shit. I'm here about these guys"—he pointed to the players. "For him it's more, I dunno how to say it." Franny paused. "It's more about the outcome of his legacy. Me, I don't give a shit. A loss teaches you a lot. And without losses you don't grow, even in life. And that's how you overcome them. It's how you become a man."

At divisionals, Arlee lost to Manhattan Christian. There were more whistles and technicals. Near the concession stand, Irma said, "I hope they can be humble. And be leaders. I feel bad for them. Everyone was with them. It spiraled out of control." Bear put the responsibility on the cameras: "It was like a zoo." But more than that, he put the responsibility on the community: "For not standing up for what we believe in. For what we are."

After the divisional final, Faith Dyksterhouse, the former school board member for Manhattan Christian, approached me wearing a hard expression. She said she had been meaning to talk to me about my article. She felt her school had been attacked because of how I'd described the team's bus. She returned repeatedly to another point: the notion that her team recruited. If the Eagles recruited, she said, they would win every year. But I had not written anything about high school recruitment—nothing about it had appeared in the article. Later, during another meeting, she apologized, saying that the suggestion had come from elsewhere. She also compared my characterization of the team's bus to the racist slur hurled Phil's way. (I'd described the vehicle as "a sleek black bus with aerodynamic curvature and tinted windows.") Faith furthermore accused an Arlee fan of showing up intoxicated—something I had not seen in two years. She brought up the officials and Pitts's prayer. "Are the refs keeping up?" she asked. "By saying that line—*if* they said it—would mean some of these refs don't keep up with what we do." She liked rules. And she allowed, "I do have a harder time with those that like to step out of it. You know, did you need to get someone's permission to wear a headdress, or not? Or is that just something you can do?" She returned to the refs: "They are in charge. Their calls will be their calls. So don't argue every single one of them." She asked, "Has it helped, in the past thirty years? You know what I mean? They say abused babies that are never picked up, they eventually quit crying. Because they know if they cry, no one comes anyway. So why put forth the effort? It's not changing. Some calls will be good. Some calls will be bad." She sighed. "There again, it's just basketball."

I ended the conversation.

In February, 406 MT Sports published another list of Montanans recruited for college athletics. It contained 222 names, 161 of them slated to attend in-state schools. Just one of eighteen in-state basketball recruits was Native American, a young woman. Not one male Indigenous ballplayer made the list.

Meanwhile, in Coeur d'Alene, the North Idaho Cardinals, with three tribal rotation players and one tribal coach, shredded opponents. They regularly won by 40 points. Phil was now entrenched as a starter alongside RayQuan Evans, the Crow kid receiving interest from top-25 programs. Phil's point totals rose—18, 12, 15, 19, 16—as did his assists and rebounds. In January, North Idaho played a team led by Damen Thacker, a guard who would go on to sign with and start for the University of Idaho. Phil guarded Thacker at the beginning of the game. Thacker scored 12 points on 4–14 shooting, with 3 rebounds; Phil scored 20, with 9 rebounds. North Idaho won by 25. Phil was among the league leaders in steals. At the small gym in Coeur d'Alene, large contingents from the Flathead Reservation came. Kids asked Phil for photos; adults came following wakes, looking for relief. Bear recounted the plays with a cleansing joy: "Phillip come clear across court last night and got a rebound or loose ball, and everybody else was just kinda standing there. Phillip was clear down over on this side of the court going west! And he turned around! And the ball was knocked loose going way over this kid's head! Phillip went across court got the goddamned thing almost out of bounds slapped it back in and turned around and picked it up and went down and dished it off for a slam!"

Toward the end of the season, Bear and Irma were able to attend fewer games. Their daughter Jennifer had been diagnosed with cancer. Together, after doctor's appointments, they all watched the games on TV, a rare and reliable source of joy then. North Idaho reached the Northwest Athletic Conference (NWAC) championship game. Their starting lineup consisted of Nate Pryor (committed to the University of Washington), Alphonso Anderson (Utah State), Jarod Greene (Dixie State University), and RayQuan Evans, who would soon join Florida State University, one of the nation's top teams. The fifth starter, and easily the smallest, was Phil. In the final, he went scoreless. But in the closing minutes, he chased down a rebound and in one motion slung a no-look pass around his back for a dunk. Back in Arlee, Bear threw things. The Cardinals' coach, Symons, later said, "Nobody on our team makes that play but Phillip." Phil had won three consecutive titles. After the game, he, Emmit Taylor III, and RayQuan Evans posed for a photograph with the trophy, an image of inspiration for those coming next. In it, Phil's cheeks were drawn, his eyes soft. He looked like a man.

A couple of weeks later, Salish Kootenai College competed in the American Indian Higher Education Consortium tournament at Crow Agency. The crowd was small, the media absent. Chasity and the kids sat courtside, all of them well behaved as ever save for the youngest, who repeatedly attempted to join his older brother on the court. Will played his heart out, with 14 points and 8 rebounds. His team lost. He said it was okay because the victorious team, from Pine Ridge, contained some relatives.

25

Where It All Began

March 2019

T he Metra in Billings hummed. In the locker room, Lane Johnson said, "Let's go be legends."

"Let's go make history," said Greg.

Zanen spoke next. "Right now I want you to just soak this in." He seemed genuinely shocked. "This is awesome, guys!"

Over the previous weeks, something unexpected had happened. The Arlee Warriors had returned. They had qualified for state when Dar hit a free throw with no time remaining during a play-in game in a snowstorm. On the first day of the state tournament, they took out an undefeated Scobey team. Greg scored 23, including a spectacular four-point play. Isaac added 13 points to go with 11 tough rebounds. In the semifinal, Arlee was again an underdog, this time against an undefeated Chinook team led by a slashing point guard named Isaac Bell, a Gros Ventre kid who would, after the season, accept an offer to play for Steve Keller at the University of Providence. Before the game, Greg told the boys he wanted it for the team—not for him.

Lane Johnson decided to guard Bell, hoping to hold him scoreless. Bell would score just 5; LJ scored 16; Isaac Fisher scored 14, along with

6 rebounds and 2 soaring blocks. When he picked up his fourth foul, Lane Schall asked to guard Isaac's man. The game's final minutes were a familiar sight, with Isaac and LJ flying around and Greg flipping in shots from all angles on the way to 29 points. On the bench, Franny started to dry heave. In the stands, Inj said, "I was so proud of all of 'em." Superintendent Baldwin watched courtside. As though nothing had happened in recent weeks, he said, "I wouldn't bet against Zanen, I'll tell ya that much!" The Warriors were back in the state finals, with a chance to three-peat. Their opponent was no surprise: Manhattan Christian awaited. That night, I walked into Zanen's hotel room and said, "I can't believe you guys are there again."

He looked up from whomever he was frantically texting and said, "I can."

Franny said, "I haven't had butterflies in like three years," adding, "They were all working for each other. Holding each other accountable. Asking each other for help. Finally made my heart tingle a little bit."

The next morning, he went for a coffee at an urban joint with brick walls and exposed ductwork. Wearing a salmon-colored hoodie and a ball cap bearing the image of a large firearm over the Stars and Stripes, Franny ordered a caramel latte. He was joined by Arlee's new bus driver, Luke Lacey, a devout Christian who wore the Warrior Movement hat everywhere. "So many Montanans have no idea what life is like," Lacey said. He'd grown up in the Bitterroot Valley. He nodded at Franny: "His homeland." When Lacey was young, he said, he and his friends drove to Whitefish to ski, taking care to avoid stopping on the reservation. He didn't truly understand his home state, he said, until he went to postapartheid South Africa to serve on a Christian mission: "It took us going over there to see it here. These same dynamics were at play. I was just oblivious and unaware. I'm over there saying there's a big need for reconciliation right in my backyard. I just don't know if us white people are wanting to suppress how much blood is on our hands.

The majority of white Montanans, they have no idea what we need to seek reconciliation and forgiveness for."

Lacey and Franny started talking about the kids' college prospects. LJ had football interest but wanted to play basketball. Within Montana, neither he, Isaac, nor Greg had any offers. Wherever they went, Franny said, it wouldn't be easy. "These kids can go anywhere and they're out of bounds." He was glad Phil was at North Idaho with Ty, Emmit Taylor III, and Zachary Camel Jr. "He would be *really* out of bounds at the University of Montana," Franny said. For it to become easier, he said, something fundamental would have to change. In Franny's mind, the kids just had to do what made them happy. His mind turned back to tonight. Another title game. Franny sipped his latte. "I'm proud of 'em." He paused. "It took all season to say that. Really am proud of 'em."

The crowd for the first games had been thin. The tournament had coincided with the annual Celebrating Salish Conference in Spokane. Many people had spent the weekend there, including the Hayneses. Sophie was recognized for her efforts to preserve the language. Will escorted her, placing an honorary jacket on her shoulders and walking her to her seat. She smiled to the skies. Afterward, he drove eight hours to Billings.

The Malatares had been watching North Idaho eviscerate some opponent north of Seattle. Following the game, they offered to take Phil to Billings. Exhausted, he declined, and his parents dropped him in Coeur d'Alene. Becky felt sad that he wouldn't make it for Dar's appearance at state. But when she woke early the next morning, she discovered a text message from Phil—a photo showed a green highway sign: BILLINGS. He'd hitched a ride with a friend, and they drove all night. He asked her to keep his presence quiet.

That afternoon, at a sporting goods store, I ran into Bing Matt. He'd decided to come, after all, attending every game. "I got to thinking about it," he said. "I been supporting these kids many years. I love these boys. I know everything about 'em." And now, he said, "It felt like it's back. They're back together again." He smiled. "It's the old team."

A few hours before the game, Bill Swaney revealed something large on Native Hoops Hub: "To the Arlee Warriors," he wrote.

> *You may not know that I started this page for 2 reasons—as a tribute to my dad and his love of Indian basketball and so I could follow you, the Arlee Warriors team and help others follow your journey. You have accomplished so much more than consecutive state championships, and you have done it as a TEAM. Last night there were moments when you didn't play for each other, and it could have cost you the game. Remember that you have a motto as the Warrior Movement: Together We Rise. Tonight will be the biggest challenge you face on the court, but you have EACH OTHER and if you play together and play for each other, you will win. No one can measure your heart, the heart of a champion. Manhattan Christian wants what you have and they are going to try to take it away from you. Stay together, play for each other on the court and you will emerge victorious. Hold yourself to the highest standards that have been set by yourselves and previous Warrior teams and you will make us proud regardless of the score at the end. A historic 3-peat is in front of you, but you will have to work together to take it. No one will hand it to you. You have the most heart of any team here, that much is clear. Now finish this and make history.*

In the second deck of the Metra, a group of boys from White Sulphur Springs wore Warrior Movement shirts. They said they were rooting for Arlee because mental health was an issue where they lived, too. One boy said, "Their message is pretty cool." Willie Stevens sat near a fan from elsewhere in the state, an older man who had lost someone close to suicide. He, too, was moved by Arlee's prevention efforts.

So were the boys from Plenty Coups, a Crow team who had announced plans to join the Warrior Movement.

Near the hot dog stand I saw an old man in sweats moving with a blocky gait: Don Wetzel Sr., the founder of the Montana Indian Athletic Hall of Fame and former Griz MVP, who is widely recognized as the first Native player to compete for four years in a Division I program in the state. On one foot he wore a hard walking boot that creaked with every step. He beckoned for me to join him. He was in a confrontational mood. "The college coaches in this state have literally forgot about the Montana Indian athlete," he'd told me the previous day. He'd been thinking about Phil and the Griz: "What a bunch of bullshit. I know the junior-college system and I know why guys send 'em there. Coaches. Because they're chickenshit." He added, "It's a way of getting rid of the kid if you want to know the truth. They never bring 'em back." He said he wanted to start a coaching camp on every reservation to diversify the ranks of those in charge at the next level: "They better wake up because I'm coming after them." Tonight he wanted to see Arlee join Lodge Grass among the state's legends. "Arlee's got the kids to do it," he said. "I really want 'em to win." He said it came down to Greg and Isaac, who would have to battle Manhattan Christian's height.

As chance would have it Les, Inj, and the Fisher boys entered just then. I excused myself to greet them. Les saw Don Wetzel and his eyes widened. He asked me to introduce Wetzel and Isaac. When I asked Wetzel, he nodded and moved toward the Fishers. A reverent silence set in as he crossed the walkway. Les's eyes softened. Inj took a breath. Then two young men moving quickly, former Manhattan Christian players, darted around Wetzel, one in front, one in back, cutting him off. They appeared oblivious and in a rush. Inj and Les stood, mouths agape, as though they had never witnessed anything so profane. Wetzel paused, then continued. He looked Isaac in the eye and said, "Show 'em who's got it."

Les had a frantic energy. "Usually I realize I can do something to make

something happen. Right now I can't. I just don't know how to explain it."
Across the arena, Senator Daines took his seat. John Malatare gathered
Dar, Isaac, and Billy and said, "I'm proud of you no matter what happens.
I'll always be proud of you boys." In the locker room, Zanen assigned
Lane Johnson to guard Caleb Bellach. Zanen told him not to go for ill-
advised steals because the refs, he said, were "gonna take care of him. So
you're just containing him. Respecting his ability." Zanen was worried
about the officials. Arlee's recent string of technicals loomed in everyone's
mind. Earlier in the day, at a shootaround, Zanen had asked for "the kind-
est, most respectful game you've ever played." He had also given specific
instructions in the event of a bad call. When it inevitably came, the boys
were to pick the ball up, walk it to the official, and say, *"Here you go, sir."*

In the locker room now, Zanen said something familiar: "You are
not gonna hear me. I promise you. There'll be about nine thousand
people here tonight. It'll be the biggest crowd you ever played in front
of. And it's—*that's why!*" My head snapped up. "People say, 'Why
would you put pressure on boys like that? 'Cause that's why I freaking
go up every day and dribble! So that I can go out and put a show on in
front of nine thousand people. I'm a showman. I'm doing the game of
basketball so people can see all the fruits of our labors. You feel me?"
The boys reacted with silence. The moment passed, and Zanen prayed.

Our Father in heaven,
Our Creator,
We are beyond grateful for

His voice cracked.

This blessing that we've been given

He started to cry.

Don't want this ride to end.

Give us the ability to focus

To go out here and take care of our assignments

To play together as a team and remember that no one man can win a game.

It's gonna take a team to win a championship.

Let our opponents play to their full potential so that if we can get this dub

We know we did it the right way.

Bless the refs to keep up.

Take care of our fans.

His tone changed:

Hey, we've put in way too much time. I'm tired of the haters!

In the name of Jesus Christ, amen.

In the first quarter, Manhattan Christian whipped the ball, playing as a team, while the Warriors made unforced errors, throwing bad passes. At the end of the quarter, the score was 19–11, Eagles. In the second quarter, Dar hit a three, then Greg a runner, and it was a three-point game. The refs called two successive fouls, one on Cody Tanner as he moved across the lane. "Two fouls away from the basketball, not really sure, I didn't see either one of them," said one TV announcer. It was Arlee's ninth foul, sending Manhattan Christian to the free-throw line. Caleb scored on a beautiful leaping move, then Greg hit a three, and Caleb answered with a jumper. An official called another foul on Cody, his third, and the crowd booed. Caleb took off on a fast break, on a play where in previous years he might have forced his way to the basket. He threw a precise bounce pass for a layup. Following a reach-in foul on Manhattan Christian, Greg inbounded the ball under the basket. When his defender turned, he threw it off the boy's back, grabbed it, scored, and was fouled.

On the next possession, Greg pressured the Eagles' point guard the length of the court. When the boy tried a crossover, Greg stuck his hand where he knew the ball would come—the move Phil had taught him. There it was, and Greg took off, one step in the other direction toward a clear layup. A whistle stung the air—an official named Tim Polk called a reach-in foul. As Zanen had instructed, Greg picked the ball up and walked it over to Polk. According to both Greg and Zanen, the player said nothing. The ref glared at him and made an exaggerated symbol with his hands: technical foul. The margin swelled to ten, then eleven, and with just over one minute remaining in the half, Zanen pulled Greg and LJ out of the game, as each had three fouls. Isaac and Cody were also on the bench. The Eagles scored five unanswered points.

At halftime, in the locker room, Greg addressed the team. "We're doing good, boys. They're balling. We have a lot of good moments." He added that Caleb Bellach was playing a dominant game; that they needed to acknowledge it and respond to the challenge. LJ grimaced and shook his head, frustrated at the officials. "I get it, bro," Greg said, trying to calm him. "We're playing five on eight all year"—a reference to the three referees on the floor. "All we got is each other in here."

The teams took the court again.

Far away, out of the public eye, Will, Phil, and Ty sat together quietly. Caleb, appearing determined, scored and scored, on the way to 42 points. Following another foul call against Arlee, a Manhattan Christian fan sitting nearby said she wanted the game to be fair.

Ty started to sense the probability of a loss. "Been there before."

"I haven't," said Will.

"Lotta time left," Phil said. His knee knocked up and down. "Lotta time left."

In the middle of the fourth quarter Phil grabbed me, fixed me with a stare, and said, "Time?" We walked down toward the court. A boy stopped him and asked for a photo. I asked about school. Phil had one class he liked. "Been a long eight months," he said. "It makes me appreciate home."

We descended toward the court, where a group of girls stopped him. One girl asked how she could attend North Idaho. "It's a community college." Phil laughed. "They'll accept anybody." He moved toward the court. Will showed up. They looked at the waning seconds. "This is where it all began," said Phil. "Crazy though. It all ends here. There'll never be another thing like this. I know there won't."

I asked, "Do you love college basketball as much?"

He shook his head: "No." He said it was for a different purpose. "How could you?"

Out on the court, Greg was called for a foul, his fifth, resulting in his ejection. He took a breath, pointed at the Arlee crowd, and walked off. A couple of minutes later, Manhattan Christian's boys rushed the court and wept. The two teams posed together for a photo in a graceful moment. Caleb draped one of the nets around his neck. He and Greg embraced and bowed their heads gently. It was not the kind of thing sports stars do for cameras. Then they separated. Off to the side, someone asked Greg where he was going to college. He said he had no offers. Out on the court, Caleb stood near his father, the lights shining on them both.

26

Where We're Gonna Be

Following the championship, David Whitesell congratulated the boys and told them to focus on graduation. Privately, he was livid about the officiating. The final attempted free-throw count was 40–7. The Eagles, he acknowledged, played a great game. "We just didn't get to play great with them." I suggested that the question he raised also hurt Manhattan Christian, who looked far hungrier, and, after all, had already beaten Arlee during divisionals. But that's the curse of uneven playing fields. No matter how much you give, you never know how much you've earned. Whitesell was uninterested in that line of thought: "I think it does a disservice more to our boys." He added, "There are so many biases. Implicit or institutional."

"I don't want to take away from Manhattan Christian," Zanen told me. "They beat us. I'm happy for them." Then I asked if it was fair to say—as I'd heard from multiple Arlee fans—that Bellach outcoached him. "You can't say that," he said, citing the foul-shot disparity.

Mark Beckman, the head of the MHSA, saw no problem with the officiating. He did not make Tim Polk available for an interview and noted that any school taking issue with officiating could file a complaint. Arlee did not. In April, when I asked Amy Bartels, the athletic director, about the matter, she answered indirectly: "MHSA's pretty well aware of what's going on. Everyone communicates a lot between the reffing pool, between the Montana officials coordinator. Everyone has a fairly good understanding of what goes on at those, just because MHSA is present at the event. So I mean, I don't know. That's a hard one." She said no one had made a formal complaint to her. A month later, she announced she was leaving Arlee for a position at the MHSA, working on social media and overseeing the training of officials. After taking the new role, she said, of the championship, "I do think overall it was a well-officiated game." She moved on. "Arlee," she said, "was a great stepping-stone for me."

In May, Jennifer Jilot led a Warrior Movement talk for grade-schoolers at Arlee. Her preparation was rushed, but beforehand, as she gathered the kids, Greg spoke. According to Jilot, he said that they were "going into a group of kids who have real issues and have been judged heavily and really needed their support. And this is their time to give the kids the support they need." It was a profound moment, unscripted and real, a forum for kids to tell their own stories. "If you don't explore things," she said, "talk through things, different points of view, then nothing ever progresses. And sometimes for things to progress you have to take a step back before you take five steps forward."

Following the season, Zanen received multiple inquiries about other coaching jobs. But, he said, "I don't want to coach anymore." The school board, unaware of his plans, rehired him. Zanen and Kendra applied for 501(c)(3) status for the Warrior Movement, so it could receive tax-deductible donations. N7 invited Zanen to bring a team to the Native American Basketball Invitational tournament, in Arizona, a prestigious event that attracts college scouts. New and large ideas began to form: perhaps a Warrior Movement recreation center or a Native American invitational tournament in Montana. Nike filmed the boys in a new

N7 video, and many people in town thought it was a classy representation. Shortly afterward, when Doug Lefler left the Warrior Movement board of directors—it was just time to move on, he said—Zanen invited a Nike employee to take his place.

On June 12, the Warriors held their team banquet. There was one new presence: a sports reporter from the *Missoulian*. Before the team watched the video and ate ice cream, Zanen announced that he would not be returning to coach. He apologized to the boys. Then he unleashed, airing some long-held grievances. The *Missoulian* published an explosive story that night, quoting Zanen as saying, "I'm sick and tired of this administration. The administration literally just tore my passion apart for the game." And: "It's constant aching. My gut twists every time I get phone calls. . . . I'm not going to put up with it anymore. I'm tired of it." Some of what he said was true: "They threatened to fire me and they told me to go different places. I don't want to coach anywhere else. It doesn't even interest me. I literally love Arlee." But his pent-up frustrations also resulted in hyperbole: "They destroyed me and my family."

The Malatares were home when the story broke. Phil was shocked. He left to find Ty. Becky was sad. The piece was so divisive that she felt she couldn't support the school and the coach at once. On social media she shared a photo of Zanen and Phil at the state tournament with Phil wearing the original Warrior Movement shirt—the black one made by his cousin. "Thanks Pitts for the memories, sacrifice & passion for the game," she wrote. Becky said, "I'm not going to be ashamed because I love my community and my school." John's feelings were more complicated. He couldn't believe Zanen said those things at a celebration of the kids.

The *Missoulian* acted the way news outlets do when a gossip story gains traction, running three successive articles. For nearly a week, they remained 406 MT Sports' most popular stories. In one of the articles,

Arlee Schools leveled murky accusations at Zanen. A reporter also called David Whitesell, who defended Zanen and recounted in detail a story about Gardner and another board member, in 2015, trying to remove the coach without cause. "Maybe it has to do," Whitesell said, "with the crabs-in-the-bucket phenomena." The matter was litigated on social media, and public opinion across the state overwhelmingly sided with Zanen. Some boys expressed their allegiance to their coach. "Wouldn't have wanted to be coached by anyone else but this man right here," wrote Ivory.

Greg wrote, "It will always go unheard but it wasn't even about winning games or championships with you, it was about our education and our growth that you prided yourself in. I could thank you 1000x for the 2 championships, the Warrior Movement that saved my life, or the countless other opportunities you gave me. . . . But most importantly, thank you for being a friend, and someone always willing to help in any way shape or form."

But discontent bubbled beneath the surface. Within the community, some expressed frustration with both the *Missoulian* and the coach. Bing Matt said, "He did a good job with those kids. He brought 'em a long ways. You have people who say, 'He didn't teach my kids, they learned it all from three-on-threes.' No. You need that guidance from someone to show you how to be a state champion. He did that." But, Bing said, "He quit 'em. It pulls 'em down. They don't know what to think—should I follow our school or the coach? A guy is stronger if he can take it on the chin and let it go by. But he didn't. And it hurts the school most of all."

That Bing—the historian of Arlee basketball—would be so critical was surprising. Even Ty Tanner said, of the *Missoulian* stories, "There was no need to say all that." He added that maybe Zanen was "trying to stay relevant." It seemed the coach's need for others to remember his name had carried him across an unspoken but sacrosanct cultural line. You were not to brag, you were not to focus on yourself, and you were never to bring shame. "He was handed the keys to a Ferrari and told not to wreck it," said Bill Swaney. "To his credit, he didn't." But, Swaney added, "Zanen wanted to be: 'Look what I've done.' You should remain humble. Other people can sing your praises."

If Zanen carried any regret, he didn't let on. When I first spoke to the coach in the midst of the news storm, on Thursday, June 13, he was checking cows. "Man, I could float up to the sky right now. Feel so good. Finally called those guys out." He said he wasn't paying much attention to the reaction. Out there, under the stunning peaks, the on-line maelstrom felt distant. "I could care less 'cause I'm not gonna be on there to look at it." Good coaches know how to position people and anticipate behavior. Zanen could go from being antagonistic to measured, calm, and cool in a smooth pivot. He saw two plays ahead and lured opponents into traps. By the time they realized where they were, it was often too late.

"You know, he did a lot for Arlee," Bear said. "I'll give him credit for that." But Bear didn't like the way the coach went out. "We talk about maturity. There again that's where I think he really faltered. I don't think he was mature enough to go out on top." Bear was worried about how the public infighting made the community look. "Jesus Christ, people. We just got all this respect. We accomplished a ton here. Let it be."

Bear had recently been asked to speak to some students who had visited from the East Coast. He met them at a church. "Some of the kids were all ears and lookin' at me. What was going on and where everything was at. It was almost noontime. I told Sister, 'Yeah, I'll talk about something.'"

Then Bear told the kids about the undefeated team. "They got all the pressure on the world on 'em. To go make it to state. To add more pressure to themselves. To dedicating that to suicide, how amazing. I said, plus they were all sick. All of 'em had the flu. Three of our starters running to the trash can every chance to throw up. I said my grandson and Will run off the court. But they did it."

They did it. No amount of noise and cameras could ever take away the moment, after the championship, when Phil stopped a television interview to point at a young fan and say, "This is who we do it for. Because they're the next generation coming up. And if we can prove to them that anything's possible like this, then we did our job."

Bear continued on with his story about the church kids. "I said you know that's where our leadership is. It's not with me. With our old people. It is you people. You're our leadership in the future. It's okay for me to give you some ideas. But you are the future." That sounded familiar. He had one more thing to say: "What you decide is where we're gonna be."

In April, Will drove Lane Johnson and Greg across the state to North Dakota. Their destination was United Tribes Technical College (UTTC), in Bismarck. The basketball coach, Pete Conway Jr.—the former Montana State University star—had already offered Greg a spot. "He said a lot of good stuff," Greg said, "about how I've been overlooked." For the other boys, it was a chance to prove themselves against the college team's players. Zanen was optimistic, anticipating that Conway would sign "all three this week.'"

David Whitesell thought Conway was just the kind of coach Greg needed. Raelena wasn't so sure about the distance from home, but she figured that at least Greg wouldn't be alone. Lane Schall was going to play football at Minot State University, just two hours from UTTC. It was so flat, he said, that you could "watch your dog run away for three days."

In March, Montana State's coach, who had recruited Caleb Bellach, departed the program. Jeff Bellach didn't seem worried. The university's athletic director, Leon Costello, had personally reached out to Caleb, as well as the team's other incoming recruits. "He's been very reassuring," Jeff said. When it came to the next coach, he said, "I also have a pretty good pulse for who's interested and who's in the mix." Scott Wolf, the former Manhattan Christian girls' coach who played Division I ball, found the discrepancy between Caleb's and Phil's recruitment astonishing. He was careful to say that Caleb was a terrific kid with Division I talent who deserved his opportunity. Also, he clearly had a gripe with Manhattan Christian, as his contract had not been renewed. But, he said, "Phillip schooled Caleb Bellach. He was taking IVs at halftime and schooled him. Caleb has a full ride to MSU." Of Phil, Wolf said, "So why didn't MSU recruit him? Is it because he's six feet? My God, I played against Muggsy Bogues. . . . You can't have all players be five foot ten but you certainly can have two or three of them." Wolf said, "If Phillip was looking at a school in LA or New York, nobody would care. Those guys wouldn't care if he's Native American." He concluded, "I think there's an institutional bias against Native kids in this state."

Ivory Brien earned a 3.78 in his second trimester at Salish Kootenai College, then a 3.68 in the spring. He was irritated by his single B. He hoped to eventually become a trauma therapist. "As Native youth we go through a lot of stuff," he said. "We're so resilient. But the resiliency throws a blanket over all these problems that are unresolved." He wanted to do some resolving. "I find it exciting. There's not a lot of Native male therapists."

Before graduation, Nate Coulson stayed with relatives. Kendra and Zanen often drove him to school. It came down to the wire, but he graduated. "Jenn helped me a lot," he said. "She's good like that." Jilot, for her part, said, "Nate is *so* smart." After graduating he moved to Pablo to be near his girlfriend, but they broke up, and he started to think about going to the oil fields. He felt down. Then, without fanfare or publicity, Zanen and Kendra invited him to stay at their home.

The week after graduation, Dar played in a football all-star game in Butte full of college prospects. He was named defensive MVP. "He played some good football," said John. The University of Montana

Western offered Dar a partial scholarship and the chance to redshirt for his freshman year. In July, he held a signing, wearing a beaming smile, just as they do in the pros. "I'm ready," he told me. Then he asked after my family.

Isaac kept talking about bullying at Warrior Movement speeches. He said he wanted to "give kids that didn't have a chance a chance. Kind of like how me and my brothers are, and what my auntie and uncle did for us. I just want to do that for other kids." On the court, UTTC reached out, as well as another tribal school in Arizona and Miles Community College. Jeff Bellach had advocated for Isaac with the coach there. But, said Les, "He don't wanna go anywhere." He felt comfortable in Arlee. "If you can't understand that, you'll never understand that." Isaac spent afternoons working on his dunks. Pretty soon he could throw the ball off the backboard and do a 360; he leaped over three motorcycles. He enrolled at the University of Montana; he later made a get-out-the-vote video with a hip-hop artist from the reservation, showing him soaring through the air.

Pete Conway extended offers to all three Warriors: Will, Greg, and Lane. The latter two accepted. "It's just crazy," Lane messaged me, "my dream came true." Will didn't sign. The drive was too far. "I also want to do other tryouts closer to home. Because also I want my family to be able to come watch some games, too, without me having to worry about them being on their own forever."

Phil spent the summer at home, sharing his room with Jordyn, who was preparing for an intensive nursing program. He got a job at the National Bison Range, where he and Alex Moran fixed fence, sprayed weeds, and chased buffalo. John drove Phil to work every day. In the car, with the Mission Mountains rising, they talked about sports, hunting, life. John looked forward to those drives. He prayed every day. "I think it's as I've gotten older," he said, "I've realized I'm not an angel.

And I need help. I ask for protection. I realize what kind of job I do. I travel this highway every day. I have a couple guardian angels to look out for us. I look out for my kids." He continued, "I pray for their health every day. And that they bury me, I don't bury them." Whitney graduated from Salish Kootenai College, got an accounting job, and had a baby—John and Becky's first grandchild. Morgan earned a prestigious nursing scholarship to work with underprivileged communities. When John considered their accomplishments, he thought back to when he started at the Forest Service, to the dense thickets he'd sought out. "You look back at where they were, and what they were, and what they've become, and what they're becoming. These are the best years of my life."

Becky thought Phil looked taller. To her dismay, he kept playing three-on-threes with Ty and Will. But, he told her, anytime he left the driveway, anything could happen. At a tournament in Bigfork, he and Ty discussed the toughest players they'd ever faced. They listed JR Camel and their North Idaho teammates Nate Pryor and RayQuan Evans. Then Phil said, "I'd like to play against Ray." He'd competed against him in practice and in a postseason Native tournament where, Phil said, Evans had taken it easy. Phil wanted to play against the Montana kid who had made it to Florida State. In case the point wasn't clear, Phil assumed his most transparent expression—brow forward, mouth pursed, eyes hard—and said, "Like, full."

Becky signed a lease on a new place in Coeur d'Alene for Phil, Ty, and Emmit Taylor III. Bear envisioned Phil running the team with Ty and Emmit starting. "Why not take the chance to do something fantastic?" he asked. "If they could only get the understanding of that style of ball." But in August, the NWAC announced sanctions of the North Idaho men's basketball team. An investigation had revealed that the booster club had reserved apartments for players—a practice that was legal within North Idaho's previous athletic conference, but not the NWAC. The league also expressed concern that the booster club operated without sufficient over-sight. No players, the NWAC determined, had received financial bene-fit. Still, the league stripped the program of its past two championships, docked North Idaho by four scholarships per year, and banned the team from postseason play for three seasons. "It's unfortunate for the boys that are still there," John said, "because ultimately they're the ones that have to suffer."

The forward-looking penalties especially seemed severe when con-sidered in a historical context. In one of the most high-profile cases of college sports sanctions in memory, it was revealed that, in the 1990s, a booster had made large payments to University of Michigan basketball players. The Federal Bureau of Investigation got involved, as did a grand jury; afterward, Michigan forfeited five years of wins, expunged records of players, and paid back hundreds of thousands of dollars. But the Uni-versity of Michigan lost only one scholarship per year, for four years, and served a one-year postseason ban. Marco Azurdia, the NWAC execu-tive director, said such comparisons were of no use. The sanctions, he said, were "severe." But, he added, they were "what the board believed was right." I pointed out that the sanctions seemed likely to hurt mar-ginalized youth, both the young men on the current team and those who would now be ineligible for scholarships.

"The sanctions," Azurdia said, "are in response to the people who are leading these young men, whether they're white or inner city or Native American. And I don't think these kids are going to lose opportunities. For scholarships, we all know how if you're a really good player, you're going to get the opportunity." On that point, we agreed to disagree.

In June, right around when everything blew up between Zanen and Arlee Schools, Will attended a field camp focused on traditional skills. On the day after news of Zanen's resignation broke, he emerged from the mountains. "Been living up in the woods like the old days," he said, when he called. "Scraping, tanning hides, making hand drums. Tough work." When he found out about his coach's decision, he simply said, "Whatever is best for him." Will hadn't known about the firestorm. He was spending time with his family, he said, "before I head out to school."

To school?

Will said he was going to go to UTTC with Greg and Lane. "There's a part of me doesn't want to leave this place. Been here my whole life. I just feel comfortable, I feel wanted here. If I go somewhere else, I feel out of place." He continued, "It's going to be tough for me at first. But I gotta get used to it." He knew he would have to earn playing time. "I gotta work for it. I ain't gonna go expecting to be starting." He also made one thing clear: "After, I'm coming back here to live." He was going to be a role model. "So everything's coming together as planned, as I seen it in my head." The world has a way of diverting the routes we set in our teenage minds, but Will had a powerful way of navigating those centripetal forces.

In his sophomore season, Phillip Malatare averaged 10.2 points, 5.2 rebounds, and more than two steals per game. He shot more than 48 percent from the field, 31 percent on three-pointers, and 77 percent on free throws. He led his team in assists, despite the stat keepers missing at least 18 of them. In one game, he registered 22 points and 10 assists, then stopped shooting so much. His coaches once told him that if he didn't shoot more, he wouldn't get recruited. Phil told his parents he was just going to play the right way—team ball—and see what happened. In December, he attended a wake, then traveled all night to Utah for a tournament. North Idaho played a team led by a prolific scorer named Mike Hood, who had signed with the Montana State University Bobcats on a full scholarship. Hood scored 28 points, Phil 2. But in the final minute, with North Idaho holding a four-point lead, Phil guarded Hood. Out of a time-out, a play was called for Hood. Phil saw it coming and darted around multiple screens, taking an elliptical route to the ball, the sort of pattern a child might draw if asked to represent the movements of a bee. He flew to the corner, blocked the three-point shot, and soared out of bounds. Then, with just over thirty seconds remaining, he stole the ball from Hood, sealing the victory. In the season's final game, about fifty people from home were present, including Zanen and Kendra. Phil sat out with the flu and Ty started, playing well. Afterward, I looked back at the tape from the previous game, Phil's last on the court. In the final minutes, he passed repeatedly to Ty. Over his varsity high school and college career, he had more than 150 wins and 9 losses.

Despite North Idaho's 28–1 record, it was a hard year, with intrateam squabbling, a focus on individual stats, and no postseason. "I just hope," said John, "they didn't ruin those boys' love for the game." Following the season, the University of Washington honored its previous commitment to Nate Pryor, signing him on scholarship. Emmit Taylor III received an offer to play Division I ball in his home state, at Idaho State University. Ty received interest from a Frontier Conference school in Idaho, but it didn't offer the scholarship he was looking for. He earned his associate's degree in business administration and moved home to work on the ranch. He enrolled in online classes, working toward a marketing degree, and took a year off from basketball, hoping he'd get a chance to play the following season. Phil received scholarship offers from multiple Division II programs. On the Division I level, South Dakota State and Montana State University reached out. The Bobcats didn't offer a scholarship for Phil's first year, but rather a walk-on spot. Phil was intrigued, but the lack of a scholarship bothered him. Besides, Bozeman, the tech boomtown, was pretty far out of bounds. "I'm rezzy," he told his mom. Danny Sprinkle, the head coach, never spoke with Phillip and no one contacted John or Becky. For Phil, it wasn't enough to break his internal attachment to the Griz. He had started for two years on a team that matriculated nine Division I players. "In Montana," said Becky, "you're only as good as your word." Phil waited to hear from DeCuire.

The Arlee boys found their way slowly with the UTTC team. At first, Will barely played, and Greg came off the bench behind two talented point guards. Lane Johnson, however, had grown, to six foot three. He played good defense, battling bigger players, and soon earned a starting position. A new dream crept in—he hoped to go play Division I basketball. When I asked what he thought it meant to make it, he said, "Going somewhere that wants you." Greg scored 22 points in a game in December, then came home for Christmas break. He did not return to North Dakota. "College isn't for everybody," he said. I asked if he missed ball, and he corrected my assumption. He regularly played pickup. But he needed to find himself outside of sport. He loved Arlee—he said it was "where I learned to respect the land and the people." But he still hoped to live in a big city someday. He started a business designing and painting custom shoes. Dar also returned home, moved out of the Malatares', and went to work in construction. He said, "I really want to take care of myself now."

At UTTC, Will fought his way into the rotation. His defense was tough. He scored 11 points against Dawson Community College in January, almost leading a comeback. In February, Zanen drove 1,030 miles round trip in a day to watch him and Lane play. Chasity, who had been promoted at work, kept posting, optimistically, about how her son was playing "Division I ball" on social media. UTTC won one playoff game before its season ended. Afterward, Will wrote, "Glad I had this opportunity to experience new parts of the game and new brotherhoods." He also found something good: a relationship with a young woman from Montana, a basketball player. He planned to continue studying at UTTC to get his associate's degree even though his junior-college basketball eligibility had elapsed. After that, he said, maybe he'd keep playing if he got an opportunity at a four-year school.

Zanen's resentments faded with time. His optimism returned. He arranged Warrior Movement speeches with kids from multiple schools and said he planned to apply for Nike grants to fund a tribal AAU team that he would oversee, to help kids get recruited. Eventually, he even took responsibility for Phillip's ineligibility with the Griz: "I unfortunately didn't do my homework, and neither did a few other chosen people." Locally, things seemed to marginally improve: Dawson Community College recruited a player from the Blackfeet Reservation, a Crow star from Hardin committed to Rocky Mountain College, and Montana Tech signed a guard with connections to Arlee.

Because Arlee's enrollment had increased in previous years, the Warriors moved up to Class B. In the regular season, with a new coach, they did not defeat a single conference opponent. They had to win a game just to make the playoffs and lost in the district tournament. Then, in divisionals, with Phil and Ty cheering them on, and Cody Tanner, Tapit Haynes, and Billy Fisher starting, they came out of nowhere and won the whole thing. They earned a place at state, knocking out the defending champion on the way. The state tournament was scheduled for early March. In the days beforehand, the coronavirus erupted across America. The NCAA and NBA canceled their seasons; Zanen's Warrior Movement talks were also sidelined. But the MHSA continued on, making Montana the last state in the union to attempt to hold its high school tournament without restrictions. Fans blamed the media for overhyping the virus's threat. On Friday, four cases of coronavirus were announced within the state. The next day, the MHSA canceled the tournament and fans turned apoplectic. Zanen got to work for the Tribal Lands Department from home and be with his family. Kendra delivered their first daughter in April. Shortly afterward, Zanen took a job managing a bison ranch in Idaho. He said he planned to return home in time for his kids to win state in Montana.

Phil waited on the Griz. Snowmelt rushed down from the Missions, magpies chased mayflies, the hills turned fat and green, and deer filled the hayfields. Still he waited. "I can't really do anything about it," he said. "It is what it is." Maybe there had been a miscommunication.

Maybe, as some suggested, that's just the way it goes in Division I ball. Or maybe that's just the way it's gone for too long in a state built on broken promises. Phil finished his coursework from home and horn hunted. Out there, he was free. "Phillip Malatare does not need basketball," Zanen said. "Basketball on the reservation needs Phillip Malatare."

Phil still had options in other places where the game was business rather than family, statistics rather than art. One night, he went to the Lyles courts and shot until late, as though working something out. Becky wondered if his fire had been lit again. "Your child's dreams," she said, "are your dreams." But upon returning, he didn't talk much about it. John suggested to Becky that it was time to let it go. The Malatares turned the field of dreams into a garden. Bear and Irma watched tapes of Phillip's old games. Sometimes, when Bear watched the first championship, he felt something rising in his chest and he thought the team might lose. But then they won. And the tape flattened everything.

Phil decided to stop playing. "I thought about it long and hard. I think it's what'll make me happy." He emphasized one point: "I'm glad I went off and did it." He noted the high quality of competition at North Idaho, and said that some of his teammates might play professionally. But he saw little point in lingering on how far he had made it. You can get stuck that way. He got his associate's degree and thought about pursuing more school that would further a career working on the land—maybe something in the trades or in range management. He also did not rule out a return to college ball under the right circumstances. There were so many possibilities. People who saw Phil after that, at the Store or around town, noted something open about his manner. He smiled a lot, a huge, easy smile.

Will made his conference's all-academic team and was honored at college for maintaining a grade point average between 3.5 and 3.99. He returned to Arlee and took Sophie to lunch. There followed a season of illness that shattered the American fantasy, forcing the nation to confront the truth that no one is promised tomorrow. Montana was flooded with newcomers. They came from cities and coasts, fleeing places where life felt desolate in search of some solace or connection to the land, something they didn't know they'd been missing. For the boys, it was time to navigate the terrain where expectation ended and adulthood began. They went where they could do that in private. They went where the earth was beautiful. They went home.

Epilogue

We're Still Playing

Summer

A three-on-three tournament in Missoula, heat seeping from the blacktop. Phil, Will, and Greg formed a team with one of Will's former college teammates. There were no cameras, save for the smartphone that Chasity held up. Greg kept defenders off-balance, tiptoeing the baseline. Phil made opponents stagger and the crowd gasp. His hair was almost shoulder-length, tailing out of a backward cap. At first, Will looked gassed. But by the final day of the tournament he caught his wind. The boys made it to the championship. People surrounded the court: Bear and Irma; Becky and Raelena; Phil's auntie Jennifer; Zanen and Kendra; Big Will and his wife, Ashley; Allen and Kelly Pierre and Tomi Brazill. Some said it felt like 2018, the year when everything had come together so cleanly.

Greg scored first, then Will, then Phil. Greg guarded the other team's leader, a stocky man with tattoos. Greg and Will missed some shots. They got down. On defense, they turned it up: switching, rotating, putting their hands in the empty spaces where the ball would come. "Pressure, Greg!" Chasity yelled. "Pressure him."

Down by one, Phil ripped off a blistering crossover and drove. He planted his left foot and floated toward the rim. It was the same move he'd tried at Polson, the one that ended up with him crumpled on the blacktop. Now he landed solidly, but his shot rolled off. Will missed his next three shots, too. Greg brought them back, crossing over, driving baseline. He made a shot to tie the game at 16, checking out for good shortly afterward. The score was 19–18 in favor of the other team when Phil split the defense for a layup. Tie game. One of the other players drove past Phil. Chasity yelled, "Help!"

Will collapsed, but the man scored. The other team was one point from victory. Then Phil and Will started to switch onto each other's defensive assignments, locking in, saying nothing. A shot bounced off the rim to an opponent and the boys descended. Their arms moved in sync, like a net, and the ball handler stumbled. One ref called a travel, another a foul. "He traveled!" yelled Chasity. The officials agreed, awarding the ball to the Arlee boys.

Then something curious happened. The tattooed man picked up the ball and held it, refusing to accept the ruling. The grimace on his face reflected astonished fury. The refs conferred with a mediator, a man in a striped shirt and cargo shorts. "He traveled," said Chasity. "He traveled." The Arlee crowd started to chant, "Tra-vel! Tra-vel!"

The refs appeared indecisive. The way the boys moved was almost too fast to see, and now the slow heat beat down and the moment hovered and faded. To litigate and harden it into something like fact, all turned to their memories, seeing what they wanted to see. The man with the tattoos clutched the ball like a treasure bestowed at birth. Phil made the hand signal for a travel, then backed off, arms akimbo, smirking. Will swept his hair back and said nothing. The mediator pondered, then said, in a most reasonable voice, "All right . . ."

When he awarded the ball to the other team, Phil and Will did not appear surprised. They switched between defensive assignments. They gave no room. Time wound down. Chasity saw something and yelled, "Take it, Phil!"

Phil went for a steal, forcing the ball handler to throw a pass. Will read his eyes and jumped the passing lane, intercepting the ball.

Chasity yelled, "We're still playing!"

Phil sliced for another layup. Tie game. Following another defensive stop, Will tossed the ball down low. Phil darted in that direction, hands up. The defense collapsed, anticipating the pass. Everyone always paid so much attention to him. But no one looked at Will. He ran to the three-point line and caught the ball. He crouched, bent his legs, jumped, and snapped his wrist. He landed with his shooting arm outstretched, just as he had when he was a boy on the Lyles courts, with only Sophie watching. The ball spun in the sky. For a moment, everything was still.

Author's Note

In March 2017, I saw a small wooden sign in Arlee, Montana, about a championship basketball team that would change my life in ways that are difficult to describe. I spent the next year reporting on a remarkable group of kids for *The New York Times Magazine*, living on the Flathead Indian Reservation for much of that time. What happened during that year could only be characterized as astounding. When the opportunity arose to write a book following the publication of the article, I was thrilled, flattered, and terrified. Here was a chance to expand a story of rare importance. The challenges the Arlee boys faced took on many forms, from overt and glaring racism to trauma to deeply complex and subtle forms of institutionalized discrimination that stymied their ambitions and paths toward self-actualization. At the same time, they lived in a beautiful, free place, with powerful community bonds and a deep and rooted value system. Not to mention perhaps the most thrilling basketball team in the nation. I'd rather watch the 2017–18 Arlee Warriors play than Duke. This was the sort of material that even a long magazine article cannot adequately convey. On the other hand, maybe this was just not what the world needed in 2018—another white guy in Indian Country. This ground had been trod before, and not always with good results. One of the things I came to more deeply understand in the time I spent in Arlee is that one hundred years is nothing. Three years represents a hiccup.

Some, such as David Whitesell and Jennifer Jilot, thought I should expand the story into a book. Jilot thought Native people should write these stories. But, she said, I was there, and the story was large and mattered. She also hoped it would be good for Will. But not everyone was in favor. One silly and prevalent form of anti-Indigenous sentiment is an assumption—in my experience, one often found within wealthy liberal enclaves—that tribal people agree in some harmonious monolith. Small towns don't work that way. Some in Arlee were disappointed by how much the magazine article I'd written focused on Phil. Someone mentioned that I didn't cover their kid's birthday. Zanen Pitts was gracious and noted that he wasn't on the cover of the magazine. He said he was loyal to me, but also mentioned that another book writer was in touch along with, it seemed, half of Hollywood. He was candid, funny, honest, and full of heart and he wanted more; always more.

What mattered was the boys, some of whom were now becoming young men. I was grateful when Will told me that speaking to me helped him. He is one of the more remarkable people I've met—smart and self-possessed, mature beyond his years. In May 2018, I had told him that if I extended the story, I'd have to include both the good and the complicated. He'd said, "I want the book." His parents, who didn't agree on much, were in favor, Chasity saying, "I'd like to see what comes of it," Big Will saying that it would be good as long as it contained deeper truths. He cited the Kent Nerburn book *Neither Wolf Nor Dog*. Greg Whitesell also wanted a book about the team. Talking about what he'd been through was good for him. He was in favor of that continuing. He liked being seen. Ty Tanner just said not to spin it; to tell the truth. Ivory Brien wanted a more complete and correct account of recent events—and of his character—in the world. The Fishers checked in regularly, sending me photos of Isaac's dunks and Billy's graduation. They took me fishing. Isaac caught a huge bass. I fell in. The Malatares seemed by turns wary and excited, as they were with all the attention surrounding their son. John said it was not his place to tell a writer what to do, but added, "You have an opportunity." Becky wasn't sure she wanted her life out there so fully, but said the obvious: "It's a great story." Bear was initially concerned. He doubted if I could understand it all. "No one can know," he said, "what it's like to be Indian." But he would support his grandson. Phil said, "I think it would be a good story," and asked that it more fully include the other players. When I expressed worry it could add to the intense pressure on him, he said, "I'm gonna have pressure." He cut that conversation short—something about the ranch—and said he'd call back. He didn't. Then things got complicated for him. He could be enigmatic, untethered to the schedules of the world—or, say, his mother, father, and girlfriend—never mind that of a journalist. He is also deeply intuitive. Once he landed in college, he popped up occasionally to tell me, "Keep writing." I suspected he knew that his career would end at a certain point, and he wanted the Warriors' efforts commemorated—as well as his own. Stories mattered, and certain things he could not say. The Malatares and I developed a deep and close relationship. My father, a huge basketball fan and a high school coach, accompanied me to watch one of Phillip's college tournaments. Phil sat and visited with him. Bear tried to help me. He prayed for me. My gratitude cannot be expressed.

With a deep breath I moved forward. I tried to keep my heart steady and good, tried to be respectful while still doing my job. I sought counsel from wise people who understood things: Willie, Patty, Anna, Gene, Allen, Bear, Bing, Donnie, Debra. I was invited to many places but not wakes. I eventually met with the Séliš-Q'lispé Culture Committee Elders Cultural Advisory Council. One of the elders requested that I include a picture of the entire team. Implicit in that, I thought, was a charge to try to write in a manner contrary to how many Americans tend to produce and consume stories. Perhaps we too often veer toward the individual and glory rather than community and humility. There was something to be learned from Arlee, something a lot of America could stand to hear in an age of rage and entitlement.

But following the transcendent 2017–2018 basketball season, entrenched historical forces set in. Allen Pierre once said, of Native kids, "There's just so much that ain't workin' for them," and he'd sadly been proven right. New tensions bubbled in the community, and I wondered if my work was part of that. Zanen said the Warrior Movement would have happened with or without me, but journalism does not exist in a vacuum. Nike's involvement was a direct result of the story I'd written. I felt a responsibility to see that through, but someone such as me writing a story such as this can be seen as fundamentally dubious. The overdue public interrogation of that cultural dynamic is only accumulating momentum, and I expect my work to be scrutinized. My fears lay elsewhere. I wondered if the boys were ready. I wondered if words would freeze them in time. I wondered if I could ever understand. When I conveyed some of my concerns to Aaron Brien, he said, "That's a good sign." But he also said this was a large responsibility. "Don't be afraid," he said, "to walk away."

In August 2018, I thought of doing just that. My job, ultimately, was to tell the truth. My great fear, the one that kept me up at night, was that I would fail the Arlee kids and betray a place that had come to mean so much to me. The time I spent with the community of Arlee changed the way I work, the way I think about politics and history and country, even my understanding of family. Arlee gave me a gift of sight that continues to evolve; what I'd written had given the Arlee boys something. Maybe that was enough. Quitting the story would have felt safe and cowardly. Seeking counsel, I drove to Allen Pierre's house. I talk in circles. Allen does not. He processes things quietly, then says what needs to be said. "That's power," his grandson once told me. But Allen was not home. I was turning out of his driveway when Will himself pulled in. He nodded as if he were expecting to see me; like a cool kid. We talked about his college plans, my coming marriage, his realization that he was not going to be in the NBA, and the other, more significant ideas that had entered his mind. He understood the complexities of his path—who had created it, who put up the waypoints, who made the laws, why he found it occasionally diverted, and where it was ultimately going. He just knew. I told him I was scared of the book. He took it in. He looked down, then up. "I wouldn't think about that," he said. He told me to be myself. "And write it."

Acknowledgments

I am first and foremost grateful to the people of Arlee for their patience, humor, acceptance, and grace. To Bear Malatare and Allen Pierre: it has been an honor of my life to learn from you. To John and Becky Malatare, Irma Malatare, Chasity Haynes, Sharon Haynes, Will Mesteth Sr. and Ashley Mesteth, Kelly Pierre, David Whitesell, Raelena Spencer Whitesell, Zanen Pitts and Kendra Wabaunsee Pitts, Scott and Jennifer Schall, Les Fisher and Roberta Lafley, Terry and Crystal Pitts, Diane Matt, Brad Johnson, Cody and Kathleen Tanner, Ernie Moran, Aaron and Misty Brien, Dean Nicolai, Tom and Gloria Haynes, TJ Haynes, Jennifer Jilot, and Franny Brown: thank you for this trust.

I would also like to thank those who generously shared wisdom and counsel and support when I greatly needed it: Debra Magpie Earling, Bing Matt, Anna Whiting Sorrell, Gene Sorrell, Patty Stevens, Willie Stevens, and Donnie Wetzel Jr.

Ryan Doherty, my editor, believed in this project from the beginning and saw it through with patience, forbearance, and thoughtfulness. Cecily van Buren-Freedman made precise, essential edits and provided crucial support at every turn. Ryan and Cecily—thank you for caring in such a deep way. Tarren Andrews read each line three times and interrogated every turn of phrase with patience and clarity. Tom Colligan checked every fact and provided editorial guidance. Tarren and Tom: I would go anywhere with you. Sloan Harris believed in me before others did and has a singular ability to see through the trees. A number of talented editors enabled and guided reporting that contributed to this book: Charles Homans and Jake Silverstein at *The New York Times Magazine*, Camille Bromley at *Harper's*, Elizabeth Hightower Allen and Chris Keyes at *Outside*, and Kit Rachlis at the dearly departed *California Sunday Magazine*. Good photographers help you see things differently, and I have been fortunate to work with two of the best, Tailyr Irvine and Devin Yalkin. Tailyr, I hope the words in this book do justice to your cover image.

I had many generous hosts over the past four years of travel and reporting, primarily Amanda Rice and Sean Mullins. Also: Ben and Anja, Luke and Laurie, Elliott, Pete and Tara, Fred and Anna, and Damian and Darcy. David and Katie Riester welcomed me to stay at a beautiful place where I could focus and work without interruption. As I was writing, Brian Eule at the Heising-Simons Foundation swooped in from nowhere and supported my work. I'm deeply grateful to him and everyone at the American Mosaic Journalism Prize.

A number of journalists, poets, and storytellers offered input and counsel, among them Ted Conover, Sue Halpern, Bill McKibben, Eliza Griswold, Sierra Crane Murdoch, Lauren Markham, Kyle Dickman, Anaïs Mitchell, Mark Sundeen, Elliott Woods, Anne Helen Petersen, Seyward Darby, Ian Frazier, Seth Fletcher, Daniel Wolff, Rachel Monroe, Carolyn Kormann, Anna V. Smith, Paul Solotaroff, Kevin Fedarko, and Geffrey Davis, who also took me on a needed river trip. The friends who helped me are too many to name, but Hailee Strassner and Allegra Love provided essential, caring support, as did the late Matthew Power, who is with me whenever I do this work.

An all-star team of thoughtful readers generously gave their time to scrutinize and improve early drafts of the book: Courtney Carlson, Charles Homans, Tailyr Irvine, Bridget Love, Nina McConigley, Jonah Ogles, John Okrent, Fernando Perez, Bob Shacochis, Brad Wieners, and my first and last editor, Stephanie Joyce.

Others who helped further my understanding: Johnny Arlee, Travis Arlee, Anna Baldwin, Chaney Bell, Jeff Bellach, Ethel Branch, Tammy Elser, Troy Felsman, Andrew HeavyRunner, Tony Incashola Sr., Matthew Kamps, Heather Kendall-Miller, Doug and Jordan Lefler, my cousin Nellie Lipscomb, Carlin Matt, Camas McClure, Gerald and Kassie Parson, Shandin Pete, Robin Selvig, Bill Swaney, Jennifer Malatare Swaney, Don Wetzel Sr., Charles Wilkinson, Scott Wolf, Willie Wright.

My family: Maeve Kinkead, Harry Streep III, Maud Streep, Dan Mach, Kathryn Walker, Lynn Shepherd, Valerie Joyce Heffner, Jarrett Heffner, Trevor Joyce, Maxine Joyce, Louisa Conrad, Lucas Farrell, Chris Ahern, Ellen Smith Ahern, Alex Reiser, Anna Sullivan Reiser, and Lark. All my aunts, uncles, and cousins, too many to name, ever in my heart. My love, Stephanie Joyce.

Those who came before: Eugene Kinkead, Katharine T. Kinkead, Harry Streep Jr., Mary Wilkinson Streep.

Those who come next: Oran, Olivia, Eleanor, Lana, Graham, Maisie, Minna, Max, Freddie, Jonah, Nuala, Gus, Silas, Izzy, Darren, Peter, Ida June, Luca, Henrietta, Clinton, Woody, Isla, Loic, Axel Bruce, Tyge, Zevon.

Finally, I would like to thank the young men who taught me, along with so many others, about courage—Darshan Bolen, Lane Johnson, Lane Schall, Alex Moran, Tyler Tanner, Cody Tanner, Ivory Brien, Chase Gardner, David "Tapit" Haynes, Nathaniel Coulson, Sage Nicolai, Troylin Tewawina, Treylin Tewawina, Amare Vanderburg, Shadenn Stone, Trey Malatare, Deon Haynes, Sam Phillips, Ardon McDonald, Isaac Fisher, Billy Fisher, Greg Whitesell, Phillip Malatare, and Will Mesteth Jr.

Notes

A Note on Sources
This book is a work of nonfiction. Since 2017, I've spent a great deal of time reporting in person in Montana and surrounding states with a recorder and a notebook. I've also relied upon the public record and the work of many authors, journalists, and scholars, as noted in the pages to come. I've confirmed statements of fact about the personal histories of living people and the ancestors of living people through detailed corroborating interviews, trips to the Montana Historical Society and the National Archives at Broomfield, Colorado, and publicly available records, including marriage licenses, census rolls, obituaries, military service records, basketball box scores, newspaper archives, and court and property records. I have not cited all those records with specificity in the notes to prevent unnecessary intrusiveness. Tarren Andrews, a writer and scholar from the Flathead Indian Reservation who is a documented descendant of the Confederated Salish and Kootenai Tribes, read the manuscript closely multiple times to critically examine assumptions, and an independent journalist, Tom Colligan, exhaustively checked every fact. I couldn't have written this book without their tireless efforts. Any errors are mine. I'm grateful to all the people who spoke and corresponded with me during the reporting of this book, both those who are named here and those who aren't:

Jason Adams, Emily Adamson, Jesse Allan, Brenda Amunrud, Brent Amunrud, Matthew Amunrud, Johnny Arlee, Travis Arlee, Pat Armstrong Jr., Marco Azurdia, Anna Baldwin, James Baldwin, Amy Bartels, Mark Beckman, Tina Begay, Chaney Bell, Caleb Bellach, Carly Danhof-Bellach, Jeff Bellach, Kimberly Blush, Darshan Bolen, Ammon Boswell, Ethel Branch, Brad Brazill, Colt Brazill, Tomi Brazill, Aaron Brien, Ivory Brien, Misty Brien, Francis Brown LoneBear, Steve Bullock, Zachary Camel Jr., Jordyn Clairmont, Leon Costello, Nathaniel Coulson, Devon Cox, Wade Davies, Travis DeCuire, Matea DePoe, Amy Doom, Bill Dreikosen, Meghan Durham, Jeff

Dyksterhouse, Faith Dyksterhouse, Parker Dyksterhouse, Tammy Elser, employees of Tricon Timber (now Idaho Forest Group), David Evans, Trina Fyant Felsman, Troy Felsman, Louis Fiddler, Jolene Field, Mark Field, Pilar Field, Cheryl Finley, Darrin Finley, Billy Fisher, Isaac Fisher, Les Fisher, Walter Fleming, Phyllis Haynes Foster, Ralph Foster, Chase Gardner, Kris Gardner, Gerald Gray, Charles Gross, Michelle Guzman, Jordan Hansen, Chasity Haynes, David Haynes, Deon Haynes, Erma Haynes, Gloria Haynes, Sharon Haynes, Sophie Cullooyah Stasso Haynes, TJ Haynes, Tom Haynes, Andrew HeavyRunner, Adam Hiatt, Sophia Hitti, Don Holst, Clint Hordemann, Kyle Houghtaling, Kevin Howlett, Shawn Huse, Tony Incashola Sr., Jennifer Jilot, Brad Johnson, Lane Johnson, Matthew Kamps, Steve Keller, Erin Lacey, Luke Lacey, Roberta Lafley, Mike Larsen, Doug Lefler, Jordan Lefler, Logan Lefler, Amy Lisk, Bear Malatare, Becky Malatare, Clayton Malatare, Irma Malatare, John Malatare, Morgan Malatare, Phillip Malatare, Trey Malatare, Whitney Malatare, Carlin Matt, Clark Matt, Diane Matt, James "Bing" Matt, Sam McCracken, Ardon McDonald, Rob McDonald, Elaine Meeks, Ashley Mesteth, William Mesteth Jr., William Mesteth Sr., Camas McClure, Carmen McClure, Kenny McClure, Tom McClure, Hilly McGahan, Scott McGowan, Heather Kendall-Miller, Donna Mollica, Alex Moran, Austin Moran, Ernie Moran, Kody Morigeau, Dean Nicolai, Sage Nicolai, Shawna Olsen, Erin O'Reilly, Shelley Otoupalik, Shannon Patton, Gerald Parson, Kassie Parson, Hunter Pauli, Kurt Paulson, Linda Peavy, Andrew Pedersen, Shandin Pete, Joe Peterson, Sam Phillips, Allen Pierre, Kelly Pierre, Patlik Pierre, Crystal Pitts, Kendra Wabaunsee Pitts, Terry Pitts, Zachary Pitts, Zanen Pitts, Jesse Repay, Bob Ricketts, Jennifer Schall, Lane Schall, Scott Schall, Stephany Seay, Derek Selvig, Robin Selvig, Stephen Small Salmon, Thompson Smith, Rhett Soliday, Anna Whiting Sorrell, Gene Sorrell, Danny Sprinkle, Laurencia Rose Starblanket, Joe Stevens, Patty Stevens, Willie Stevens, Bill Stockton, Shadenn Stone, Bill Swaney, Jennifer Malatare Swaney, Ron Swaney, Corey Symons, Chase Tait, Ashley Tanner, Cody Tanner, Tyler Tanner, Jim Taylor, Lena Tewawina, Treylin Tewawina, Troylin Tewawina, Walden Tewawina, Julie Tonkin, Marc Umile, Amare Vanderburg, Frances Vanderburg, Derek Von Heeder, Jill Wabaunsee, Jeff Welsch, Noelle West, Don Wetzel Jr., Don Wetzel Sr., Justin Wetzel, Ryan Wetzel, David Whitesell, Greg Whitesell, Raelena Spencer Whitesell, Charles Wilkinson, Scott Wolf, Rachi Wortham, Frankie Lynn Wright, Willie Wright, Izzy Yasana.

Prologue

1   *On the wall of her hospital room:* Poster by Bob Gunderson, of Gundy Artistry in Polson. Image emailed to the author November 13, 2020.

3   *somewhere between escape and religion: Class C: The Only Game in Town.* Directed by Justin Lubke. Montana PBS, February 2008, https://www.montanapbs.org /programs/ClassC/, accessed January 31, 2021; Shann Ray, "The Artistry of Montana Basketball Legend Jonathan Takes Enemy," *Nervous Breakdown,* April 2011, http://thenervousbreakdown.com/sray/2011/04/the-artistry-of-montana -basketball-legend-jonathan-takes-enemy/; Gary Smith, "Shadow of a Nation,"

Sports Illustrated, February 1991, https://vault.si.com/vault/1991/02/18/shadow
-of-a-nation-the-crows-once-proud-warriors-now-seek-glory-but-often-find
-tragedy-in-basketball.

3   *an estimated population:* "Arlee, Montana," United States Census Bureau, 2019
American Community Survey Demographic and Housing Estimates, https://
data.census.gov/cedsci/all?q=arlee%20mt, accessed February 1, 2021.

3   *no one locally does:* Nick Martin, "Can the Census Be Saved in Indian Country?"
New Republic, September 2020, https://newrepublic.com/article/159458/can
-census-saved-indian-country; Anna V. Smith, "An Inaccurate Census Has Major Implications for Indian Country," *High Country News,* October 2020, https://
www.hcn.org/issues/52.10/indigenous-affairs-an-inaccurate-census-has-major
-implications-for-indian-country.

5   *Over a three-game span:* "Arlee Boys Basketball, Varsity 16–17," Max Preps,
February 16–18, 2017, https://www.maxpreps.com/high-schools/arlee-(arlee,mt)
/basketball-winter-16-17/schedule.htm, accessed February 1, 2021.

7   *"Ladies and* gennnnnnnntlemen*":* Details from the pregame introductions, including announced player height, are sourced from archived video at NFHSNet-
work.com.

1: We Just Know

11   *"where Montana began":* Historic St. Mary's Mission and Museum, accessed
January 31, 2021, saintmarysmission.org; Stevensville Historical Society, *Mon-
tana Genesis* (Missoula: Mountain Press Publishing Company, 1971); Jamie
Kelly, "Main Street Jitters," *Missoulian,* October 11, 2008, A1.

11   *near ground that was once:* Salish–Pend d'Oreille Culture Committee and Elders
Cultural Advisory Council, Confederated Salish and Kootenai Tribes, *The Salish
People and the Lewis and Clark Expedition* (Lincoln: University of Nebraska Press,
2005), 46–47.

12   *a $3 million:* Interview with Marc Umile of Sirius Construction, November 13,
2020. Rob Chaney, "Arlee School District Asks Voters for Financial Help," *Missoulian,* October 31, 2006, B1.

19   *that holds ten thousand:* "First Interstate Arena," MetraPark, www.metrapark.com
/p/facilties/firstinterstatearena, accessed February 1, 2021.

20   *build a spiritual retreat:* Rob Chaney, "Buddhist Teacher Expands Tibetan Tradition
in Montana," *Missoulian,* April 3, 2016, https://missoulian.com/news/local/buddhist
-teacher-expands-tibetan-tradition-in-montana/article_2e3d32fa-b241-5022-b30f
-d5aaf39defab.html; Sarah Van Gelder, "How an American Lama Finds Joy in
Turbulent Times," *Yes!,* February 12, 2014, https://www.yesmagazine.org/health
-happiness/2014/02/12/how-an-american-lama-finds-joy-in-turbulent-times/;
Namchak Foundation Form 990-PF for period ending December 2018, accessed via
ProPublica's "Nonprofit Explorer," https://projects.propublica.org/nonprofits/display
_990/264712157/02_2020_prefixes_26-27%2F264712157_201812_990PF
_2020020717125080, January 31, 2021.

2: They're Following You

23   *first state finals appearance:* Rial Cummings, "Fairfield Stymies Arlee," *Missoulian,* March 12, 1995, D1.

23   *run track at the University of Wisconsin:* L. E. Skelley, "Texas Stars Shine in Drake Relays Prelims: Set 2 Marks; Badgers Qualify in Three," *Capital Times* (Madison, WI), April 26, 1941; Monte Mack, "Coach Jones Will Take 17 Badgers on Vacation Trip," *Wisconsin State Journal,* April 16, 1941.

24   *According to available records:* The figures as reported here are from MaxPreps.com, which keeps records and statistics for high school games. For the Arlee teams, those records occasionally vary from those reported by news outlets including the *Missoulian* by one or two games per season. According to the records from various *Missoulian* stories, the Warriors went 93-35 from 2009 to 2013—a discrepancy of five wins and one loss over four seasons.

24   *earned a scholarship:* "Western Women Sign Arlee's Malatare," ButteSports .com, May 19, 2014, https://buttesports.com/western-women-sign-arlees -malatare/; "Arlee High School," *Missoulian,* June 10, 2014, https://missoulian .com/arlee-high-school/article_d221d2bc-f0bf-11e3-8099-0019bb2963f4 .html.

24   *formally apologized after cursing:* Tetona Dunlap, "Arlee Superintendent, Elementary Principal Resign," *Valley Journal,* March 21, 2012, http://www.valleyjournal .net/Article/1009/Arlee-superintendent-elementary-principal-resign; "Weeklies Reader: Arlee School District Sees Resignations, Banishments," *Ravalli Republic,* March 25, 2012, https://ravallirepublic.com/news/state-and-regional/article _a77a7f61-55f8-5042-b055-9f1a37ed0fde.html.

24   *inheriting a team:* "Montana High School Association 2013 State Class C Boys Basketball Tournament," Montana High School Association (MHSA) archives, https://www.mhsa.org/page/show/2172039-archives, accessed February 2, 2021.

24   *But during his first year:* "2014 State Class C Boys Basketball Tournament," MHSA archives, https://www.mhsa.org/page/show/2172039-archives, accessed February 2, 2021; Carrie Pichler, "Arlee Warriors End Season Upbeat," *Valley Journal,* March 12, 2014, http://www.valleyjournal.net/Article/8470/Arlee -Warriors-end-season-upbeat.

25   *lost just one game before:* "Skyview Boys Nab First State AA Crown. . . . Belt Finishes Atop Class C," *Independent Record* (Helena), March 15, 2015, https:// helenair.com/sports/high-school/basketball/skyview-boys-nab-first-state-aa -crown/article_ccc70a5e-ed5b-5efa-879e-9a61985c0c0f.html.

27   *advanced to the state championship:* AJ Mazzolini, "State C Boys' Basketball: Box Elder Denies Arlee in Title Game, 95–73," *Missoulian,* March 5, 2016, https:// missoulian.com/sports/high-school/state-c-boys-basketball-box-elder-denies-arlee -in-title-game-95-73/article_30063be9-dd61-52e1-87d8-089c7e07b874.html.

3: We Need Her

30   *ten probing questions:* Laura Starecheski, "Take the ACE Quiz—And Learn What It Does and Doesn't Mean," National Public Radio, March 2, 2015, https://

www.npr.org/sections/health-shots/2015/03/02/387007941/take-the-ace-quiz
-and-learn-what-it-does-and-doesnt-mean.

30   *According to ACE data collected:* M. T. Merrick, D. C. Ford, K. A. Ports et al.,
"Vital Signs: Estimated Proportion of Adult Health Problems Attributable to
Adverse Childhood Experiences and Implications for Prevention—25 States,
2015–2017," *Morbidity and Mortality Weekly Report,* Centers for Disease Control and Prevention 68 (2019): 999–1005, http://dx.doi.org/10.15585/mmwr
.mm6844e1.

31   *50 percent of Arlee's third graders:* Data from Office of Public Instruction, "Growth
and Enhancement of Montana Students," emailed to the author in June 2019.

31   *readers had fallen more than fourfold:* Ibid.

35   *Phil scored nine points in just over:* Video provided to the author by Jordan Lefler
and Zanen Pitts. Accessed in 2018 and 2019.

4: This Crazy Feeling of Infinity

36   *boomed the* Billings Gazette: Jeff Welsch, "Class C Boys: Arlee's Malatare
Shows Again He's 'One of a Kind,'" *Billings Gazette,* March 9, 2017, https://
billingsgazette.com/sports/high-school/basketball/boys/class-c-boys-arlees
-malatare-shows-again-hes-one-of-a-kind/article_50b8046b-1a86-56bd-84ed
-732662efe893.html.

36   *poured in 28 points:* Jeff Welsch, "State C Boys: Arlee Outlasts Hays-Lodgepole,
Moves into Final," *Missoulian,* March 10, 2017, https://missoulian.com/sports
/high-school/basketball/boys/updated-state-c-boys-arlee-outlasts-hays
-lodgepole-moves-into-final/article_ec952d53-8db7-51a4-b13d-b4ae1f3c9464
.html.

37   *had come in second:* John Smithers, "Colstrip Nips Polson Boys," *Missoulian,*
May 28, 1995, D3; Montana High School Association, "State Boys' Basketball Champions of the Past, 1911–2019," https://www.mhsa.org/page/show
/2173443-archives, accessed February 2, 2021.

37   *His brother, the all-state guard:* Fritz Neighbor, "Browning Too Much for Ronan
in Title Game," *Missoulian,* February 24, 2002, C1; "Athletes of the Week," *Missoulian,* February 26, 2002, D4.

37   *said the right things:* Cummings, "Fairfield Stymies Arlee."

37   *Both of those players had transferred:* Dan Chesnet, "MC's Lodine, Ramirez Ink
with In-State Colleges," *Belgrade News,* April 28, 2017, http://www.belgrade
-news.com/sports/mc-s-lodine-ramirez-ink-with-in-state-colleges/article
_61cb7318-2c50-11e7-b0e6-5bfe2248386e.html.

39   *Montana had the nation's highest suicide rate:* "Suicide Rates Rising Across the
U.S.," CDC Newsroom, Centers for Disease Control, June 7, 2018, https://www
.cdc.gov/media/releases/2018/p0607-suicide-prevention.html; Chris McG-
real, "Financial Despair, Addiction, and the Rise of Suicide in White America,"
Guardian, February 7, 2016, https://www.theguardian.com/us-news/2016/feb/07
/suicide-rates-rise-butte-montana-princeton-study?CMP=Share_AndroidApp
_Tweet_with_Plume; Karen Sullivan, "State, County Working to Reduce Suicide

Rate," *Montana Standard,* September 8, 2015, https://mtstandard.com/lifestyles /health-med-fit/state-county-working-to-reduce-suicide-rate/article_1a5c1e82 -3738-576b-bcc7-61067f7aba2c.html.

39   *its most vulnerable demographic:* Montana Department of Health and Human Services, "2016 Suicide Mortality Review Team Report," https://dphhs.mt.gov /Portals/85/suicideprevention/2016SuicideMortalityReviewTeamReport.pdf; Seaborn Larson, "Montana Leads National Suicide Rate Growth in Latest Report," *Great Falls Tribune,* June 8, 2018, https://www.greatfallstribune.com/story /news/2018/06/08/montana-leads-national-suicide-rate-growth-latest-report /686036002/.

39   *brought in $57,000 in ticket sales:* Interview with Mark Beckman, Montana High School Athletic Association, February 21, 2018.

39   *Phil raised his arms:* The game details come from archived tapes from the subscription NFHS Network, the Montana High School Athletic Association, videographer Jordan Lefler, and multiple interviews.

5: Keep Up

48   *build computer materials used for military equipment:* "About Us," S&K Electronics, Inc., https://skecorp.com/about-us/, accessed February 2, 2021; David Erickson, "S&K Electronics Lands $1.8M Deal with Military Contractor," *Missoulian,* April 22, 2014, https://missoulian.com/news/local/s-k-electronics -lands-1-8m-deal-with-military-contractor/article_a18b177e-ca5b-11e3-b75e -0019bb2963f4.html.

48   *once an affront, now property of the Tribes: The Place of the Falling Waters.* Directed by Roy Bigcrane and Thompson Smith (Pablo: Salish Kootenai College Media and the Native Voices Public Television Workshop, 1990); "Montana Tribes Realize Long-Held Vision of Acquiring Kerr Dam: Interview with Energy Keepers, Inc. CEO Brian Lipscomb," US Department of Energy Office of Indian Energy Policy and Programs, September 16, 2015, https://www.energy .gov/indianenergy/articles/montana-tribes-realize-long-held-vision-acquiring -kerr-dam-interview-energy; Kim Briggeman, "Genesis of a Dam's Name: Pend d'Oreille Fight for Their Identity," *Missoulian,* October 31, 2015, https:// missoulian.com/news/local/genesis-of-a-dams-name-pend-doreille-fight-for -their-identity/article_6ada093d-d299-525f-aec4-e5538c24072c.html.

48   *Nyack is named:* James F. Leiner, "A Brief History of Nyack, Part One," Patch .com, January 1, 2012, https://patch.com/new-york/nyack/bp--a-brief-history -of-nyack-part-one; Robert Knight, "History Notebook," *Rockland County Journal News,* January 25, 1969, 5.

48   *the town's Native population:* "Nyack, New York," United States Census Bureau QuickFacts, https://www.census.gov/quickfacts/fact/table/nyackvillagenewyork /INC110219, accessed January 31, 2021.

48   *the Indianettes*: Lanning Taliaferro, "Nyack School Board Retires Indian Name for Sports Teams," msn.com, August 14, 2020, https://www.msn.com/en-us

/sports/ncaafb/nyack-school-board-retires-indian-name-for-sports-teams/ar
-BB17Yebb; Peter D. Kramer, "Nyack Bids Farewell to MacCalman Field," *Journal News*, October 18, 2016, 1A.

48   *named for the Q'lispé:* "Kalispell," *Encyclopedia Britannica*, https://www.britannica
.com/place/Kalispell, accessed January 31, 2021. "Historic and Architectural Properties of Kalispell, Montana," US Department of the Interior National Park Service, National Register of Historic Places, https://npgallery.nps.gov/GetAsset/d0d1358a
-5b0d-4c81-9606-47cdba1d2821, accessed March 3, 2021.

48   *Kalispell is 93.5 percent white:* "Kalispell city, Montana," United States Census Bureau QuickFacts, https://www.census.gov/quickfacts/fact/table/kalispellcitymontana
/INC110219, accessed March 3, 2021.

48   *a number of far-right ideologues:* Anne Helen Petersen, "Neo-Nazis Came for This Small Town. Can You Keep Them from Coming to Yours?" *Buzzfeed News*, February 12, 2017; Abe Streep, "The Last Best Place," *Harper's*, June 2018, https://
harpers.org/archive/2018/06/the-last-best-place/.

48   *the presence of a coach:* AJ Mazzolini, "Prep Notebook: Arlee's Phillip Malatare a Quadruple-Double Waiting to Happen," *Missoulian*, January 11, 2017, https://
missoulian.com/sports/high-school/basketball/boys/prep-notebook-arlees
-phillip-malatare-a-quadruple-double-waiting-to-happen/article_3e9792ae
-fe2b-5d0c-9495-301989be579e.html.

49   *since shuttered by: Missoulian* staff, "Lee Enterprises Closes the Indy," *Missoulian*, September 12, 2018, A1.

49   Lake County Leader, *adorned with a photo:* Jason Blasco, "Plains Game Cited as Turning Point of Warriors Season," *Lake County Leader*, March 30, 2017, B4.

50   *which had enabled his great-grandfather's arrival:* Fifty-eighth Congress of the United States, Session II, "An Act for the Survey and Allotment of Lands Now Embraced Within the Limits of the Flathead Indian Reservation, in the State of Montana, and the Sale and Disposal of All Surplus Lands After Allotment," April 23, 1904, https://www.loc.gov/law/help/statutes-at-large/58th-congress
/session-2/c58s2ch1495.pdf, accessed February 2, 2021.

50   *Zanen had told a reporter:* Richie Melby, "Arlee's State Championship for 'All of Indian Country,'" MontanaSports.com, March 12, 2017, https://www
.montanasports.com/high-school/boys-basketball/2017/03/12/arlees-state
-championship-for-all-of-indian-country/.

52   *made the curious choice:* Peter Friesen, "Arlee Welcomes Home Its First State Champion Basketball Team," *Missoulian*, March 12, 2017, https://missoulian
.com/news/state-and-regional/arlee-welcomes-home-its-first-state-champion
-basketball-team/article_4b231b28-30d1-5252-8f4a-40594167ca64.html.

54   *a town named for the legislator:* Robert J. Bigart, *Getting Good Crops* (Norman: University of Oklahoma Press, 2010), 218; "Flathead Reservation Timeline," Montana Office of Public Instruction, Indian Education Division, https://opi.mt.gov/Portals
/182/Page%20Files/Indian%20Education/Social%20Studies/K-12%20Resources
/Flathead%20Timeline.pdf, accessed January 31, 2021.

55   *defined their enrolled membership:* Tailyr Irvine, "Reservation Mathematics: Navigating Love in Native America," National Museum of the American Indian, Smithsonian Institution, https://americanindian.si.edu/developingstories/irvine.html, accessed January 31, 2021; Ronald L. Trosper, "Native American Boundary Maintenance: The Flathead Indian Reservation, Montana, 1860–1970," *Ethnicity* 3, no. 4 (1976): 265–67.

55   *to preserve the property and power of those:* Paul Spruhan, "A Legal History of Blood Quantum in Federal Indian Law to 1935," *South Dakota Law Review* 51, no. 1 (2006): 1–50; Ryan W. Schmidt, "American Indian Identity and Blood Quantum in the 21st Century: A Critical Review," *Journal of Anthropology* 2011 (2011): 1–9, https://www.hindawi.com/journals/janthro/2011/549521/, accessed March 3, 2021; Cedric Sunray, "Blood Policing," in *Native Studies Keywords*, ed. Stephanie Nohelani Teves et al. (Tucson: University of Arizona Press, 2015), 209–20. I was directed to the above texts by Charles Wilkinson and Tarren Andrews. See also: David Turner, "'Purity of Blood' and the Spanish Inquisition (1492)," *Jerusalem Post*, July 17, 2011, https://www.jpost.com/blogs/the-jewish-problem---from-anti-judaism-to-anti-semitism/purity-of-blood-and-the-spanish-inquisition-1492-366992.

55   *In colonial states, tribal ancestry:* Schmidt, "American Indian Identity," 4; Spruhan, "A Legal History," 4–6.

55   *in eighteenth-century North Carolina:* Spruhan, "A Legal History," 4–5.

55   *"The Dawes rolls were based on blood":* David Treuer, *Rez Life* (New York: Grove Press, 2012), 288.

56   *In some parts of the West:* Sixtieth Congress of the United States, Session I, "An Act for the Removal of Restrictions from Part of the Lands of Allottees of the Five Civilized Tribes, and for Other Purposes," May 27, 1908, https://www.loc.gov/law/help/statutes-at-large/60th-congress/session-1/c60s1ch199.pdf, accessed February 2, 2021.

56   *"full bloods" were permitted to do so:* Ibid.

56   *updated its constitution:* Trosper, "Native American Boundary Maintenance," 267.

56   *"Adopt their conquerors'":* Trosper, "Native American Boundary Maintenance," 258.

56   *an account he once gave:* "Eugene Pitts Interview, September 28, 1984" (1984), *Smokejumpers 1984 Reunion Oral History Project*, OH 133-087. Archives and Special Collections, Mansfield Library, University of Montana.

6: Never Do It for Yourself

62   *a young Blackfeet teacher:* Linda Peavy and Ursula Smith, *Full-Court Quest: The Girls from Fort Shaw Indian School, Basketball Champions of the World* (Norman: University of Oklahoma Press, 2014), 65–69.

63   *scholars have noted:* Wade Davies, *Native Hoops: The Rise of American Indian Basketball, 1895–1970* (Lawrence: University Press of Kansas, 2020), chapter 1.

63   *The Indian boarding-school era:* Mary Annette Pember, "Death by Civilization," *Atlantic,* March 8, 2019, https://www.theatlantic.com/education/archive/2019/03/traumatic-legacy-indian-boarding-schools/584293/.

63   *described his plan:* Richard Pratt, "Kill the Indian, and Save the Man: Capt. Rich-

ard H. Pratt on the Education of Native Americans," Carlisle Indian School Digital Resource Center, http://carlisleindian.dickinson.edu/teach/kill-indian -and-save-man-capt-richard-h-pratt-education-native-americans, accessed January 31, 2021.

63   *did not assimilate: Playing for the World.* Directed by John Twiggs. Montana PBS, 2010.

63   *recited passages from:* Ibid.

63   *"objects on display":* Peavy and Smith, *Full-Court Quest,* xii.

63   *Native theater that was widely known:* Deanne Stillman, *Blood Brothers: The Story of the Strange Friendship between Sitting Bull and Buffalo Bill* (New York: Simon and Schuster, 2017), 1–3, 155–72; "George Catlin," Virginia Museum of Fine Art, https://www.vmfa.museum/learn/resources/george-catlin/, accessed January 31, 2021.

64   *"As the nineteenth and twentieth centuries":* Philip J. Deloria, *Playing Indian* (New Haven, CT: Yale University Press, 1998), 8.

64   *home to twelve individual nations:* "Montana Indians: Their History and Location," Division of Indian Education, Montana Office of Public Instruction, http://opi.mt.gov/Portals/182/Page%20Files/Indian%20Education/Indian%20 Education%20101/Montana%20Indians%20Their%20History%20and%20Location.pdf, accessed March 3, 2021.

64   *citizens were overrepresented:* Walter Echo-Hawk, "Study of Native American Prisoner Issues," National Indian Policy Center, The George Washington University, Washington, D.C., 1996, 5, https://narf.org/nill/documents/NARF_PRISONER _ISSUES.pdf, accessed March 3, 2021; "Montana Counties Among Poorest in United States," *Billings Gazette,* December 8, 2000, 2B.

64   *89 percent white:* "Montana," United States Census Bureau QuickFacts, https://www.census.gov/quickfacts/MT?, accessed January 31, 2021.

64   *won back-to-back high school state championships:* Montana High School Association, "State Boys' Basketball Champions of the Past, 1911–2019."

64   *Wolf Point, won four titles:* Ibid.

64   *Larry Pretty Weasel averaged 32 points:* Jeff Welsch, "Above the Rim: Six Decades Later, Larry Pretty Weasel Still Stands Tall in Indian Basketball Lore," *Billings Gazette,* July 9, 2016, https://billingsgazette.com/sports/high-school /basketball/above-the-rim-six-decades-later-larry-pretty-weasel-still-stands -tall-in-indian-basketball/article_9d4db790-5018-522d-a43e-fd1f35b833e0 .html.

64   *turned down universities like Utah:* Smith, "Shadow of a Nation."

64   *averaged 18 points per game in two seasons:* "Willie Weeks," Sports Reference, https://www.sports-reference.com/cbb/players/willie-weeks-1.html, accessed January 31, 2021; "Willie Weeks Quits Bobcats," *Daily Interlake,* January 4, 1972, 3.

64   *would later write:* Willie Weeks, "Letters," *Sports Illustrated,* April 15, 1991, https://vault.si.com/vault/1991/04/15/letters.

65   *In 1967, Don Wetzel:* University of Montana-Missoula, Office of University Relations, "1967–68 University of Montana Freshman Basketball Statistics (Two

Games)," 1967. University of Montana News Releases, 1928, 1956–present. 3166. https://scholarworks.umt.edu/newsreleases/3166, accessed March 3, 2021.

65   *won the team's MVP:* University of Montana—Missoula. Athletics Department, "Grizzly Basketball Yearbook, 1971-1972," 1971. *Grizzly Basketball Yearbook, 1955-1992.* 6. https://scholarworks.umt.edu/grizzlybasketball_yearbooks_asc /6, accessed March 3, 2021.

65   *consist largely of teams from ranching:* "Member Schools," Montana High School Association, https://www.mhsa.org/memberschools.

65   *boys' teams from reservations:* Montana High School Association, "State Boys' Basketball Champions of the Past, 1911–2019."

65   *thrilled crowds:* Smith, "Shadow of a Nation"; Jeff Welsch, "One on One: A Conversation with Basketball Coaching Legend Gordon Real Bird Sr.," *Billings Gazette,* May 19, 2016, https://billingsgazette.com/sports/high-school/basketball /boys/one-on-one-a-conversation-with-basketball-coaching-legend-gordon -real-bird-sr/article_f8db1961-5297-5dd2-9ef1-44024b7c98c5.html; Slim Kimmel, "MTTop50 No. 5: Elvis Old Bull a Legendary Figure in Montana Basketball History," MontanaSports.com, June 1, 2020, https://www.montanasports .com/high-school-sports/boys-basketball/mttop50-no-5-elvis-old-bull-a -legendary-figure-in-montana-basketball-history.

65   *In 1991, Gary Smith wrote:* Smith, "Shadow of a Nation."

66   *she once said:* Kim Briggeman, "Deep Roots: Lady Griz Have Not One, But Two Native American Stars," *Missoulian,* March 10, 2007, A1.

66   *made ten NCAA tournaments:* Cary Rosenbaum, "38 Years of Recruiting Native Players: Indian Hall of Famer Robin Selvig," *Indian Country Today,* February 9, 2017, https://indiancountrytoday.com/archive/38-years-recruiting-natives-robin -selvig. National Collegiate Athletic Association tournament archives.

66   *He publicly suggested he might leave:* Tony Castleberry, "Conway Hedging at Return to MSU," *Bozeman Daily Chronicle,* July 1, 2001, https://www.bozemandailychronicle .com/sports/bobcats/conway-hedging-at-return-to-msu/article_a09d2229-222f -5489-b30f-e1efd5ad6a7a.html.

66   *said to* The New York Times: Selena Roberts, "Off-Field Hurdles Stymie Indian Athletes," *New York Times,* June 17, 2001, A1.

66   *taken out of context:* George Geise, "Conway May Leave MSU Program," *Great Falls Tribune,* July 3, 2001, 1S–2S.

66   *averaged more than 14 points:* "Pete Conway," Sports Reference, https://www .sports-reference.com/cbb/players/pete-conway-1.html, accessed January 31, 2021.

67   *under intense scrutiny:* Bob Meseroll, "Chavez Parts Ways with Griz," *Missoulian,* October 11, 2003, D1; *Tribune* staff, "UM's Chavez Leaves Team, Quits School," *Great Falls Tribune,* October 11, 2003, 1S.

67   *Since then, no Montana tribal members:* Reporting confirmed by emails sent by Andrew Pedersen, assistant director, athletics communications, Montana State University Bobcats, December 16, 2020, and by Julie Tonkin, program coordinator, University of Montana Grizzlies, January 26, 2021.

67   *those seven schools' men's basketball programs':* "Men's Basketball Coaching Staff," 2017–18 Men's Basketball Roster, Montana State University Billings, https://msubsports.com/sports/mens-basketball/roster/2017-18#sidearm-roster-coaches, accessed November 12, 2020; "Men's Basketball Coaching Staff," 2017–18 Men's Basketball Roster, Carroll Athletics, https://carrollathletics.com/sports/mens-basketball/roster/2017-18#sidearm-roster-coaches, accessed November 12, 2020; "Men's Basketball Coaching Staff," 2017–18 Men's Basketball Roster, Official Site of Montana State University Northern Lights & Skylights Athletics, https://golightsgo.com/sports/mens-basketball/roster/2017-18, accessed November 12, 2020; "Men's Basketball Coaching Staff," 2017–18 Men's Basketball Roster, Go Diggers, https://godiggers.com/sports/mens-basketball/roster/2017-18#sidearm-roster-coaches, accessed November 12, 2020; "Men's Basketball Coaching Staff," 2017–18 Men's Basketball Roster, Rocky Men's Basketball, https://gobattlinbears.com/sports/mens-basketball/roster/2017-18#sidearm-roster-coaches, accessed November 12, 2020; "Men's Basketball Coaching Staff," 2017–18 Men's Basketball Roster, Official Athletic Website of the Montana Western Bulldogs, https://umwbulldogs.com/sports/mens-basketball/roster/2017-18#sidearm-roster-coaches, accessed November 12, 2020; "Coaching Staff," 2017–18 Men's Basketball Roster, Offical Athletics Site of the University of Providence Argonauts, https://upargos.com/roster.aspx?roster=1583&path=mbball#coaches_anchor, accessed November 12, 2020.

68   *started a basketball league:* Myers Reece, "Tribal Hoop Dreams Continue," *Missoulian,* October 30, 2011, E13.

68   *improved recruitment and retention:* "Native American Freshman Retention/Graduation Rates," Montana State University Office of Planning and Analysis, https://www.montana.edu/opa/students/nativeamerican/nativefroshretentiongraduation.html, accessed March 3, 2021.

70   *tuition-fee waivers available at Montana's public universities:* "Paying for College," American Indian Student Services, University of Montana, http://www.umt.edu/aiss/Paying%20for%20College/default.php, accessed March 3, 2021.

72   *suicides often come in waves:* Sari Horwitz, "The Hard Lives—and High Suicide Rate—of Native American Children on Reservations," *Washington Post,* March 9, 2014, https://www.washingtonpost.com/world/national-security/the-hard-lives--and-high-suicide-rate--of-native-american-children/2014/03/09/6e0ad9b2-9f03-11e3-b8d8-94577ff66b28_story.html; Julie Bosman, "Pine Ridge Indian Reservation Struggles with Suicides Among Its Young," *New York Times,* May 1, 2015, https://www.nytimes.com/2015/05/02/us/pine-ridge-indian-reservation-struggles-with-suicides-among-young-people.html.

72   *according to the Centers for Disease Control:* Sally C. Curtin, Margaret Warner, and Holly Hedegaard, "Suicide Rates for Females and Males by Race and Ethnicity: United States, 1999 and 2014," NCHS Health E-Stat, National Center for Health Statistics, April 2016, https://www.cdc.gov/nchs/data/hestat/suicide/rates_1999_2014.htm, accessed February 1, 2021.

7: Almost Exactly the Same

74   *Every June, the University of Montana basketball program:* "Camp Information," University of Montana, Montana Grizzlies, https://gogriz.com/sports/2015/3/3 /GEN_201401012.aspx, accessed January 31, 2021.

75   *The first Black head coach:* "Black History Month Q&A—Travis DeCuire— Montana Men's Basketball," Big Sky Men's Basketball, February 2018, https:// bigskyconf.com/news/2018/2/12/black-history-month-q-a-travis-decuire -montana-mens-basketball.aspx, accessed February 1, 2021.

75   *hired by his alma mater in 2014:* Keila Szpaller, "Krakauer's 'Missoula' Reignites Debate over Local Rape Response," *Missoulian,* May 4, 2015, https://missoulian .com/news/local/krakauers-missoula-reignites-debate-over-local-rape-response /article_70800285-079a-5462-b666-4db2a3cc6194.html; Rebecca Martin, "Jon Krakauer Tells a 'Depressingly Typical' Story of College Town Rapes," National Public Radio, April 19, 2015, https://www.npr.org/2015/04/19/400185648/jon -krakauer-tells-a-depressingly-typical-story-of-college-town-rapes.

75   *contributed to an eight-year span:* Dan Bauman and Sarah Brown, "The U. of Montana Has Lost More Students This Decade Than Any Other Flagship. What's Going On?" *Chronicle of Higher Education,* September 26, 2019, https://www .chronicle.com/article/the-u-of-montana-has-lost-more-students-this-decade -than-any-other-flagship-whats-going-on/.

75   *was a needed bright spot:* Bill Speltz, "Speltz: Good News Not Available in Hardcover," *Missoulian,* February 28, 2015, https://missoulian.com/sports /college/montana/speltz-good-news-not-available-in-hardcover/article _21bb4473-4b2c-5dc9-85fc-120d40c759b8.html.

75   *"make my stamp with recruiting":* Kyle Sample, "DeCuire Follows Long, Winding Road Back to Montana," 406 MT Sports, February 19, 2016, https:// 406mtsports.com/college/big-sky-conference/university-of-montana/decuire -follows-long-winding-road-back-to-montana/article_9adc5ae8-efdb-5112 -89dc-0bcf862ee250.html.

75   *picked to finish in the middle:* "Griz Picked Fifth and Eighth in Big Sky Preseason Polls," Montana Grizzlies Men's Basketball, October 23, 2014, https:// gogriz.com/news/2014/10/23/Griz_picked_fifth_and_eighth_in_Big_Sky _preseason_polls.aspx.

75   *repeated that performance:* "2016 Big Sky Men's Basketball Championship," Big Sky Conference, https://bigskyconf.com/tournaments/?id=390, accessed February 1, 2021; Ryan Gaydos, "Big Sky Conference Men's Basketball Championship History," Fox News, February 19, 2020, https://www.foxnews.com/sports/big-sky -conference-mens-basketball-championship-history.

75   *Just one of DeCuire's first:* Interview with Travis DeCuire, December 27, 2020.

75   *Zack competed at Polson for three years:* Lindsay Schnell, "From the Rez to the Griz: Zack Camel Jr. Follows in His Uncle's Footsteps to Play for Montana," *Sports Illustrated,* February 17, 2016, https://www.si.com/college/2016/02/17/montana -walk-zack-camel-jr-seeks-set-example-his-tribe.

78   *more than 20 percent:* "Missoula City," United States Census Bureau QuickFacts,

https://www.census.gov/quickfacts/fact/table/missoulacitymontana,missoulacountym
ontana/AGE295219, accessed March 3, 2021.

79   *During the previous two seasons:* "2016–17 Men's Basketball Roster," Carroll Athletics, https://carrollathletics.com/sports/mens-basketball/roster/2016-17, accessed
February 1, 2021; "2015–16 Men's Basketball Roster," Carroll Athletics, https://
carrollathletics.com/sports/mens-basketball/roster/2015-16, accessed February 1,
2021; "2016–17 Women's Basketball Roster," Carroll Athletics, https://carrollathletics
.com/sports/womens-basketball/roster/2016-17, accessed February 1, 2021; "2015–16
Women's Basketball Roster," Carroll Athletics, https://carrollathletics.com/sports
/womens-basketball/roster/2015-16, accessed February 1, 2021.

80   *For thousands of years:* Salish–Pend d'Oreille Culture Committee and Elders
Cultural Advisory Council, Confederated Salish and Kootenai Tribes, *The Salish People and the Lewis and Clark Expedition* (Lincoln: University of Nebraska
Press, 2005), xi–9; Salish–Pend d'Oreille Culture Committee, *A Brief History of
the Salish and Pend d'Oreille Tribes* (St. Ignatius, MT: Salish–Pend d'Oreille Culture Committee, Confederated Salish and Kootenai Tribes, 1982; rev. ed., 2003),
8–14. Citations refer to the 2003 edition.

80   *returned to the Bitterroot Valley:* Salish–Pend d'Oreille Culture Committee and Elders Cultural Advisory Council, *The Salish People,* 19–25.

80   *traded with the Nez Perce:* Culture Committee, *A Brief History,* 6–7, 22–24.

80   *known to them as Saáptniša:* Tachini Pete, *seliš nyoʔnuntn: Medicine for the Salish
Language: English to Salish Translation Dictionary,* 2nd ed. (Pablo, MT: Salish
Kootenai College Press, 2010), 350, 415. In the cited edition of the dictionary,
tribe names are lowercased. In accordance with the current practice of the Séliš-
Q'lispé Culture Committee (previously the Salish–Pend d'Oreille Culture Com-
mittee), I am capitalizing proper names, including tribe names.

81   *Archaeological research in western Montana:* Adam N. Johnson, Regina Sievert, Michael Durglo Sr., Vernon Finley, Louis Adams, and Michael H. Hofmann, "Indigenous Knowledge and Geoscience on the Flathead Indian Reservation, Northwest
Montana: Implications for Place-Based and Culturally Congruent Education,"
Journal of Geoscience Education 62, no. 2 (2014): 187–202.

81   *numbered in excess of:* Culture Committee, *A Brief History,* 21–23.

81   *who had brought guns:* Culture Committee and Elders Cultural Advisory Council,
The Salish People, xiv, 83.

81   *a group of haggard travelers:* Culture Committee and Elders Cultural Advisory
Council, *The Salish People,* xi, 85–110; Bernard DeVoto, *The Journals of Lewis and
Clark* (Cambridge: Houghton Mifflin, 1953), 233–37.

81   *appeared to have misinterpreted:* Culture Committee and Elders Cultural Advisory
Council, *The Salish People,* 85–87; DeVoto, *The Journals of Lewis and Clark,* 233–34.

81   *"band of the Flathead nation":* "September 4, 1805," Journals of the Lewis and
Clark Expedition, University of Nebraska–Lincoln, https://lewisandclarkjournals
.unl.edu/item/lc.jrn.1805-09-04#n22090402, accessed February 1, 2021.

81   *according to tribal history:* Culture Committee and Elders Cultural Advisory
Council, *The Salish People,* 107–9.

81   *where they survived by eating:* Ibid., 87; DeVoto, *The Journals of Lewis and Clark,* 239; "September 16, 1805," Journals of the Lewis and Clark Expedition, University of Nebraska–Lincoln, https://lewisandclarkjournals.unl.edu/item/lc.jrn .1805-09-16, accessed February 1, 2021.

81   *trappers and traders arrived:* Alvin M. Josephy Jr., *The Nez Perce Indians and the Opening of the Northwest* (New Haven, CT: Yale University Press, 1965; reiss., New York: Houghton Mifflin, 1997), 40–78. Citations refer to the Houghton Mifflin edition.

81   *Christian influence spread:* Robert J. Bigart, *Getting Good Crops* (Norman: University of Oklahoma Press, 2010), 26–29; Culture Committee and Elders Cultural Advisory Council, *The Salish People,* 109–12; Josephy Jr., *The Nez Perce Indians,* 81–119; Claude Schaeffer, "The First Jesuit Mission to the Flathead, 1840–1850: A Study in Culture Conflicts," *Pacific Northwest Quarterly* 28, no. 3 (July 1937): 227–50.

81   *coming ecological destruction:* Schaeffer, "The First Jesuit Mission," 231–32; Leslie Spier, *The Prophet Dance of the Northwest and Its Derivatives: The Source of the Ghost Dance* (Menasha, WI: George Banta Publishing, 1935; New York: AMS Press, 1979), 5–29. Citations are to the AMS Press edition.

81   *Iroquois fur trappers moved:* Culture Committee, *A Brief History,* 25–26; Culture Committee and Elders Cultural Advisory Council, *The Salish People,* 136; Bigart, *Getting Good Crops,* 25, 38–39; Josephy Jr., *The Nez Perce Indians,* 124–25.

82   *would bring new knowledge:* Culture Committee and Elders Cultural Advisory Council, *The Salish People,* 111–12; Culture Committee, *A Brief History,* 8–10, 25–26; Schaeffer, "The First Jesuit Mission," 229–32; Bigart, *Getting Good Crops,* 26.

82   *a group of Indigenous men traveled:* Culture Committee and Elders Cultural Advisory Council, *The Salish People,* 112; Culture Committee, *A Brief History,* 25; Josephy Jr., *The Nez Perce Indians,* 93–96; Robert J. Bigart, *Life and Death at St. Mary's Mission, Montana: Births, Marriages, Deaths, and Survival Among the Bitterroot Salish Indians 1866–1891* (Pablo, MT: Salish Kootenai College Press, 2005), 1.

82   *Two of the men died:* Josephy Jr., *The Nez Perce Indians,* 97.

82   *published a sensationalist account:* Ibid., 101.

82   *Before long, wrote the historian Alvin M. Josephy Jr.:* Ibid.

82   *Big Ignace himself led:* Culture Committee and Elders Cultural Advisory Council, *The Salish People,* 136; Josephy Jr., *The Nez Perce Indians,* 124; Pierre-Jean De Smet, Hiram Martin Chittenden, and Alfred Talbot Richardson, *Life, Letters and Travels of Father Pierre-Jean de Smet, S.J., 1801–1873* (New York: Francis P. Harper, 1905), 28–29, https://catalog.hathitrust.org/Record/008721153, accessed February 1, 2021.

82   *killed by a Lakota party:* Peter Ronan, *Historical Sketch of the Flathead Indian Nation from the Year 1813 to 1890* (Helena, MT: Journal Publishing, 1890), 24–25. Accessed February 1, 2021, via the University of California libraries digital archive, https://archive.org/details/university_of_california_libraries; Josephy Jr., *The Nez Perce Indians,* 167–68; Edmond Mallet and Francis X. Reuss, "The

Origin of the Flathead Mission of the Rocky Mountains," *Records of the American Catholic Historical Society of Philadelphia* 2 (1886–1888): 193–96.

82   *In 1839, two more emissaries:* De Smet, Chittenden, and Richardson, *Life, Letters and Travels*, 29–30; Ronan, *Historical Sketch*, 26–27; Culture Committee, *A Brief History*, 25.

82   *In 1840, De Smet traveled:* De Smet, Chittenden, and Richardson, *Life, Letters and Travels*, 31–33.

82   *arrived in the Bitterroot Valley:* Ibid., 39–40; Ronan, *Historical Sketch*, 30; Culture Committee and Elders Cultural Advisory Council, *The Salish People*, 62.

82   *Nez Perce were baptized:* De Smet, Chittenden, and Richardson, *Life, Letters and Travels*, 331–40; Ronan, *Historical Sketch*, 31.

82   *But the priests' dogmatism:* Culture Committee, *A Brief History*, 26; Bigart, *Life and Death*, 1–3.

82   *Smallpox also persisted:* Katherine Mitchell and Ellen Baumler, "The St. Ignatius Mission," *Montana: The Magazine of Western History* 57, no. 3 (2007): 66-69, http://www.jstor.org/stable/25485638, accessed March 4, 2021.

82   *left St. Mary's Mission:* Salish and Pend d'Oreilles Culture Committee, "Indian Time #10," YouTube video, October 11, 2018, accessed February 1, 2021; Culture Committee and Elders Cultural Advisory Council, *The Salish People*, 62, 112.

82   *"As it was told to me":* Culture Committee, "Indian Time #10."

83   *in the heart of Q'lispé:* Culture Committee, *A Brief History*, 26; Joseph L. Obersinner, SJ, and Judy Gritzmacher, *St. Ignatius Mission: National Historic Site* (Missoula: Gateway Printing & Litho, 1977), 1–4; Ronan, *Historical Sketch*, 37.

83   *make way for a railroad:* Kent Richards, "The Stevens Treaties of 1854–55," *Oregon Historical Quarterly* 106, no. 3 (Fall 2005): 342–50, http://www.jstor.org/stable/20615553, accessed March 4, 2021; Josephy Jr., *The Nez Perce Indians*, 292-32; Lonny Hill, "Blast from the Past: Treaty of Hellgate 164 Years Old Today," *Char-Koosta News*, July 18, 2019, http://www.charkoosta.com/news/blast-from-the-past-treaty-of-hellgate-164-years-old-today/article_9aa93da4-a9a9-11e9-bb18-7b71d639c06d.html.

83   *"Not a tenth of it":* Bigart, *Getting Good Crops*, 31; Culture Committee, *A Brief History*, 29.

83   *ceded 20 million acres:* "Treaty with the Flatheads, Etc.," July 16, 1855, in *Indian Affairs: Laws and Treaties*, Vol. II (Treaties). Compiled and edited by Charles J. Kappler (Washington, D.C.: Government Printing Office, 1904), https://www.fws.gov/pacific/ea/tribal/treaties/flatheads_1855.pdf, accessed February 1, 2021.

83   *it broke its treaty obligations:* Bigart, *Getting Good Crops*, 29–37.

84   *Officials assigned Natives:* Culture Committee, *A Brief History*, 48; Bigart, *Life and Death at St. Mary's*, 31–39.

84   *as the economy changed, grazing cattle:* Culture Committee, *A Brief History*, 37; Culture Committee and Elders Cultural Advisory Council, *The Salish People*, 117; Robert J. Bigart, *Providing for the People: Economic Change Among the Salish and Kootenai Indians, 1875–1910* (Norman: University of Oklahoma Press, 2020), 21–24, 40–41.

84   *driving down game populations:* Bigart, *Getting Good Crops*, 37–47, 78–81; Ronan, *Historical Sketch*, 65.

84   *merchants opened a trading post:* "Early Missoula History," Historical Museum at Fort Missoula, https://fortmissoulamuseum.org/exhibit/early-missoula-history/, accessed February 1, 2021; "Historical Notes," City of Missoula, https://www.ci .missoula.mt.us/401/Historical-Notes, accessed February 1, 2021.

84   *died on a buffalo hunt:* Culture Committee, *A Brief History*, 30–31; Bigart, *Getting Good Crops*, 47–48.

84   *Claw of the Small Grizzly Bear:* Ibid.

84   *issued an executive order:* Culture Committee, *A Brief History*, 31; Bigart, *Getting Good Crops*, 119.

84   *The Oglala Lakota chief Red Cloud had only recently:* Dee Brown, *Bury My Heart at Wounded Knee* (New York: Henry Holt, 1970), 121–46.

84   *militias formed:* Bigart, *Getting Good Crops*, 120, 124.

84   *sent the Ohio Congressman James Garfield:* Ibid., 121; Ronan, *Historical Sketch*, 57.

84   *warned Charlo and two subchiefs:* Bigart, *Getting Good Crops*, 120.

84   *Arlee and Adolph worried:* Ibid., 123.

84   *"We should be everlastingly cursed":* Ibid. Board of Indian Commissioners, *Fourth Annual Report of the Board of Indian Commissioners to the President of the United States* (Washington, D.C.: Government Printing Office, 1872), 173, https:// catalog.hathitrust.org/Record/100154357, accessed March 4, 2021.

84   *Garfield offered $55,000:* Ronan, *Historical Sketch*, 57–61; "Agreement Drawn Up by James A. Garfield, Special Commissioner, Flathead Ind. Agency, Jocko Reservation, August 27th, 1872," Historic St. Mary's Mission and Museum, http://www.stmarysmission.com/BitterrootSalish-GarfieldAgreement.html, accessed February 2, 2021.

84   *Charlo again refused:* Bigart, *Getting Good Crops*, 123–24.

84–85 *the head chief's signature had been forged on it:* Culture Committee, *A Brief History*, 31–32; Bigart, *Getting Good Crops*, 124; Ronan, *Historical Sketch*, 62–64.

85   *Arlee left for the Jocko Valley:* Bigart, *Getting Good Crops*, 125; Father Philip Rappagliosi, *Letters from the Rocky Mountain Indian Missions*, ed. Robert Bigart (Lincoln: University of Nebraska Press, 2003), 55–58.

85   *"What is he?":* Culture Committee and Elders Cultural Advisory Council, *The Salish People*, 88. Versions of this oft-cited speech vary slightly in different translations and attributions. I am including verbatim sections quoted by the Séliš-Q'lispé Culture Committee in *The Salish People and the Lewis and Clark Expedition*. On page 135, the Culture Committee writes, "We do not know who translated the speech or how accurate the printed text was, but years later, elders who had heard Chief Charlo's words as passed down through tribal oral tradition gave similar accounts of what the chief said; the text is accurate at least in expressing Chief Charlo's basic message."

85   *defeated General Custer's forces:* Dee Brown, *Bury My Heart*, 288–302; Thomas Powers, "How the Battle of Little Bighorn Was Won," *Smithsonian Magazine*,

November 2010, https://www.smithsonianmag.com/history/how-the-battle-of
-little-bighorn-was-won-63880188/.

85   *came east over the Bitterroot Range:* Ronan, *Historical Sketch,* 65; Culture Committee,
      A *Brief History,* 32–33; Bigart, *Getting Good Crops,* 96–106; Josephy, Jr., *The Nez
      Perce Indians,* 563-572..

85   *government expressed its gratitude:* Culture Committee, *A Brief History,* 33; Bigart,
      Getting Good Crops, 128–29.

85   *In 1882, senators pushed:* William Kittredge and Annick Smith, *The Last Best Place:
      A Montana Anthology* (Helena: Montana Historical Society Press, 1988; Seattle:
      University of Washington Press, 1991), 354–64. Citations refer to the University
      of Washington Press edition.

85   *a Missouri senator met with Charlo:* Bigart, *Getting Good Crops,* 129–31.

85   *He traveled to Washington, D.C.:* Ronan, *Historical Sketch,* 66–72.

85   *led prayers in the evening:* Bigart, *Getting Good Crops,* 211.

86   *fared well in developing agriculture:* Culture Committee, *A Brief History,* 37; Cul-
      ture Committee and Elders Cultural Advisory Council, *The Salish People,* 117. For
      more on this period, see Robert J. Bigart, *Providing for the People: Economic Change
      Among the Salish and Kootenai Indians, 1875–1910* (Norman: University of Okla-
      homa Press, 2020).

86   *broke Garfield's word:* Fifty-eighth Congress, Session II, "An Act for the Survey and
      Allotment of Lands Now Embraced Within the Limits of the Flathead Indian
      Reservation, in the State of Montana, and the Sale and Disposal of All Surplus
      Lands After Allotment," April 23, 1904, https://www.loc.gov/law/help/statutes
      -at-large/58th-congress/session-2/c58s2ch1495.pdf, accessed February 2, 2021.

86   *allotment was a remarkably effective tool:* David Treuer, *The Heartbeat of Wounded
      Knee: Native America from 1890 to the Present* (New York: Riverhead Books,
      2019), 143–51.

86   *"a mighty pulverizing engine":* Theodore Roosevelt, "26th President of the United
      States: 1901–1909, First Annual Message," December 3, 1901, American Pres-
      idency Project, University of California–Santa Barbara, https://www.presidency
      .ucsb.edu/documents/first-annual-message-16, accessed February 1, 2021.

86   *the government planned to sell off:* Fifty-eighth Congress, Session II, "An Act for
      the Survey."

86   *deem individual Natives "competent":* Fifty-ninth Congress, Session I, "An Act To
      to Amend Section Six of an Act Approved February 8, 1887, Entitled 'An Act
      to Provide for the Allotment of Lands in Severalty to Indians on the Various
      Reservations, and to Extend the Protection of the Laws of the United States and
      the Territories over the Indians, and for Other Purposes,'" May 8, 1906, https://
      www.loc.gov/law/help/statutes-at-large/59th-congress/session-1/c59s1ch2348
      .pdf?loclr=bloglaw, accessed February 2, 2021.

86   *Subsequent legislation increased:* Sixtieth Congress of the United States, Session
      II, "An Act to Provide for an Enlarged Homestead," February 19, 1909, https://
      www.loc.gov/law/help/statutes-at-large/60th-congress/session-2/c60s2ch160
      .pdf, accessed February 2, 2021; Digital Public Library of America, "Boom and

Bust: The Industries That Settled Montana," https://dp.la/exhibitions/industries
-settled-montana/early-settlement/homestead-act, accessed February 2, 2021.

86   *enabled the government to sell off:* Sixtieth Congress, "An Act for the Removal of
Restrictions from Part of the Lands of Allottees of the Five Civilized Tribes,
and for Other Purposes," May 27, 1908, https://www.loc.gov/law/help/statutes
-at-large/60th-congress/session-1/c60s1ch199.pdf, accessed February 2, 2021.

86   *Taft signed a proclamation opening:* William Howard Taft, "Proclamation
874—Opening Lands in the Flathead, Coeur d'Alene, and Spokane Indian Reservations," May 22, 1909, American Presidency Project, University of California–
Santa Barbara, https://www.presidency.ucsb.edu/documents/proclamation-874
-opening-lands-the-flathead-coeur-dalene-and-spokane-indian-reservations,
accessed February 1, 2021.

86   *The government claimed and fenced off:* Culture Committee, *A Brief History,* 53–55;
Anna V. Smith, "Reclaiming the National Bison Range," *High Country News,* January 26, 2021, https://www.hcn.org/issues/53.2/indigenous-affairs-tribes-reclaiming
-the-national-bison-range; Steven Rinella, *American Buffalo* (New York: Spiegel &
Grau, 2008), chapter 3.

86   *Mercantile owners offered Natives:* Culture Committee, *A Brief History,* 51–52.

86–87 *priests and nuns started boarding schools:* Peter Ronan, *Justice to Be Accorded to the Indians: Agent Peter Ronan Reports on the Flathead Indian Reservation, Montana, 1883–
1893,* ed. Robert J. Bigart (Pablo, MT: Salish Kootenai College Press, 2014), 70–71.

87   *a Catholic school opened at St. Ignatius:* Robert Bigart and Clarence Woodcock,
"St. Ignatius Mission, Montana: Reports from Two Jesuit Missionaries 1885
& 1900–1901 (Part II)," *Arizona and the West* 23, no. 3 (1981): 267–78, http://
www.jstor.org/stable/40169164, accessed February 2, 2021; St. Ignatius Mission,
100 Years in the Flathead Valley: The St. Ignatius Centennial (Whitefish, MT:
Kessinger Publishing), 47.

87   *One boosterish account of the Ursulines':* John Merlin Trepp, "Music at St. Ignatius
Mission, 1854–1900" (Master of Music Thesis, University of Montana, 1966), 35.

87   *most of the allotted property:* Culture Committee, *A Brief History,* 50–51; Culture
Committee and Elders Cultural Advisory Council, *The Salish People,* 116–17;
"Flathead Reservation Timeline," Indian Education Division, Montana Office
of Public Instruction, https://opi.mt.gov/Portals/182/Page%20Files/Indian%20
Education/Social%20Studies/K-12%20Resources/Flathead%20Timeline.pdf,
accessed February 1, 2021.

88   *In his junior year:* "Arlee 2016–17 Basketball Player Stats," Max Preps, https://
www.maxpreps.com/high-schools/arlee-(arlee,mt)/basketball-winter-16-17
/stats.htm, accessed February 1, 2021.

8: He Don't Like to Go Far

91   *The courts spread over:* "Spokane Hoopfest," https://www.spokanehoopfest.net
/3on3basketball.

91   *promoting a new Nike sneaker:* Sean Quinton, "Kevin Durant Attends Hoopfest in
Spokane, Shows Love to Washington," *Seattle Times,* June 26, 2017, https://www

.seattletimes.com/sports/kevin-durant-attends-hoopfest-in-spokane-shows-love
-to-washington/.

100   *Since its founding in the nineteenth century:* Church of Jesus Christ of Latter-day
Saints, "Lamanites," https://www.churchofjesuschrist.org/study/scriptures/gs
/lamanites?lang=eng, accessed February 1, 2021; Daniel H. Ludlow, *Encyclopedia of
Mormonism* (New York: Macmillan, 1992; Brigham Young University, 2001), 804–5,
981–85. Brigham Young University Library Digital Collections, https://lib.byu.edu
/collections/encyclopedia-of-mormonism/, accessed February 1, 2021.

9: A Brutal Truth

107   *and an air-quality specialist:* Kim Briggeman and Peter Friesen, "'Spiral of Misery
and Despair,'" *Missoulian,* September 7, 2017, A1.

108   *a tiny town known for fly-fishing:* Ross Purnell, "A Part of Fly-Fishing History Is
Gone," *Fly Fisherman,* May 8, 2017, https://www.flyfisherman.com/editorial/a
-part-of-fly-fishing-history-is-gone/152147.

108   *Twin Bridges is more than 95 percent white:* "Twin Bridges Town, Montana" United States Census Bureau, https://data.census.gov/cedsci/profile?g
=1600000US3075475, accessed March 3, 2021.

108   *left the district with a settlement:* Vince Devlin, "Polson School Board Approves $120K
Settlement with Superintendent," *Missoulian,* March 16, 2012, https://missoulian
.com/news/state-and-regional/polson-school-board-approves-120k-settlement
-with-superintendent/article_310ca520-6f82-11e1-8316-0019bb2963f4.html.

109   *He held to the increasingly prevalent:* Olga Khazan, "Inherited Trauma Shapes
Your Health," *Atlantic,* October 16, 2018, https://www.theatlantic.com/health
/archive/2018/10/trauma-inherited-generations/573055/; Benedict Carey, "Can
We Really Inherit Trauma?" *New York Times,* December 10, 2018, https://www
.nytimes.com/2018/12/10/health/mind-epigenetics-genes.html.

10: Who's Tired?

123   *wrote Wildcat:* Vine Deloria Jr., and Daniel R. Wildcat, *Power and Place: Indian
Education in America* (Golden, CO: Fulcrum Publishing, 2001), 29.

125   *journalists have described:* Michael Powell, "Games on a Reservation Go By in a
Blur," *New York Times,* March 2, 2015, https://www.nytimes.com/2015/03/03
/sports/amid-the-red-rock-a-fever-pitch-for-rez-ball.html; Abe Streep, "What
the Arlee Warriors Were Playing For," *New York Times Magazine,* April 4, 2018,
https://www.nytimes.com/2018/04/04/magazine/arlee-warriors-montana
-basketball-flathead-indian-reservation.html; Matthew Bain, "'Rez Ball' Works
in NBA, Provides Opportunity for Kids," *AZ Central,* June 28, 2016, https://
www.azcentral.com/story/sports/high-school/2016/06/28/rez-ball-works-nba
-provides-opportunity-kids/86476614/; Russell Contreras, "'Basketball or
Nothing' Covers Hoop Dreams on Navajo Nation,'" Associated Press, August 1, 2019, https://apnews.com/article/79577afacec5460d9a7d2490ef8bc7b1;
Jeff Welsch, "One on One: A Conversation with Basketball Coaching Legend
Gordon Real Bird Sr.," *Billings Gazette,* May 19, 2016, https://billingsgazette

.com/sports/high-school/basketball/boys/one-on-one-a-conversation-with
-basketball-coaching-legend-gordon-real-bird-sr/article_f8db1961-5297-5dd2
-9ef1-44024b7c98c5.html.

129   *focused on the amount of vomit:* Kyle Houghtaling, "Warriors' Way," *Missoulian,*
December 1, 2017, D1.

129   *reputation for cutting editorial costs:* Montana News Guild, "Lee Enterprises
Continues to Cut Staff at Montana Newspapers," October 8, 2020, https://
montananewsguild.org/2020/10/08/lee-enterprises-continues-to-cut-staff-at
-montana-newspapers/.

131   *a transplant from Ohio:* "Paul Mushaben," Cat Country, https://catcountry1029
.com/author/paulmushaben/, accessed January 28, 2021.

131   *segregate its basketball tournaments:* Des Bieler, "Radio Host Suggests Indian
Teams Have Separate Tournament. Listeners Want Him Fired," *Washington Post,*
February 22, 2017, https://www.washingtonpost.com/news/early-lead/wp/2017
/02/22/radio-host-suggests-indian-teams-have-separate-tournament-listeners
-want-him-fired/.

131   *ran an op ed:* Mike Chavez, "Mike Chavez: Radio Personality's Comments
About Native Americans Toxic," *Billings Gazette,* February 28, 2017, https://
billingsgazette.com/sports/high-school/basketball/boys/mike-chavez-radio
-personalitys-comments-about-native-americans-toxic/article_118c4881-8722
-5349-a60c-b10e0cbbac42.html; Mike Chavez, "Native Americans and Montana Hoops Intertwined," *Missoulian,* March 1, 2017, B2.

131   *published a lengthy story on:* Mike Kordenbrock, "Protesters March in Billings
to Support Suspended Cat Country Radio Host," *Billings Gazette,* February 28, 2017, https://billingsgazette.com/news/local/protesters-march-in-billings-to
-support-suspended-cat-country-radio-host/article_3c47def6-72fd-54dc-b747
-6e62ddcab501.html; Mike Kordenbrock, "Protest Supports Radio Host," *Missoulian,* March 2, 2017, A7.

131   Lake County Leader's *season preview:* Jason Blasco, "Warriors Prepare to Defend
Class C," *Lake County Leader,* November 2017.

11: This Is the Right Now

139   RETURN OF THE KINGS: Kyle Houghtaling, "Return of the Kings," *Missoulian,*
December 9, 2017, D1.

140   *the vast majority:* George Geise, "Number of American Indian Basketball Referees
Growing," *Montana Standard,* March 30, 2007, B6.

140   *series of listening sessions:* "MOA to Meet on Cultural Diversity," *Montana Standard,* January 30, 2012, 3B; Montana Officials Association, "Cultural Diversity Training Information," http://www1.arbitersports.com/front/106278/Site
/Cultural%20Diversity%20Training/Cultural-Diversity-Training-Information,
accessed March 4, 2021.

142   *out of Bozeman to a scholarship:* Frank Gogola, "Bozeman's Mack Anderson Makes
'Right Decision,' Commits to Montana Grizzlies Men's Basketball over Montana
State," *Missoulian,* September 5, 2017, https://missoulian.com/sports/college

/big-sky-conference/university-of-montana/bozemans-mack-anderson-makes
-right-decision-commits-to-montana-grizzlies-mens-basketball-over-montana
-state/article_574872cf-d80f-5105-bd7f-b42ef2754ce5.html.

142   *somehow, already committed:* Frank Gogola, "Worster Commits to Griz," *Missoulian,* October 23, 2017, B1.

12: Why Do You Care What Other People Think?

144   *the board had self-reported:* Arlee Schools Board of Trustees, School Board Meeting Minutes, September 18, 2017, accessed July 2019.

144   *a series of images:* Tommy Martino, "Photos: Arlee Edges Rocky Boy in Native American Classic," *Missoulian,* December 9, 2017, https://missoulian.com/sports/high-school/basketball/boys/photos-arlee-edges-rocky-boy-in-native-american-classic/collection_c190a48a-4ef8-5429-99c6-6da84bd0cf7e.html.

149   *St. Regis, a town of about:* "Montana 2010: Population and Housing Unit Counts," United States Census Bureau, 2010 Census of Population and Housing, Population and Housing Unit Counts, CPH-2-28, Montana (Washington, D.C.: Government Printing Office, 2012), https://www.census.gov/prod/cen2010/cph-2-28.pdf.

149   *largest employer, a lumber mill:* Edward O'Brien, "Tricon Timber Lays Off 90 in St. Regis," Montana Public Radio, September 28, 2015, https://www.mtpr.org/post/tricon-timber-lays-90-st-regis.

149   *unemployment rate was 7.4 percent:* Montana Department of Labor and Industry, "Local Area Unemployment Statistics," Mineral County 2017 unemployment rate, https://lmi.mt.gov/Home/DS-Results-LAUS, accessed February 1, 2021.

14: How Can It Be Business?

156   *scored 43 points while shooting 57 percent:* "Arlee Boys Basketball," MaxPreps, December 21, 2017; January 2, 2018, https://www.maxpreps.com/high-schools/arlee-(arlee,mt)/basketball-winter-17-18/schedule.htm, accessed February 1, 2021.

156   *story had just come out:* Kyle Houghtaling, "Phil in the Family: Arlee's Phillip Malatare Shines Bright Among Talented Squad," *Missoulian,* January 3, 2018, https://406mtsports.com/high-school/basketball/boys/phil-in-the-family-arlees-phillip-malatare-shines-bright-among-talented-squad/article_e3dbecda-bde6-5c52-ae5e-240db63b8f22.html.

159   *told a newspaper: Lake County Leader,* "Vikes Get Ready to Take On Arch Rival Arlee," January 2018.

163   *tribal hunting grounds in a treaty:* Washington State Historical Society, "Treaty with the Blackfeet, 1855," https://www.washingtonhistory.org/wp-content/uploads/2020/04/blackfeetTreaty-1.pdf, accessed January 31, 2021; Montana Office of Public Instruction, Indian Education Division, "Blackfeet Reservation Timeline," https://opi.mt.gov/Portals/182/Page%20Files/Indian%20Education/Social%20Studies/K-12%20Resources/BlackfeetTimeline.pdf, accessed January 31, 2021.

163   *before gold was discovered:* Kim Briggeman, "First Gold Strike in Territory That Became Montana Was 150 Years Ago," *Independent-Record,* August 5, 2012, 8A;

Digital Public Library of America, "Boom and Bust: The Industries That Settled Montana," https://dp.la/exhibitions/industries-settled-montana/mining.

163   *to accommodate settlers:* Brown, *Bury My Heart*, 103–74; *The Bozeman Trail: A Rush to Montana's Gold.* Directed by Tom Manning (Montana PBS, 2019), https://www.montanapbs.org/programs/BozemanTrail/, accessed February 2, 2021.

163   *so named for a man:* Merrill G. Burlingame, "John M. Bozeman, Montana Trailmaker," *Mississippi Valley Historical Review* 27, no. 4 (1941): 541; *The Bozeman Trail;* Michael Cassity, "Bozeman Blazed His Trail Against All Odds," *Jackson Hole Guide,* March 28, 1990, 6; "Tributes Given Guide to Montana Settlers," *Billings Gazette,* Friday, June 18, 1926, 3; Gail Schontzler, "John Bozeman Descendant Pays His Respects," *Bozeman Daily Chronicle,* October 13, 2014, https://www.bozemandailychronicle.com/news/john-bozeman-descendant-pays-his-respects/article_2ff2e980-5330-11e4-887d-539ece5d3ad9.html.

163   *Then came the railroad:* Gilbert King, "Where the Buffalo No Longer Roamed," *Smithsonian Magazine,* July 17, 2012, https://www.smithsonianmag.com/history/where-the-buffalo-no-longer-roamed-3067904/; Steven Rinella, *American Buffalo,* chapter 10.

163   *different sort of boom:* Abe Streep, "Bullock, Daines, and Montana's Growing Pains," *High Country News,* October 27, 2020, https://www.hcn.org/articles/election2020-bullock-daines-and-montanas-growing-pains.

163   *settled by Dutch farmers:* Rob Kroes, "Windmills in Montana: Dutch Settlement in the Gallatin Valley," *Montana: The Magazine of Western History* 39, no. 4 (1989): 40–51.

163   *has received funding:* Gail Schontzler, "Gianfortes Give $4.6 Million for Private-School Choice," *Bozeman Daily Chronicle,* April 12, 2012, https://www.bozemandailychronicle.com/news/education/gianfortes-give-4-6-million-for-private-school-choice/article_65e078d4-8432-11e1-84cb-0019bb2963f4.html.

164   *funded it with donations:* Slim Kimmel, "Montana Gym Rankings: Manhattan Christian," *Billings Gazette,* July 24, 2013, https://billingsgazette.com/sports/high-school/blogs/gazprepsports/basketball/bonus-montana-gym-rankings-manhattan-christian/article_162a552e-ae45-5962-98a5-9e793a9aa66c.html.

166   *tuition is around $10,000:* Manhattan Christian School, 2020–2021 Family Tuition K-12 Rate, https://www.manhattanchristian.org/admissions/tuition.cfm, accessed January 31, 2021.

166   *Three starters from the previous:* Mike Brandt, "Eagles Cruise to Victory to Tip Off Season," *Belgrade News,* December 8, 2015, http://www.belgrade-news.com/sports/eagles-cruise-to-victory-to-tip-off-season/article_44717e62-9d26-11e5-8a7a-d39a6e7d2847.html; Chesnet, "MC's Lodine, Ramirez Ink."

16: A Perfect World

171   *five Indigenous nations:* Michael Wright, "Blackfeet to Join Bison Hunt Outside Yellowstone," *Bozeman Daily Chronicle,* February 1, 2018, https://www.bozemandailychronicle.com/news/environment/blackfeet-to-join-bison-hunt-outside-yellowstone/article_c780904a-e215-536a-a539-37432fc3b73a.html.

171   *under the watch of environmental protesters:* "About BFC," Buffalo Field Campaign, https://www.buffalofieldcampaign.org/about-buffalo-field-campaign; Hal Herring, "The Killing Fields," *High Country News,* February 6, 2006, https://www.hcn.org/issues/315/16076.

171   *showed up in buckskin:* "Montana's Off-the-Grid Bison Scavengers," *Outside,* June 2016, https://www.outsideonline.com/2086566/montanas-grid-bison-scavengers.

171   *man named Latati: In the Spirit of Atatice.* Directed by Daniel Glick (Pablo, MT: Confederated Salish and Kootenai Tribes, 2018).

171   *populations were falling:* Gilbert King, "Where the Buffalo No Longer Roamed," *Smithsonian Magazine,* July 17, 2012, https://www.smithsonianmag.com/history/where-the-buffalo-no-longer-roamed-3067904/; Steven Rinella, *American Buffalo,* chapter 10.

171   *With their territories diminishing:* Bon I. Whealdon et al., *"I Will Be Meat for My Salish": The Montana Writers Project and the Buffalo of the Flathead Indian Reservation,* ed. Robert Bigart (Pablo and Helena, MT: Salish Kootenai College Press and the Montana Historical Society Press, 2001), 36–41; Rinella, *American Buffalo,* chapter 10.

171   *Lassaw Redhorn was once quoted:* Whealdon et al., *I Will Be Meat,* 37–38.

172   *number over five hundred:* Rinella, *American Buffalo,* chapter 3; John Elfreth Watkins, "Many New Game Laws, Perplexing to Nimrods, to Go into Effect This Season," *Evening Star* (Washington, D.C.), October 25, 1908, 6.

172   *called the largest:* "Last Buffalo Hunt," *Allentown Daily Leader,* November 24, 1903, 2.

172   *remained in private hands:* Rinella, *American Buffalo,* chapter 3.

172   *revive the flagging:* P. J. White, Rick L. Wallen, and David E. Hallac, "Yellowstone Bison: Conserving an American Icon in Modern Society," Yellowstone Association (2015), 46, 120, https://www.nps.gov/yell/learn/nature/upload/Yellowstone_Bison_ForWeb.pdf, accessed February 1, 2021.

172   *symptoms of brucellosis:* "Brucellosis," National Park Service, Yellowstone National Park, https://www.nps.gov/yell/learn/nature/brucellosis.htm, accessed January 31, 2021; Amy Martin, *Threshold* (podcast), season 1, episode 1, https://www.thresholdpodcast.org/s1e1-transcript, accessed January 31, 2021.

172   *held "brucellosis-free" status:* "USDA Downgrades Montana's Brucellosis-Free Status," *Tri-State Livestock News,* September 5, 2008, https://www.tsln.com/news/usda-downgrades-montanas-brucellosis-free-status/.

172   *In the early days of the hunt:* Joshua Kurlantzick, "American Buffalo: The Hunt Is On," *New York Times,* January 27, 2006, https://www.nytimes.com/2006/01/27/travel/escapes/27bison.html; Herring, "The Killing Fields."

172   *"open and unclaimed land":* "Confederated Salish and Kootenai Tribes Off-Reservation Wild Bison Hunting Regulations," Department of Natural Resources, Confederated Salish and Kootenai Tribes, https://csktbisonhunt.org/Orientation/Regulations/, accessed January 2021; Whitney Angell Leonard, "Habitat and Harvest: The Modern Scope of Tribal Treaty Rights to Hunt and Fish," *American Indian Law Journal* 3, no. 1 (2014): 311–22.

17: As Good As Your Word

181   *announced his resignation:* Arlee Schools Board of Trustees, School Board Meeting Minutes, January 10, 2018, accessed July 2019.

183   *On January 25:* Videotape provided by Jordan Lefler, February 2018; Slim Kimmel, "Energy, Enthusiasm Drive Arlee Boys Basketball Coach Zanen Pitts," MontanaSports.com, February 21, 2018, https://www.montanasports.com/high-school/2018/02/21/energy-enthusiasm-drive-arlee-boys-basketball-coach-zanen-pitts/.

184   *"a shell-shock factor":* Richie Melby and Slim Kimmel, "MTN Sports' Richie Melby and Slim Kimmel Discuss the Montana Winter Sports Landscape," Facebook, January 31, 2018, https://www.facebook.com/watch/live/?v=774342112759116&ref=watch_permalink, accessed February 1, 2021.

19: It Can Also Break Your Heart

198   *Billy Fisher led the scoring:* MontanaSports.com, "Western C Boys; Arlee, Manhattan Christian Set Up Anticipated Semifinal; Plains, Twin Bridges Advance," February 22, 2018, https://www.montanasports.com/high-school/2018/02/22/western-c-boys-arlee-manhattan-christian-set-up-anticipated-semifinal-plains-twin-bridges-advance/.

199   *resistance to regulation:* Marshall Swearingen, "Will a Twice-Burned County Change Its Ways?" *High Country News,* October 2016, https://www.hcn.org/issues/48.22/will-a-twice-burned-county-change-its-ways.

201   *since the school shooting:* Julie Turkewitz, Patricia Mazzei, and Audra D. S. Burch, "Suspect Confessed to Police That He Began Shooting Students 'in the Hallways,'" *New York Times,* February 15, 2018, https://www.nytimes.com/2018/02/15/us/florida-shooting.html.

201   *had recently been arrested for making:* Michelle McConnaha, "Darby High School Student in Custody After Threatening Social Media Posts," *Ravalli Republic,* February 19, 2018, https://ravallirepublic.com/news/local/article_36732d73-1738-588c-9ec6-4e22e9ce4af1.html; Michelle McConnaha, "Wednesday's Darby Snapchat Threats Traced to California," *Billings Gazette,* February 23, 2018, B2.

201   *"Big Sky got shut down":* Lucy Tompkins, "Missoula's Big Sky High Under Perimeter Lock-in Due to Graffiti Threat, Students Allowed to Leave," *Missoulian,* February 22, 2018, https://missoulian.com/news/local/missoulas-big-sky-high-under-perimeter-lock-in-due-to-graffiti-threat-students-allowed-to/article_2972b415-061d-5588-9469-21b02b711c5e.html.

201   *that teachers should be armed:* Amanda Holpuch, "Trump Insists on Arming Teachers Despite Lack of Evidence It Would Stop Shootings," *Guardian,* February 22, 2018, https://www.theguardian.com/us-news/2018/feb/22/donald-trump-insists-arming-teachers-guns-shootings.

203   *Manhattan Christian scored first:* Video by Jordan Lefler, accessed December 2020.

20: "Love You" on Three

213   *staying in hotels for weeks:* Kim Briggeman, "Paralyzing Winds and Snow Have

Turned Heart Butte's Basketball Teams into Road Warriors," *Missoulian,* February 27, 2018, https://missoulian.com/news/state-and-regional/paralyzing-winds-and-snow-have-turned-heart-buttes-basketball-teams-into-road-warriors/article_18bf9295-24e2-5843-97ba-cc65fd6f0bc6.html.

213   *Greg replied with:* Heidi Meili, "Arlee Basketball Player Goes Live with NBC Montana Today," NBC Montana, March 2, 2018, https://nbcmontana.com/news/local/arlee-basketball-player-goes-live-with-nbc-montana-today.

214   *took its name from an Indian agent:* "Scobey Objects to Letter from Pratt to Uncle of Student," Carlisle Indian School Digital Resource Center, http://carlisleindian.dickinson.edu/documents/scobey-objects-letter-pratt-uncle-student; accessed February 1, 2021; Linda Peavy and Ursula Smith, *Full-Court Quest: The Girls from Fort Shaw Indian School, Basketball Champions of the World* (Norman: University of Oklahoma Press, 2014), 27.

214   *Scobey had beaten Arlee:* Fritz Neighbor, "Scobey Cools Off Arlee in Title Game," *Missoulian,* March 13, 2011, C1.

218   *seats about six thousand people:* "Information for Promoters," Butte Civic Center, https://www.butteciviccenter.com/promoters, accessed January 31, 2021.

220   *won the opening tip-off:* Game details from archived video at NFHSNetwork.com.

226   *secured a grant:* "Tester Secures $50,000 to Combat Suicide Epidemic in Indian Country," U.S. Senator Jon Tester, March 16, 2018, https://www.tester.senate.gov/?p=press_release&id=6016, accessed January 31, 2021.

21: The Cracks

233   *led all scorers:* "Class C Reigns at HIT," *Great Falls Tribune,* March 24, 2018, https://www.greatfallstribune.com/story/sports/high-school/2018/03/24/class-c-reigns-hit/456510002/.

234   *Will had averaged:* "Arlee Boys Basketball Varsity 17–18," MaxPreps, https://www.maxpreps.com/high-schools/arlee-(arlee,mt)/basketball-winter-17-18/schedule.htm, accessed February 2, 2021.

234   *The honor went to:* "2017–2018 Montana Boys Basketball Player of the Year," Gatorade, https://playeroftheyear.gatorade.com/winner/sam-beighle/36441, accessed January 31, 2021.

234   *Phil averaged 22.3 points:* "Arlee 2017-18 Basketball Player Stats," MaxPreps, https://www.maxpreps.com/high-schools/arlee-(arlee,mt)/basketball-winter-17-18/stats.htm, accessed March 3, 2021.

234   *a Native American student population above:* "Census Enrollment Numbers," University of Montana, https://www.umt.edu/institutional-research/metrics/enrollment/census-enrollment.php, accessed January 31, 2021.

234   *the university published data:* "2010–2011 Diversity Report," University of Montana Office of Equal Opportunity and Title IX, https://www.umt.edu/eo/equal-opportunity/diversity/reportlong.php, accessed January 31, 2021.

234   *covered the university's struggles to retain:* Keila Szpaller, "UM Adjusts to Support Its Native American Students," *Missoulian,* July 29, 2018, A1.

235   *graced the home page:* Dillon Kato, "University of Montana Student, Former Student Arrested in Convenience Store Shooting," *Missoulian,* March 8, 2018, https://missoulian.com/news/state-and-regional/crime-and-courts/university -of-montana-student-former-student-arrested-in-convenience-store-shooting /article_b22d57e0-da23-590d-ab77-5e70cd6f71ff.html.

236   *it appeared in newspapers:* Dillon Kato, "2 UM Students Suspected in Shoot- ing," *Billings Gazette,* March 9, 2018, B4; Dillon Kato, "Bail Set at $1M Each for Pair in Shooting," *Missoulian,* March 10, 2018, B1; Dillon Kato, "Bail Set at $1M Each for Pair Charged in Store Shooting," *Independent Record,* March 11, 2018, A10.

236   *According to the nonprofit:* "Montana Profile," Prison Policy Initiative, https://www .prisonpolicy.org/profiles/MT.html, accessed January 31, 2021.

239   *Other Griz recruits had:* Slim Kimmel, "RayQuan Evans Officially Signs with Florida State," MontanaSports.com, April 22, 2019, https://www.montanasports .com/more-college/2019/04/22/rayquan-evans-officially-signs-with-florida -state/; Ryan Collingwood, "RayQuan Evans Draws Interest from Big Colleges as North Idaho Basketball Career Nears End," *Spokesman-Review,* February 20, 2019, https://www.spokesman.com/stories/2019/feb/19/rayquan-evans-draws -interest-from-big-colleges-as-/.

240   *the area was known for white supremacism: Our Private Idaho: America by the Num- bers with Maria Hinojosa.* Directed by Billy Shebar (Futuro Media Group, 2014), https://www.pbs.org/wgbh/america-by-the-numbers/episodes/episode-103/, accessed January 31, 2021; Doug Struck, "The Idaho Town That Stared Down Hate—and Won," *Christian Science Monitor,* August 31, 2017, https://www .csmonitor.com/USA/Society/2017/0831/The-Idaho-town-that-stared-down -hate-and-won.

240   *nearly 94 percent white:* "Coeur d'Alene, Idaho," United States Census Bureau QuickFacts, Population Estimates, July 1, 2019, https://www.census.gov/quickfacts /coeurdalenecityidaho, accessed January 31, 2021.

240   *Another incoming recruit:* Dan Ninham, "Emmit Taylor III (Yakama/Nez- Perce): Heading to Idaho State University Next Season," NDNSports, January 8, 2020, https://www.ndnsports.com/emmit-taylor-iii-yakama-nezperce-heading -to-idaho-state-university-next-season/.

242   *CNN reached out:* Scott Mansch, "'Warrior Movement' Comes to Great Falls," *Great Falls Tribune,* April 19, 2018, 1S.

242   *Tester made a video:* "We're Joining the #WarriorMovement," Senator Jon Tester, Facebook, March 15, 2018, https://www.facebook.com/watch/?v =10156226141301665, accessed January 31, 2021.

22: The Singing

245   *an effort to quantify the Tribes' water rights:* "Confederated Salish and Kootenai Tribes Compact," The Montana Department of Natural Resources & Con- servation, http://dnrc.mt.gov/divisions/water/water-compact-implementation

-program/confederated-salish-and-kootenai-tribes-compact, accessed March 3, 2021.

247   *in a white ranch town:* "Beaverhead County, Montana," United States Census Bureau QuickFacts, Population Estimates, July 1, 2019, https://www.census.gov/quickfacts/beaverheadcountymontana, accessed January 31, 2021.

248   *the division started:* "About the N7 Fund," Nike, https://n7fund.nike.com/about/, accessed January 31, 2021.

248   *the kind now being sold:* "Warrior Movement Store," Join the Warrior Movement, https://www.jointhewarriormovement.com/product-page/wm-hoodie-gray-white, accessed January 31, 2021.

249   *the designer of many of:* "Tinker Hatfield 1977," University of Oregon, College of Design, https://design.uoregon.edu/tinker-hatfield-1977, accessed January 31, 2021.

252   *Only five boys' teams in Montana:* MHSA archives, "Montana High School Association State Boys' Basketball Champions of the Past 1911–2019."

257   *had announced the hiring:* Joe Kusek, "Mick Durham Hired as New Montana State Billings Men's Basketball Coach," 406MTSports, March 28, 2018, https://406mtsports.com/college/gnac/msu-billings/mick-durham-hired-as-new-montana-state-billings-mens-basketball-coach/article_7ca9f558-6b18-5c22-a4c1-ce482dd2c66a.html.

257   *406 MT Sports published a list:* Kyle Hansen, "Class of 2018 College Recruit Tracker," 406 MT Sports, May 29, 2018, https://406mtsports.com/high-school/class-of-2018-college-recruit-tracker/article_c4ee6e48-563d-5a7d-ade2-45e8a8def741.html.

257   *told 406 MT Sports:* Frank Gogola, "Montana Grizzlies Get Commitment from Washington High School Sharpshooter Freddy Brown III," 406 MT Sports, June 8, 2018, https://406mtsports.com/college/big-sky-conference/university-of-montana/montana-grizzlies-get-commitment-from-washington-high-school-sharpshooter-freddy-brown-iii/article_7f669a06-a479-5335-a050-1cb5be73f05c.html.

259   *called Elizabeth Warren "Pocahontas":* Jonathan Allen, "Trump Challenges 'Pocahontas' Warren to DNA Test to Prove She's Native American," NBC News, July 5, 2018, https://www.nbcnews.com/politics/politics-news/trump-challenges-pocahontas-warren-dna-test-prove-she-s-native-n889206.

260   *on a football scholarship:* Kyle Hansen, "Hardin's David Evans Is a Humble Star," 406 MT Sports, June 7, 2018, https://406mtsports.com/high-school/basketball/boys/hardins-david-evans-is-a-humble-star/article_57217cd7-eaa4-5d23-aba6-3f113aed8c50.html.

260   *Bellach had signed:* Slim Kimmel, "Manhattan Christian's Caleb Bellach Fulfills Dream, Commits to Montana State Bobcats," MontanaSports.com, August 8, 2018, https://www.montanasports.com/high-school/boys-basketball/2018/08/08/manhattan-christians-caleb-bellach-fulfills-dream-commits-to-montana-state-bobcats/.

24: Must Be the New Shoes

265   *made four three-pointers:* "Salish Kootenai College vs. Eastern Oregon University," Eastern Oregon University Sports, October 12, 2018, https://eousports .com/sports/mens-basketball/stats/2018-2019/salish-kootenai/boxscore/3248, accessed January 31, 2021.

267   *scored 18 points against:* "Salish Kootenai College vs. Montana Western," Official Athletic Website of the Montana Western Bulldogs, October 20, 2018, https://umwbulldogs.com/sports/mens-basketball/stats/2018-19/salish-kootenai -college/boxscore/691, accessed January 31, 2021.

267   *played thirteen minutes and scored 1 point:* "Phillip Malatare #4," 2018–2019 Game Log, Official Website of the Northwest Athletic Conference, https://nwacsports .com/sports/mbkb/2018-19/players/phillipmalatareoz8a?view=gamelog&pos =sh, accessed January 31, 2021.

267   *play substantial minutes:* Ibid.

269   *began to wind its way:* Seaborn Larson, "Alleged Shooter Gets New Trial Date, Still Time for Plea Agreement," *Missoulian,* October 2, 2018, https://missoulian .com/news/local/alleged-shooter-gets-new-trial-date-still-time-for-plea -agreement/article_af420a5c-ec80-5003-985e-5323acb78a14.html.

271   *a boy brought a gun to school:* Seaborn Larson, "Arlee Student Cited for Bringing Gun to School, Officials Schedule Meeting to Hear Concerns," *Missoulian,* November 2, 2018, https://missoulian.com/news/state-and-regional/crime-and -courts/arlee-student-cited-for-bringing-gun-to-school-officials-schedule -meeting-to-hear-concerns/article_c9b74fd2-5ade-559e-9bd4-e192a91cda66 .html.

271   *portraying Arlee's kids:* Cameron Evans, "Arlee's Warrior Movement Brings Message of Hope to Big Sky Native American Heritage Event," *Missoulian,* September 26, 2018, https://missoulian.com/news/local/arlees-warrior-movement -brings-message-of-hope-to-big-sky-native-american-heritage-event/article _c61a7205-6db9-5306-b401-a89f71553286.html.

272   *When speaking to high school students in Missoula:* Evans, "Arlee's Warrior Movement."

273   *as well as NBA TV: Beyond the Paint: Arlee Warriors* (NBA TV, 2019), https:// www.nba.com/watch/video/beyond-the-paint-arlee-warriors, accessed January 31, 2021.

278   *published another list of Montanans:* Kyle Hansen, "Class of 2019 College Recruit Tracker," 406 MT Sports, https://406mtsports.com/high-school/class-of-2019 -college-recruit-tracker/article_badd61e5-07da-52e4-9dfd-fdd8b337fd3a.html, accessed February 12, 2019.

278   *shredded opponents:* Ryan Collingwood, "RayQuan Evans Draws Interest from Big Colleges as North Idaho Basketball Career Nears End."

278   *Phil's point totals rose:* "Phillip Malatare #4," 2018–2019 Game Log.

278   *played a team led by Damen Thacker:* "NIC MBB Host Walla Walla," NIC Athletics YouTube channel, January 12, 2019, accessed January 31, 2021.

278   *league leaders in steals:* "Ball Control," Men's Basketball 2018–2019 Season Statistics, Official Website of the Northwest Athletic Conference, https://nwacsports

.com/sports/mbkb/2018-19/players?sort=treb&view=&pos=bt&r=0, accessed January 31, 2021.

279   *Their starting lineup consisted of:* "Walla Walla vs. North Idaho, March 17, 2019," Official Website of the Northwest Athletic Conference, https://nwacsports.com/sports/mbkb/2018-19/boxscores/20190317_yj2a.xml?view=boxscore, accessed January 31, 2021.

279   *with 14 points and 8 rebounds:* The author kept statistics.

25: Where It All Began

280   *Dar hit a free throw:* "Arlee Boys Edge Out Twin Bridges to Earn Bid at State," MontanaSports.com, February 27, 2019, https://www.montanasports.com/high-school/boys-basketball/2019/02/27/arlee-boys-edge-out-twin-bridges-to-earn-bid-at-state/.

280   *Greg scored 23:* Game details from archived video at NFHSNetwork.com.

280   *would, after the season, accept an offer:* "Chinook's Isaac Bell to Play Basketball at University of Providence," MontanaSports.com, April 22, 2019, https://www.montanasports.com/frontier/university-of-providence/2019/04/22/chinooks-isaac-bell-to-play-basketball-at-university-of-providence/.

286   *In the first quarter:* Game details from archived video at NFHSNetwork.com.

26: Where We're Gonna Be

289   *The final attempted free-throw count was 40–7:* "Manhattan Christian vs. Arlee High School," Box Score produced by DakStats, emailed by the MHSA, March 9, 2019.

290   *applied for 501(c)(3) status:* "Warrior Movement," Charity Navigator, https://www.charitynavigator.org/ein/830958791, accessed January 2021.

291   *in a new N7 video:* "N7: Rezball's Finest," Nike YouTube channel, June 21, 2019, accessed January 31, 2021.

291   *airing some long-held grievances:* Frank Gogola, "Zanen Pitts, Warrior Movement Founder, Resigns as Arlee Boys Basketball Coach," 406 MT Sports, June 12, 2019, https://406mtsports.com/high-school/basketball/boys/zanen-pitts-warrior-movement-founder-resigns-as-arlee-boys-basketball-coach/article_ba1abb8c-b59a-5094-9c91-8baf6a296f8f.html.

291   *running three successive articles:* Frank Gogola, "Arlee Administration Fires Back at Zanen Pitts over Resignation as Boys Basketball Coach," 406 MT Sports, June 13, 2019, https://406mtsports.com/high-school/basketball/boys/arlee-administration-fires-back-at-zanen-pitts-over-resignation-as-boys-basketball-coach/article_fbdd3244-8c80-538d-955d-65b72c9bf8b1.html; Kyle Hansen, "Zanen Pitts Receives Outpouring of Support over Decision to Leave Arlee Basketball Coaching Job," 406 MT Sports, June 13, 2019, https://406mtsports.com/high-school/basketball/boys/zanen-pitts-receives-outpouring-of-support-over-decision-to-leave-arlee-basketball-coaching-job/article_06891f21-017c-5a4a-a21c-f03c473c2e53.html.

297   *the NWAC announced sanctions:* "North Idaho College Men's Basketball Violations,"

letter from Marco Azurdia, Executive Director, Northwest Athletic Conference, to Richard MacLennan, President, North Idaho College, June 3, 2019, https://www.nic.edu/modules/images/websites/46/file/0603-NWAC-Letter.pdf, accessed February 1, 2021.

298   *In one of the most high-profile cases:* "Report of the National Collegiate Athletic Association Division I Infractions Appeals Committee," Report no. 208, University of Michigan (Ann Arbor), September 25, 2003. Emailed by Meghan Durham, NCAA Associate Director of Communications, January 26, 2021.

298   *The Federal Bureau of Investigation got involved:* "FBI Investigates UM Booster," CBS News, May 14, 1999, https://www.cbsnews.com/news/fbi-investigates-um-booster/.

299   *In his sophomore season:* "Phillip Malatare #4," 2019–2020 individual statistics, Official Website of the Northwest Athletic Conference, https://nwacsports.com/sports/mbkb/2019-20/players/phillipmalatare03y0, accessed February 1, 2021.

299   *missing at least 18 of them:* The author kept statistics from the video of games available on NIC Athletics' YouTube channel.

299   *played a team led by a prolific scorer:* "North Idaho College Men [sic] Basketball vs. College of Southern Idaho," NIC Athletics' YouTube channel, December 5, 2019.

300   *Ty started, playing well:* "NIC Men's Basketball Hosts Columbia Basin CC," NIC Athletics' YouTube channel, February 26, 2020.

300   *North Idaho's 28–1 record:* "2019–2020 Men's Basketball Statistics—North Idaho," Official Website of the Northwest Athletic Conference, https://nwacsports.com/sports/mbkb/2019-20/teams/northidaho, accessed February 1, 2021.

300   *honored its previous commitment:* Kim Grinolds, "Nate Pryor Talks About His Re-Commitment to UW," 247 Sports, March 31, 2020, https://247sports.com/college/washington/Article/Washington-Huskies-UW-Basketball-Nate-Pryor-talks-about-his-re-commitment-145588444/; Percy Allen, "Point Guard Nate Pryor Took a Detour on His Route to UW and Reclaimed His Career Along the Way," *Seattle Times,* December 19, 2020, https://www.seattletimes.com/sports/uw-huskies/point-guard-nate-pryor-took-a-detour-on-his-route-to-uw-and-reclaimed-his-career-along-the-way/.

300   *received an offer to play:* Dan Ninham, "Emmit Taylor III (Yakama/NezPerce): Heading to Idaho State University Next Season," NDNSports, January 8, 2020, https://www.ndnsports.com/emmit-taylor-iii-yakama-nezperce-heading-to-idaho-state-university-next-season/.

302   *recruited a player from the Blackfeet Reservation:* "Browning's Riley Spoonhunter to Continue Basketball Career at Dawson CC," 406 MT Sports, April 9, 2020, https://billingsgazette.com/sports/college/brownings-riley-spoonhunter-to-continue-basketball-career-at-dawson-cc/article_a143a9f0-b783-5c0e-8461-da377825166f.html.

302   *a Crow star from Hardin:* Victor Flores, "Hardin's Famous Lefthand Signs with Rocky Mountain College Men's Basketball," 406 MT Sports, August 22, 2019, https://billingsgazette.com/sports/high-school/basketball/boys/hardin-s

-famous-lefthand-signs-with-rocky-mountain-college-men/article_dc5f8bba
-520f-5843-8d2a-b70d12569e89.html.

302   *a guard with connections to Arlee:* Montana Tech Sports Information, "Hellgate's
LaRance, Transfer Signs with Orediggers," April 24, 2020, https://godiggers
.com/news/2020/4/24/mens-basketball-hellgates-larance-transfer-signs-with
-orediggers.aspx.

302   *Warriors moved up to Class B:* Amie Just, "Arlee Scarlets, Warriors to Move Up
from Class C to Class B in 2019–20," 406 MT Sports, April 10, 2018, https://
406mtsports.com/high-school/arlee-scarlets-warriors-to-move-up-from-class-c
-to-class-b-in-2019-20/article_95d64de1-beb6-56cf-918b-b1b566e1ea4c.html.

302   *did not defeat a single conference opponent:* Frank Gogola, "'A Cinderella Story':
How Arlee Went from Winless in Conference to State Qualifier in 1st Year in
Class B," 406 MT Sports, March 10, 2020, https://406mtsports.com/high-school
/basketball/boys/a-cinderella-story-how-arlee-went-from-winless-in
-conference-to-state-qualifier-in-1st/article_9f3b4892-0707-5ff8-a7cf
-821794f07428.html.

302   *knocking out the defending champion:* Kyle Hansen, "Western B Boys: Arlee, Deer
Lodge Advance to Championship Game," MontanaSports.com, February 28,
2020,   https://www.montanasports.com/sports/high-school-sports/western-b
-boys-arlee-deer-lodge-advance-to-championship-game.

302   *the last state in the union to attempt:* Josh Peter, "Montana Only State Allowing
Fans at High School Sports Events Despite Coronavirus Concerns," *USA Today,*
March 13, 2020, https://www.usatoday.com/story/sports/highschool/2020/03
/13/coronavirus-montana-high-school-sports-fans-games/5047967002/.

About the Author

Abe Streep has written for *The New York Times Magazine*, *The New Yorker*, *Outside*, *The California Sunday Magazine*, *Wired*, *The Columbia Journalism Review*, and *Harper's*. His writing has been anthologized in Best American Sports Writing and noted by Best American Essays and Best American Science and Nature Writing. He was a recipient of the 2019 American Mosaic Journalism Prize for deep reporting on underrepresented communities.

CELADON
BOOKS

Founded in 2017, Celadon Books, a division of
Macmillan Publishers, publishes a highly curated list
of twenty to twenty-five new titles a year. The list of
both fiction and nonfiction is eclectic and focuses
on publishing commercial and literary books and
discovering and nurturing talent.